The Dialectics
of Oppression in Zaire

The Dialectics
of Oppression in Zaire

MICHAEL G. SCHATZBERG

Indiana University Press
Bloomington and Indianapolis

Manufactured in the United States of America

Library of Congress Cataloging-in-Publication Data

Schatzberg, Michael G.
The dialectics of oppression in Zaire

Bibliography: p.
Includes index.
1. Human rights—Zaire—Lisala (Equateur)
2. Political persecution—Zaire—Lisala (Equateur)
3. Lisala (Equateur, Zaire)—History. I. Title.
JC599.Z282L577 1988   323.4'9'0967513   87-46093
ISBN 0-253-31703-7
1 2 3 4 5 92 91 90 89 88

For Doreen

Contents

Preface   ix
Acronyms   xi

1. Introduction   1
2. Triple Helix: State, Class, and Ethnicity in Africa   8
3. The State as Ear: Information, Coercion, and
   the Political Police   30
4. The State as Bandit: Armed Forces, Coercive Force   52
5. The State as Family, Mobutu as Father: Political Imagery   71
6. The Insecure State, I: Resistance Within—The Magistrature   99
7. The Insecure State, II: Resistance Without—Religious Groups   115
8. The Dialectics of Oppression   134

Notes   145
Bibliography   174
Index   190

Preface

Much of the information for this book about the Zairian state and the dialectic of oppression it exacerbates was collected in Lisala, a small town situated along the Zaire River in the northwestern corner of the country. Located in Equateur Region, Lisala is an important governmental center and headquarters of three administrative units: Mongala Subregion, the Zone of Lisala, and the Cité (collectivity) of Lisala. In the mid-1970s Mongala was composed of five zones: Lisala, Bongandanga, Bumba, Mobayi-Mbongo, and Businga. In 1977 Mongala lost the zones of Businga and Mobayi-Mbongo (now Yakoma) to the new Nord Ubangi Subregion, whose headquarters became Gbadolite, President Mobutu's ancestral village. For consistency and convenience, however, subsequent references to Mongala Subregion generally refer to the older, and larger, administrative unit. Lisala is also an educational center and in 1974 over one-third of the population (then 27,000) were students. In 1980 Lisala had approximately 35,000 people. Not noted for commercial activity, without the state and its schools Lisala would probably revert to the large village it once was because its population growth has nearly always depended on the state. As "the source of *Mobutisme*" and the president's birthplace, Lisala does not lack high-level attention.[1]

I spent 1974–75 in Lisala gathering most of the data contained in this study. Although unable to return to refresh my acquaintance with this part of the country, a period of intensive research in Brussels during the summer of 1983 enabled me to update my knowledge and complement the fruits of field research with other information. Because it is necessary to maintain the anonymity of my respondents, formal interviews are cited by number. Copies of these documents are available in Memorial Library at the University of Wisconsin-Madison. The same concern guided my handling of contemporary documentary sources, and most documents are simply cited as "administrative correspondence." Unless indicated, I consulted them in the archives of the Political Affairs Department, Mongala Subregion, Lisala. Notes indicating "Field Log" refer to my daily journal, which is available to interested scholars on request. All translations are mine unless noted otherwise.

Although only one name appears on the title page, all authors know this is profoundly misleading. Along the way institutions and individuals have contributed to this book, and I am pleased to record my gratitude. Funding for fieldwork in Zaire during the 1970s was provided by the Fulbright Hays Program, and my stay in Brussels in 1983 was supported by a grant from the Peter A. Magowan Research Fund of the Foreign Policy Institute of the Johns Hopkins University School of Advanced International Studies (SAIS). I am grateful to both institutions for their generous support. Many Zairians—ordinary and extraordinary, at home and abroad, opponents and partisans of the present regime—shared their knowledge of the way things work in their country. I thank them and hope the decent life they desire may soon be theirs. I was also privileged to receive counsel and constructive criticism on completed drafts from Jean-François Bayart, Guy Gran, René Lemarchand, Crawford Young, and Jan Vansina. Thomas Callaghy's keen eye saw both consistencies and contradictions that I did not, and I am grateful. At SAIS, Fouad Ajami and I. William Zartman also criticized and encouraged, while the African Studies doctoral seminar spiritedly assailed my ideas, as did students in my seminar on Politics and Society in Central Africa. Those who commented on parts of the work, especially in its early stages, include Bruce Fetter, Bogumil Jewsiewicki, Curtis Keim, Janet MacGaffey, Nzongola-Ntalaja, Elise Pachter, Yahya Sadowski, and Herbert Weiss. It is a joy to share whatever credit may accrue; these individuals, friends and colleagues all, have my thanks for making this a better book. But I am selfish about blame; good advice was not always followed and any remaining deficiencies or errors are therefore mine alone.

Finally, my wife, Doreen, took time from her own busy professional life to share mine. She read, commented, and then read again. She has been my most demanding critic, my most loving companion. I wouldn't want it any other way.

Acronyms

CAR	Central African Republic
CND	Centre National de Documentation
CNRI	Centre National de Recherches et d'Investigations
CPM	contribution personnelle minimum
EJCSK	Eglise de Jésus-Christ sur Terre par le Prophète Simon Kimbangu
FAZ	Forces Armées Zairoises
GDN	Gendarmerie Nationale
IMF	International Monetary Fund
JMPR	Jeunesse du Mouvement Populaire de la Révolution
MNC	multinational corporation
MPR	Mouvement Populaire de la Révolution
OPJ	Officier de la Police Judiciaire
PRP	Parti Révolutionnaire du Peuple
RDA	Ruvuma Development Association (of Tanzania)
SRB	State Research Bureau (of Uganda)
UDPS	Union pour la Démocratie et le Progrès Social
UMHK	Union Minière du Haut-Katanga

The Dialectics
of Oppression in Zaire

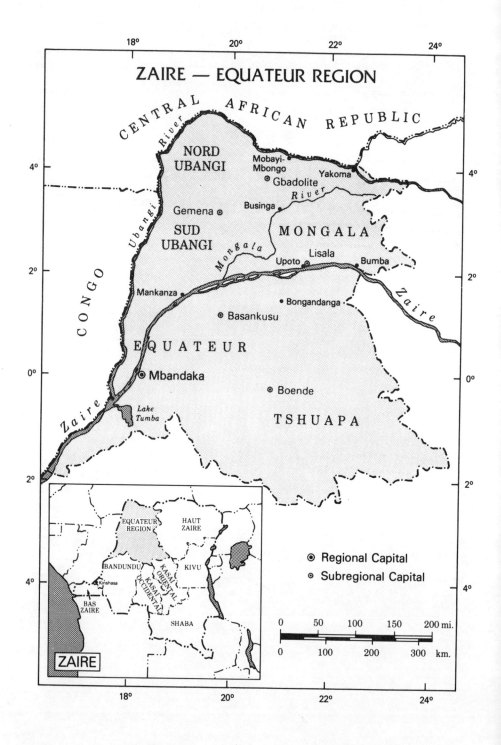

ZAIRE — EQUATEUR REGION

CENTRAL AFRICAN REPUBLIC

NORD UBANGI

Mobayi-Mbongo

Gbadolite

Yakoma

Businga

MONGALA

Gemena

SUD UBANGI

Lisala

Upoto

Bumba

Mankanza

Bongandanga

Basankusu

EQUATEUR

Mbandaka

Boende

Lake Tumba

TSHUAPA

CONGO

Ubangi River

River

Mongala

Zaire

Zaire

EQUATEUR REGION

HAUT ZAIRE

BANDUNDU

KIVU

KASAI ORIENTAL

KASAI OCCIDENTAL

Kinshasa

BAS ZAIRE

SHABA

ZAIRE

◉ Regional Capital
◎ Subregional Capital

0   50   100   150   200 mi.

0   100   200   300 km.

1
Introduction

Zaire has two faces: one smiles, the other snarls; one exudes paternal confidence and caring, the other is insecure and oppressive. In May 1983 President Mobutu Sese Seko proclaimed a general amnesty for all political prisoners. His declaration on that occasion conveyed an image of a generous, magnanimous, and forgiving father—a tantalizing glimpse of Zaire's first face.

> We live on the earth of men and the large family of the MPR [Mouvement Populaire de la Révolution] today numbers close to thirty million souls.
> In every family, bad boys—difficult children—are not absent . . .
> My constant worry has always been to give each son, each daughter of this country, the opportunity to bring his small contribution to the work of national recovery.
> The chief that I am is not only for the good citizens, but also, and perhaps even more, for those who are less so.
> And if a chief must know how to punish, I believe that a pardon is sometimes necessary.
> There is not only the prodigal child who deserts the paternal roof whose return one day is passively awaited, there is also the lost sheep who leaves the herd that the master is going to find . . . [1]

In November 1984 armed invaders opposed to the regime seized Moba, a small town in northeastern Shaba. Although the Zairian army (Forces Armées Zairoises, FAZ) quickly recaptured Moba, it immediately launched an extensive campaign of violent reprisal against the surrounding population. The testimony of a local teacher, arrested and illegally detained in May 1985, speaks to Zaire's other face.

> I was arrested at the school where I worked in Moba with two other teachers. We were taken to the FAZ headquarters in the centre of Moba without being told why we were arrested. We arrived at about 1400 hours and were put straight into a cell there which contained a total of about 20 prisoners, all of them apparently accused of some political offense or other.
> The next morning the three of us were called out and taken for questioning. I was the first and was taken into an office next to the cell. I was interrogated for about two hours. First of all they asked me about my background and were rude when they heard I was a muBembe. They then asked me whether I was in contact with a particular political party . . . and its leaders, but I did not know anything about it and told them so. They also asked me if I had ever travelled outside Zaire, but I explained that I had not.

Obviously I had not given the answers which they wanted, so they subjected me to two kinds of torture. They whipped me with barbed wire on my back, sides, and chest, which began bleeding. They also beat me on the soles of my feet with a stick.

Eventually they stopped, after about two hours, I think. Then they tied up my arms and pushed me into a corner of the room while the two others were interrogated. They were given the same treatment as me. . . .

We were eventually put back into the cell with the others and left there. We were not questioned again. I spent a further two and a half months there. During that time we never received food or drink in any systematic way and could not get food brought in from outside. Soldiers would occasionally throw in a few small bananas, which they covered with *pilipili* (chili pepper) to make them less edible. We only got tiny amounts of water to drink after repeatedly pleading or crying. We were never allowed out for exercises, but were occasionally involved in emptying the butt which served as a WC in the cell.

The most remarkable incident occurred in July 1985, when 10 prisoners, all Moba residents, were brought in one evening. Later that night five of them were taken out: these were evidently the ones the soldiers suspected seriously of being in contact with rebels. We heard a series of gunshots outside. Then some of us, including me, were told to come outside to bury the bodies. Just near the headquarters building was a tree where the five men were lying with bullet wounds all across their bodies. We dug a hole to put them in and noticed a series of other graves nearby. The soldiers laughed at our terror and nodded towards those graves, indicating what was likely to be our fate.

The next morning soldiers again came to fetch 15 of us. Fortunately, I was left behind. The 15, who included the two men who were arrested with me, were told they were to act as porters during a military operation. However, none ever came back and I am sure that they were all killed by the soldiers.

At the end of July 1985 I managed to escape.[2]

Since independence in 1960, the fortunes of the Zairian state have waxed and waned. The transfer of formal political power from the Belgian colonizers to the newly independent republic and the turbulence of the so-called Congo Crisis induced a general and thorough weakening in the sinews of the state. Multiple secessions and the erection of autonomous and competing poles of authority, external interventions, administrative decentralization, widespread rebellion, and the breakdown of order in the countryside all contributed to a bleak and unlamented period of Zairian history. Independent armies and police forces loyal to regional suzerains emerged to fill the political space which the central government could no longer occupy. Insecurity, both personal and political, was the order of the day.[3]

A resurgence of the state under President Mobutu followed this period of political upheaval as the societal crisis of the First Republic (1960–1965) gradually ceded pride of place to a strong and ostensibly centralized national government under the Second Republic (1965–present). After seizing power in a military coup in November 1965, Mobutu restored order while recentralizing the authority and power of the state as he exerted an increasingly personalized and autocratic style of rule. The then relatively high price of copper on the international market financed a shift toward administrative centralization, the institutionalization of a state-party, and ambitious development plans. For several years Mobutu was a truly popular ruler; he had reestablished order, increased personal security in much of the country, and had seemingly put paid to the harsh and difficult conditions of Zaire's early years.

The period of *Mobutiste* renewal lasted until the mid-1970s, when it again seemed the state had entered a phase of pervasive decline and dissolution. By this time Mobutu's political capital had gradually diminished, and ordinary Zairians were increasingly victims of extraction, exploitation, and oppression at the hands of the state. This was a gradual process whose starting point eludes precise dating, but the evidence was there well before the more glaring symptoms of the *mal zairois* (Zairian sickness) became visible later in the decade.[4] Ironically, Mobutu's initial success in building his own power base and stabilizing the regime to eliminate the endemic social and political instability of the First Republic has generated new forms of personal insecurity which are now characteristic of the Second Republic. Measures to strengthen the central state such as frequent rotation of officials, administrative centralization, and waves of ill-advised economic policy measures (Zairianization, radicalization, and, finally, retrocession of stores and plantations) have made most Zairians insecure in their political and economic lives. This personal insecurity helps explain why exploitation and oppression are common coin.[5]

By the late 1970s the situation had become so catastrophic that the state appeared to be lurching from one disaster to the next as it had in the past. Zaire's military intervention in Angola (1975), invasions of the copper-rich Shaba Region (Shaba I, 1977; Shaba II, 1978), and escalating indebtedness to Western banks and multilateral financial institutions compounded an already disastrous situation. Observers increasingly characterized Zaire as a land of "unending" and "continuing" crisis.[6] Each new installment of Zaire's lamentable saga has increased the insecurity of its people, its rulers, and of the Zairian state itself.

In an earlier work I argued that, at least in Zaire, insecurity and scarcity are the motoring forces behind a dialectic of oppression. As personal, political, and economic insecurity increase, people in power seek to accumulate resources as rapidly as possible from those who occupy contextually inferior positions in the social hierarchy. However they can, while they can, they extract whatever they can because those in authority know a fall from grace may be imminent. Their positions are so insecure, and Mobutu's favor so fickle, that even the president's closest collaborators must assume that a similar opportunity to convert power into wealth might not reappear. Power is quickly gained, and rapidly lost.[7] Sakombi Inongo, long Mobutu's champion, has nicely expressed this aspect of Zairian political life. As part of his defense of the regime against the onslaughts of the once-exiled opposition leader, former prime minister, and now Zaire's ambassador to the United States, Nguza Karl-i-Bond, and speaking directly to Nguza he wrote:

It is you, Nguza, who were accused, judged, condemned, then pardoned—thank God!—according to the logic of the social Order to which you belonged. Zairian political men who accede to the summit of the country's hierarchy and who, through the risks of politics, return, without striking a blow, to the ranks of other fellow citizens are legion. I am one of them. One is not born a Minister or a Prime Minister. One becomes it. And, one day, one ceases to be it.[8]

Under these conditions and according to the unstated but well-known "rules" of Zairian politics, it is better to profit while possible to insure oneself and one's family a bit of security after the fall. The dialectic of oppression ensues as this pervasive insecurity interacts with a general condition of economic scarcity induced by the fall of the price of copper, a badly managed economy, and a thoroughly corrupt polity. Still more oppression, personal insecurity, and—over the long term—new sources of instability and insecurity for both regime and state are the consequences of this dialectic.

Ultimately the state and its rulers exacerbate, if not instigate, the prevalent conditions of insecurity and scarcity, thus setting in motion the dialectic of oppression. Young notes "massive and systematic assaults upon human dignity are a function not of ideological strategy but of insecure and paranoid rulers."[9] Callaghy, too, argues the "Zairian absolutist state is an emerging organization of domination seeking to expand its domain in a very hostile and uncertain environment, both internally and externally. The survival of this early modern state never appears assured; uncertainty remains a pervasive fact for the rulers of this centralizing structure of domination."[10] When we consider the insecurity of the state, as well as the scarcity and insecurity it engenders in society, is it any wonder people describe life as "combat," or view the state as an oppressive and alien entity, or realize their ill-fortune is not due to "counterrevolutionaries," as their rulers would have them believe, but that, in the last analysis, their struggle is with the state itself?[11]

But what is this state? Where does state end and civil society begin? What is the relationship between the two? Scholars have long labored to provide answers. Others have already reviewed the rapidly expanding body of theoretical and empirical literature on this subject,[12] and chapter 2 presents my own views on the state in Africa. So instead of needlessly recapitulating this work here, suffice it to say even subtle and sophisticated thinkers such as Gramsci and Poulantzas have used the term *state* inconsistently.[13] In consequence, there is an important dispute over what, exactly, the state is—or is not. In general, however, there are two major lines of response to the definitional problem: one stresses attention to concrete institutions and organizations, while the second emphasizes theoretical and ideological considerations. Gramsci was similarly inconsistent in his attempts to delineate the notion *civil society*, a crucial matter if one is to arrive at a workable definition of the state and posit a relationship between it and civil society.[14]

This chapter cannot deal with these questions definitively, and will not try to do so. Succeeding chapters and analyses will, for the most part, focus on concrete organizational aspects of the state and be guided by the definitions of Skocpol ("states as administrative and coercive organizations"[15]) and Giddens, who maintains the "state is best seen as a set of collectivities concerned with the institutionalised organisation of political power."[16]   Although these definitions cover a significant portion of what the state is and does, there is more to it than that. No state can govern through coercion alone; there are usually ideological mechanisms to induce people to internalize the state's normative and behavioral rules. Sometimes explicitly articulated ideologies accomplish this (in Zaire these are called authenticity and *Mobutisme*), but myth, metaphor, and the symbolic dimension of politics also contribute.[17]

We thus need a definition that accommodates both the concrete organizational aspects of the state and its symbolic and metaphorical charter. In consequence, throughout this book the state will be defined as a congeries of organized repositories of administrative, coercive, and ideological power subject to, and engaged in, an ongoing process of power accumulation characterized by uneven ascension and uneven decline. Chapters 3 and 4, therefore, analytically examine the sinews of state power, the coercive arms of the Zairian state. Coercion is a major theme and will reappear frequently. Chapter 5 probes the Zairian state's political imagery and explores in detail the origins, purposes, and consequences of the paternal and familial metaphors Mobutu employed in issuing his general amnesty in May 1983.

Subsequent chapters, especially the analysis of the Zairian magistrature in chapter 6, indicate the validity of Poulantzas's observation that the state is neither "a completely united mechanism, founded on a homogenous and hierarchical distribution of centres of power," nor "a monolithic bloc without cracks."[18]   The structure of the state contains fissures and crevices between institutions, and internal pockets of resistance result. Resistance internal to the state often appears as part of a long-term and ongoing dialectical struggle for space between societal forces favoring centralization on the one hand, and those which push for decentralization on the other. I shall often refer to various aspects of this dialectic. Chapter 7 returns to the question of relations between the state and civil society in greater depth and examines the interactions between the Zairian state and certain religious organizations and groups. We shall see that the existence of groups outside the state in the realm of civil society may, under certain circumstances, result in pockets of resistance external to the state. External opposition exists in many forms and is also part of the dialectical struggle for space. Using the limited means at hand, the citizenry seeks to reassert control over some autonomous political, social, and economic space. Put simply, Zairians desire room to breathe and search for ways to resist the state's usually unpleasant and unwelcome encroachments on their lives. This opposition, both from within and without, contributes to the insecurity of the Zairian state and its rulers. Insecurity is also a principal motif that weaves its way through the entire study since, as indicated, it interacts with scarcity to create a pervasive dialectic of oppression.

Although some theorists of the state have created elegant intellectual abstractions, they have often lost sight of how the state appears to the powerless who must deal with it every day. Does it smile, or snarl? What does the state look like in up-country Zaire as its various institutional arms go about their daily business? Perhaps those who experience the state perceive it differently than those who write about it. If this is the case, then it would be wise to pause, take stock, and wonder if something is not amiss. More specifically, how do peasants and up-country townspeople perceive the state? Do their perceptions at all resemble the portraits theorists have provided? Do certain aspects of the state become clear only when viewed from a local-level perspective? If so, what are the implications for our understanding of the state? Analysts have usually elaborated their observations on the basis of national-level phenomena. Although these efforts may be stimulating and useful, without sustained attention to the local level such efforts will be at worst misguided, at best incomplete. Wherever possible, therefore, this book will present the Zairian state as people in the hinterland see it, and a major aim will be to construct a detailed empirical picture of what the state is and does away from the capital—a picture the illegally detained schoolteacher from Moba might recognize. In this way I hope to redress the balance ever so slightly by focusing on the state's patterns of interaction with its up-country population.

There are other reasons for focusing on the state at the local level. To be sure, when seen from afar the Zairian state's cycle of rise and subsequent demise stands out clearly.[19] As subsequent chapters demonstrate, however, a micropolitical and local-level perspective indicates the image of a unified, centralized, and increasingly powerful authoritarian monolith is overdrawn, as are images of the state's capacity to effect change.[20] Similarly exaggerated are recent tales of the state's decline and disappearance, for behind them is the presumption that the Zairian state is a monolith. As Jessop reminds us, "There are no valid grounds for presupposing the essential class unity of the state and various arguments suggest that it is necessarily fragmented and fissured. The state comprises a plurality of institutions (or apparatuses) and their unity, if any, far from being pregiven, must be constituted politically."[21] Because the state is fragmented, it encounters pockets of resistance from within, for it is most unlikely that all the apparatuses comprising it will subscribe to the same values or vision. In consequence, we should not think of state formation as a process destined to attain a final, predetermined goal but instead as an ongoing, continuous, and extremely uneven process of formation, consolidation, and even, occasionally, disintegration or dissolution. There will be, therefore, uneven ascendancy and uneven decline both of the state itself and of each of its component parts. Furthermore, the uncertainty of these processes contributes dramatically to the rising levels of insecurity in Zaire.

The unevenness of this process becomes most readily apparent when we shift attention from the national to the local level. For these reasons, this book deliberately interweaves local-level data gathered from the field with wider observations and information on Zaire as a whole. Only in this way will the micropolitical perspective shed light on larger, national realities, and vice versa. From this interplay between the two levels of analysis a picture of the contemporary Zairian state will emerge.

One important clarification is in order before proceeding. Both the next chapter and the remainder of this study argue the state is, at least in some ways, a fluid, contextual, and protean phenomenon. When referring to the state in succeeding chapters, I shall *not* mean the state as a territorial entity defined by its international boundaries. International frontiers—fixed by international law, convention, and formal recognition of sovereignty by other states in the international arena—today constitute an important and rarely changing grid first imposed on Africa just over one hundred years ago at the Berlin Conference in 1885. Although the internal state apparatus is not especially healthy and has all but dissolved in places like Uganda, Chad, and Ghana, the shell of the state—understood as firmly fixed territorial boundaries sanctified by international legal recognition of sovereignty—endures, a paradox that Jackson and Rosberg cogently explore.[22] Here the state refers only to the administrative, coercive, and ideological configurations that occupy the internal political space within each geographic unit featured on maps of Africa. The state's exterior shell remains fixed; the state as an internal constellation of organized repositories of power is, as we shall see, anything but immutable.

2
Triple Helix
State, Class, and Ethnicity in Africa

In Ubangi everyone is rich.

—A bureaucrat in Lisala[1]

You [Citizen President-Founder] are in the
habit of affirming that there are no small and
big Zairians. But, of a population of 25 million inhabitants, only fifty individuals "occupy
the most lucrative positions and control the entire political apparatus." This is the same as
saying that in "authentic" Zairian society, the
percentage of those who control the economy
and politics reaches 0.0002% [sic] !!!! There
is not, that we know, any country in the world
in which the concentration of economic and
political power is as scandalous.

—Thirteen dissident parliamentarians[2]

The Welfare State is dead from this moment,
and cedes its place simply to the State. . . .
The State can no longer be a milch cow, just
as it can no longer be placed before accomplished facts.

—Mobutu Sese Seko[3]

The three citations above speak to ethnicity, class, and state—the basic dimensions
of contemporary political life in Zaire, and throughout sub-Saharan Africa. Un-
derlying the first observation is a widely shared belief that Mobutu's ethnic
homeland has gained enormously from his rule because the president has used his
office to aid his kinsmen. Unstated, but clearly understood in present-day Zaire,
is the assumption that ethnic affiliation is critical in determining access to wealth.
The second citation is part of a thorough critique of the *Mobutiste* state and stresses that social classes and class conflict have appeared in Zaire. The final remark

indicates, certainly prematurely, that a major role of the Zairian state has changed, and at least in theory Mobutu will no longer permit its use as a milch cow to provide wealth.

Over the past twenty years, Africanist social scientists have developed an impressive body of literature which demonstrates conclusively that ethnic groups are neither primordial nor immutable. To the earlier pioneering work of Mercier, Vansina, and Southall, we may add the more recent studies of Young and Schildkrout.[4] Many now believe "boundaries of ethnic categories change over time as new categories emerge, and others disappear, merging into larger, more inclusive units."[5] In his current and ongoing study of the peoples of the Central African forest, Vansina has applied the same logic of historical change to both segmentary lineage systems and clans, noting, "Changes in commercial or political relations from group to group carry along modifications in the structure and constitution of clans if not even the appearance of clans where none existed."[6] In addition, scholars agree individuals do not view ethnic identities as mutually exclusive. Depending on the context of the moment, people may "migrate" from one cultural identity to a second, or even a third.[7] Ethnicity, in other words, is a protean, contextual, and intermittent phenomenon.

Similarly, although a less well established and more contentious proposition, observers are starting to recognize, as Robin Cohen argues, "the fluidity of class relationships is the dominant *motif*."[8] Samoff, although he would probably disagree with the thrust of this argument, also sees classes in flux with ambiguous and changing boundaries.[9] Recent work on Ivory Coast makes the same point and notes the "remarkable fluidity" of the ruling class;[10] and a study of Nigerian factory workers indicates their class identities may well vary depending on the context of the moment. Phrasing his argument in terms of a rural-urban continuum, Peace observes: "While in the context of Agege the migrant factory workers are underprivileged, in the context of the home-town setting they are seen as privileged young men by virtue of their having received some education."[11] Bienen also sees class in situational terms, as a product of specific contexts.[12] Leo makes a related point regarding Kenya, where "peasant and capitalist classes [are] thoroughly interpenetrated, with many an individual merging the two class identities in his or her person."[13] I have previously summarized this perspective in propositional form:

> (1) Social classes are constantly changing in response to differing sociopolitical contexts. (2) The individual actor can, and does, belong to differing class alliances at the same time. (3) The degree of class identity will vary depending upon the geographic, social, political, and economic junctures of the moment in question.[14]

Class, like ethnicity, is contextually fluid. The identity, composition, and boundaries of social class often vary according to the contexts of the moment.

Class and ethnicity coexist and interact. Which phenomenon may be most salient to political actors at any given time probably depends on the context. Mitchell's classic study of social relations on the copperbelt, *The Kalela Dance*, underscored this fundamental point almost a generation ago.

The evidence we have from Northern Rhodesia is that in certain situations Africans ignore either class differences or tribal differences (or both), and that in other situations these differences become significant. I have presented evidence to show that in their opposition to the Europeans, Africans ignore both their "class" and tribal differences. Inside a tribal association such as those found in Southern Rhodesia I would expect oppositions to be phrased in terms of "class" differences. I would expect the dissension within a teachers' or clerks' association to be phrased in terms of tribalism. The same people who stand together in one situation may be bitterly opposed in another.[15]

More recently, several authors have underlined the same contextual subtleties.[16] In a probing investigation of the Ethiopian Revolution, Keller argues the salience of class and ethnic identities "in explaining political behaviour is highly contingent on the nature of the stakes involved and the existing political climate at a given point in time. At one time and under certain circumstances, clan identities or the new ethnicity might provide the basis for action; at another, a sense of national identity or social class interest might spark conflict and change."[17] Moreover, all these factors could conceivably operate simultaneously, a point Scott makes explicitly in reference to a Malaysian village. There, as in Africa, "the messy reality of multiple identities will continue to be the experience out of which social relations are conducted."[18]

Added to the contextual interactions of class and ethnicity is a third and perhaps equally important factor, the state. Like ethnicity and social class, we may understand the state as a contextual phenomenon in constant flux as it forms, consolidates, and—in some cases—disintegrates. I shall examine the state as a contextual, fluid, and intermittent factor in the social dynamics of sub-Saharan Africa at greater length presently. For the moment, however, let us merely note that all three phenomena interact and intersect but are discrete only on the analytical plane. To unravel their interactions in practice or to provide precise weightings of their importance is extraordinarily difficult. Reality is, after all, messy. Nonetheless, previous work on the contextual nature of ethnicity and applications of a contextual approach to the political dynamics of social class formation have led me to think about how we might fruitfully apply such a perspective to the state.

This chapter has three aims. First, to discuss the nature of the state in Africa and advance the thesis that it is possible, at least in part, to understand the state both as an organization particularly susceptible to domination by a social class and as a contextual phenomenon, one which interacts with class and ethnicity in a variety of complex ways. "Perhaps the most enduring weakness of African Studies," Lonsdale argues, "is that we have not yet devised means of analyzing societies, doubly divided by both community and class, which do not seem crassly biased toward the explanation of one division alone."[19] I agree, but believe the state should be included in the quest for conceptual integration. To be sure, the three phenomena—state, class, ethnicity—are not precisely the same. Villagers and up-country townsfolk do not, and perhaps cannot, "belong" to the state in quite the same way they are members of a class or ethnic group. Nevertheless, on the structural plane, and especially in terms of their basic fluidity, these three social forces share striking similarities. Therefore, and second, I shall explore some of the interactions between these three forces by examining strategies of access and dominance. Rather than conceiving social dynamics as a dialectic of class and tribe, to use one analyst's lapidary phrase,[20] I argue it would be better to view them as a triple-stranded helix of state, class, and ethnicity.

To render the metaphor of the triple helix clearer, imagine a three-stranded braid in which each strand weaves itself around the other two. The braid, however, is imperfectly formed, for the strands are almost never of equal thickness or importance. In some situations, and at certain times, one component will be dominant. At other times, in other circumstances, a different strand (or both concurrently) will come to the fore. Each strand of the braid, or helix, is always changing. But not only is each strand a protean and intermittent phenomenon in its own right, each of the helix's component parts also forms a significant portion of the context of the other two. Frequently, therefore, social class and the state compose the context in which ethnicity becomes politically salient. Similarly, the context in which social class comes to the fore might well be a combination of ethnicity and the state. So, too, for the state. Considerations of social class, on the one hand, and ethnic factors, on the other, will probably condition the process of state formation as a factor in social dynamics. The "braiding" process, or the continual formation and reconstitution of the helix, is thus likely to be extremely uneven. This constant interaction of the strands of the helix constitutes the field of African social dynamics. The metaphor of the triple helix represents my own vision of the major dynamic social forces that form the warp and woof of politics in Africa. To be sure, since this is a book about the state, I shall devote most attention to that strand of the helix.

The final aim of this chapter is to provide a pan-African setting for the analysis of the Zairian state and the dialectics of oppression that follow. Fortunately, analysts no longer see this perpetually troubled polity as unique; occurrences there are merely considered localized manifestations of similar social processes that dominate political dynamics throughout Africa.

The State in Africa

In his study of neocolonialism in Kenya, Leys remarked wistfully, "[o]f all the real deficiencies of underdevelopment theory the most troublesome . . . was the substantial absence of a systematic theory of the state or of the nature of politics in conditions of underdevelopment."[21] Since then numerous scholars, particularly those working within a broadly defined Marxian paradigm, have responded to Leys's lament by trying to furnish a more coherent theoretical notion of the state in Africa.[22] Thus far much of the debate has concentrated on whether the postcolonial state is "overdeveloped," on the role of the state in facilitating or impeding indigenous capital accumulation, and on whether the state enjoys autonomy vis-à-vis either domestic or foreign capital. Some of these questions are of general interest, others are not.

To comprehend more fully the nature of the state in much of Africa, we need to approach the question in a slightly different way. Marx's classic description of the French peasantry is a convenient and apposite starting point.

> In so far as millions of families live under economic conditions of existence that separate their mode of life, their interests and their cultural formation from those of the other classes and bring them into conflict with those classes, they form a class. In so far as these small peasant proprietors are merely connected on a local basis, and the identity of their interests fails to produce a feeling of community, national links, or a political organization, they do not form a class.[23]

Here is the basis of Marx's distinction between a class-in-itself and a class-for-itself. The dividing line between the two concepts of class hinges on the existence of an organization capable of representing the interests of a class. Put another way, the transition from one type of class to the other presumably occurs when, for example, peasants organize and create a political-organizational arm to engage in class struggle on their behalf. In contemporary Africa, the state (or more precisely its various institutional arms and manifestations) is almost always such a class organization. Moreover, if we treat the state as a class organization, some important conundrums are resolved satisfactorily.

Many have noted that the formation of social class and class consciousness generally occurs more rapidly at the top of the social hierarchy than at the bottom and that such class formation depends more on control of the state than on ownership of the means of production. Most African states became independent in the 1960s without significant indigenous bourgeoisies. Ownership of the major means of production was, in almost every case, located in the former colonial metropole because, until the final phases of imperial rule, discouragement of productive domestic bourgeoisies was often an explicit premise of colonial policy. Since there were only restricted opportunities for capital accumulation under foreign domination, those who inherited the levers of state power first consolidated their rule and then moved to transform their political power into economic wealth. Thus, in an examination of social stratification in Guinea-Conakry, Rivière argues that in Africa we should reverse the standard Marxian formula, "those who govern do so because they are rich," to read "those who are rich are so because they govern."[24]

The same pattern is present in Ivory Coast where Michael Cohen believes "public authority precedes the acquisition of property" and government officials have used their positions in the state "to create both property and the rules for its use."[25] If Cohen is correct, and there is increasing evidence he is, Campbell's thesis that a rural bourgeoisie of indigenous plantation owners is dominant is called into question.[26] After carefully investigating the composition of the elite, an Ivorian scholar notes that, if anything, the public sector is disproportionately represented when compared to the private sector and most politicians were civil servants before entering the plantation economy.[27] In addition, Berry demonstrates convincingly that social differentiation in western Nigeria is due more to "differential access to the state (and foreign capital and markets) . . . than . . . differential access to local land and labor."[28] Or, as Lonsdale puts it, "Ready access to state institutions is therefore literally what makes classes dominant."[29]

In prerevolutionary Ethiopia, Markakis found political and administrative action primarily responsible for prompting rural class formation whereas in urban areas class formation was a consequence of formal education and political recruitment.[30] Similarly, after investigating processes of class formation among the proletariat of Lubumbashi, Zaire, in the early 1970s, Mwabila discovered that, although workers did not constitute a class-for-itself, they could nonetheless perceive the "existence of class consciousness in the superior social layers, structured around class interests and developing in the wake of political authority."[31] Mwabila's conclusions are consistent with my own evaluation of social class formation in Lisala.[32]

In general terms, then, many social scientists would probably agree with Balandier's observation that a "new class"—those who manage the contemporary state and who have been, by and large, the main beneficiaries of the transition to political independence—has emerged.[33] Put simply, those who took over the levers of state command after independence have developed class consciousness much more rapidly than those at lower levels of the social hierarchy because the state itself provided all the organizational focus they needed for their class aspirations. In other words, the political organization Marx spoke of already existed in the shape of the institutionalized state. Thus, those at society's upper levels did not need to constitute an organization to represent their class interests and potentially engage in class struggle because the state was more than adequate for the purpose. It was already there, waiting for them.

But there was certainly no requirement that class rather than ethnic, religious, linguistic, or any other set of concerns dominate the state's agendas at independence.[34] African leaders who wished to use the state to insure the dominance of a particular ethnic group found its organization perfectly capable of adapting to that objective as well (as in Rwanda and Burundi). Moreover, skilled politicians could often accommodate such disparate agendas simultaneously. In retrospect, however, and regardless of the agenda emphasized, the consequences of policy were usually consistent with the interests of the newly dominant group of politicians and bureaucrats. Furthermore, in many cases they consciously used their political power, and the state, to create for themselves the economic wealth denied them under colonial rule. This conception of the state as a class organization in waiting enables us to understand why politico-commercial bourgeoisies have developed class consciousness and implemented appropriate class actions more rapidly and effectively than those who did not inherit political power.[35]

Coupled with this emphasis on the state as an organization particularly susceptible to class domination, we must also consider the organizational difficulties encountered at lower levels of the sociopolitical hierarchy. Many have tried to explain the lack of class-based organizations, solidarity, and, by extension, consciousness among society's dispossessed by focusing on ethnicity and the existence of patron-client links which often follow ethnic lines. In his work on prerevolutionary Ethiopia, Markakis argues: "The persistence of traditional norms that emphasize kinship, and of social mechanisms that promote vertical integration, diminishes social distance and inhibits the growth of class consciousness."[36] Mwabila's later study of Lubumbashi's workers found essentially the same phenomenon. As Zaire's economic situation has become progressively worse, the workers' struggle for survival has led them to depend less on their own organizational initiatives and, concomitantly, to seek solace in their individual ethnic networks. This has been a marked trend since 1973 as better-off members of each relevant ethnic group have associated themselves with the power of the state to better preserve their own interests in the first instance, and those of their ethnic group and native region, in the second. As workers have sought survival and refuge in their ethnic enclaves, horizontal solidarity has lessened and ethnic consciousness has risen.[37] In this same vein, Bertrand's study of Congo-Brazzaville indicates "lineage society" and its numerous personal and familial relationships offer young members of the urban proletariat a bulwark against the rigors of urban misery.[38] Here, as elsewhere, this results in continued reliance on ethnic networks which, in many circumstances, vitiate urban-based class identities. In a sensitive investigation of the interactions between sex, ethnic, and class consciousness in western Kenya, Staudt—like others who have studied Kenya—finds ethnic consciousness tends to obscure class consciousness. A state which divides people and goods geographically may subsume class and gender consciousness and thus, at least, either weaken these two other possible foci of political and social identity or, at most, drives them entirely underground.[39]

Closely related, and in some senses overlapping the ethnic dimension, is the existence of patron-client distributive networks. Saul, among others, has noted these networks "tend to preempt the possible crystallization of alternative modes of (class) consciousness . . . which could see the African masses moving in the direction of consciousness of themselves as exploited peasants and workers vis-à-vis the 'baronial' class as a whole."[40] Students of politics in Kenya have studied such phenomena extensively, and one anthology characterized Kenya's political system as patron-client capitalism.[41] Senegalese politics also demonstrates a clear tendency toward this form of organization, especially where the powerful Mouride brotherhood is concerned.[42] Zaire, too, has its share of political clientelism. As we shall see in greater detail in chapter 4, in 1972 General Bobozo—long one of Mobutu's closest cronies—intervened on behalf of villagers in his home collectivity by requesting their exemption from annual taxes because of their enthusiasm in maintaining local roads.[43] The distribution of largesse through such "big men" is by no means unusual and certainly makes people more conscious of their specific links to those with power, wealth, and influence. Oftentimes these ties are ethnic, but even if not, political clientelage—as a vertical form of solidarity—cuts across horizontal identities such as social class and can thus reduce their salience.[44]

The effective emasculation of labor unions and experiments in communal farming, usually through a process of co-optation, also impedes the evolution of class-based consciousness at lower ends of the social hierarchy. In 1967 the state unified, and then absorbed, the numerous Zairian labor unions. The syndicates thus yielded their independence as organizations of potential opposition and became a single organ that supported government policy in all matters. The national syndicate's elite sits on committees of the MPR, the state-party, at all levels. They can thus participate, at least to some extent, in the decision-making process and communicate relevant decisions to the membership through union representatives in all enterprises. But the flow of communication within the union is invariably from the top down rather than from the bottom up, and the union has become more closely associated with the interests of the state than with those of the workers. In this regard, the Zairian union bears a striking resemblance to those in Eastern Europe, with the obvious exception of Poland's Solidarity.[45]

The Zairian experience is not unusual. In East Africa a similar pattern ensued, and trade unions, once defenders of workers' rights and interests, eventually became obedient pillars of the regimes. When East African labor leaders used their organizations to confront governments on behalf of their memberships, politicians interpreted this as both a political threat and a violation of trust. Neither Kenyatta nor Nyerere hesitated to dissolve confrontational unions, dismiss their leaders, and create new and more pliant unions in their place. Trade unions are thus no longer organizational tools in the hands of the workers, they are tools of governance in the hands of the state.[46]

In Tanzania's agricultural sector, bureaucratic staff and wealthier peasants often reach mutually advantageous arrangements which operate to the detriment of the poor. This was certainly the pattern von Freyhold uncovered in her study of ujamaa villages.[47] Van Hekken and Thoden van Velzen noted the same phenomenon among wealthier farmers in Rungwe District who were able both to protect and increase their relative well-being by pursuing two strategies simultaneously. First, they built up their clientele within the village; second, they created alliances with local government staff people and thus placed themselves in a position to exert partial control of the village's relations with the outside world. Wealthier peasants often sat on village development committees and occupied other important positions because of these alliances.[48]

Furthermore, when, for whatever reason, the state cannot control local organizational initiatives, its tendency is to suppress them. The fate of the Ruvuma Development Association (RDA) is an eloquent testimonial. Guided by Nyerere's ujamaa philosophy, the RDA successfully organized peasant agricultural production along communal lines, provided some welfare services for its members, and emphasized both participatory democracy in its internal organization and independence from the central government. Certain regional and national politicians perceived the RDA's political, organizational, and agricultural successes as a threat to their continued control and, in consequence, suppressed it.[49]

The suppression of autonomous unions and experiments in communal farming should come as no surprise. States in Africa are insecure—politically, economically, socially—and their leaders are likely to perceive any organization they cannot control as a direct threat. The state may thus forbid and suppress any organization which does not fall within the state-party's prescribed framework. In effect, state-parties seek to occupy all available political space, thus precluding the creation and emergence of potentially competing political and organizational foci from below. Speaking of the Union Nationale Camerounaise (UNC), Bayart expresses this point well.

> It is possible that one of its principal functions is essentially negative: to inhibit eventual counter-powers, to prevent there being "something else," to guarantee the politically monolithic nature of the regime. Thus could be explained that one speaks so much of the UNC without it ever doing anything—an excessive formulation which nevertheless expresses one of the most astonishing paradoxes of the Cameroonian political system, and which summarizes the researcher's confusion when confronted with the reality, at the same time omnipresent and ungraspable, of the single party.[50]

The MPR, we shall later see, also tries to fill all available political space, and the state's coercive arms move expeditiously against any with the temerity to establish organizations outside the officially approved scheme of things.

The state can indeed be a class organization in waiting, and its presence goes a long way toward explaining why class consciousness emerges most emphatically in the upper reaches of the social hierarchy. The state, therefore, is most certainly not the neutral arena of competition which American political scientists immersed in pluralist and Western liberal ideology like to discern. In recent years the perversion of the state in Uganda, Central African Republic (CAR), Chad, Equatorial Guinea, Zaire, Guinea-Conakry, and Ghana has convinced some who still view politics in Africa through the prism of a Western liberal perspective that the state is neither neutral nor benign. Young, for example, has argued "The state is not necessarily a neutral and benevolent purveyor of development," and, in relation to Touré's Guinea, Nkrumah's Ghana, and Keita's Mali, "the ideological leadership failed to ponder the class nature of the state itself and the latent conflict of interest between the state and the rural population, indigenous commercial groups, and others not part of the nascent politico-bureaucratic bourgeoisie."[51] From the related, but not identical, public choice perspective Bates affirms "Through the public management of economic resources, the bureaucracies help to institutionalize a structure of relative advantage—a structure within which they themselves occupy positions of privilege and power."[52]

In addition to viewing the state in Africa as a tool, some Western observers also perceive it as an arena. At base, both notions spring from a liberal, pluralist world view. Pluralists see the state as an arena for the dramas of distributional politics; developmentalists find the state an instrument to provide the greatest good for the greatest number, at least in theory. These views are not necessarily incompatible with the argument that the state often operates as an organization of class. Of necessity, however, if the state is viewed as an implement under these circumstances, we need to consider both who controls it and for what purposes. If used as a class-based organization, its rulers may well employ it in ways liberal theorists might deplore. In this light it will be a tool in the hands of the politico-commercial bourgeoisie and used mostly to further the interests of this class. But here one must exercise great caution. States in Africa, as elsewhere, enjoy a measure of relative autonomy and often develop independent institutional interests which may or may not conform to those of the dominant politico-commercial

bourgeoisie. Under no circumstances should we assume the state will always, inevitably, and simplemindedly do the bidding of the politico-commercial bourgeoisie—even making the improbable assumption this class speaks with a single
voice. Greenberg and Springborg have empirically demonstrated this proposition
in both South Africa and Egypt.[53] And, as Bates has argued, "Politicians want
power. And they use the instruments of the state to secure and retain it by
manipulating the economy to political advantage."[54] Moreover, the suppression
of the RDA in Tanzania is certainly a relevant example of the state exerting its
autonomous power. Even the most totalitarian state is not a monolithic entity but,
rather, a collection of organized repositories of administrative, coercive, and
ideological power. In consequence, however centralized the state appears on
paper, its various organizational components often have lives—not to mention interests, ideologies, traditions, procedures, and practices—of their own resulting
in both independent action and a struggle for dominance within the state.[55] Chapter 6 will explore the role of the Zairian magistrature, an occasionally autonomous
branch of the state.

The state is also an arena, but a special kind of arena. As Samora Machel once
said, "The State is not an eternal and immutable structure."[56] It is without fixed
or constant shape, exists in flux, and may be transformed according to the context of the moment. Perhaps it would be best to envisage the state as an ice hockey arena. Normally the ice is level, the goals are equidistant from the center-ice
line, and both goals are the same width. But the state in Africa, unlike this normal hockey arena, does not maintain its size and shape. Imagine, for example, a
sudden tilt in the ice in favor of one team, or the expansion of one goal mouth
while the other contracts, or the creation of a rippling effect on the ice as one side
tries to skate forward, or, finally, the vast extension of the distance one must skate
even to reach center ice. This is one sense in which the state as an arena changes constantly according to social, political, and economic contexts. Those who
control the state can, and do, alter the nature of the playing field while the game
is underway. The state is protean in another important sense as well. Regardless of the state's present effective shape, people within it will more than likely
perceive its actual contours differently, and these perceptions will also vary
depending on both the specific context and, especially, their placement in the social hierarchy. In the words of one Zairian analyst:

> People at different levels of the society have different views of the State depending
> on where they stand on the social ladder. For the local level . . . the notion that the
> present State is most distinguished by what it takes from peasants [rather] than what
> it gives, as well as by its repeated and unrealized promises, is particularly high.[57]

It is scarcely earthshaking to observe that people ascribe different normative values to their state. Some think it good; others find harsher adjectives. That is
not the point. I wish to advance the related, but somewhat different, idea that
people have varying perceptions of the very nature of the state governing them
regardless of how they evaluate it normatively. This leads me to conclude state
formation is not a process destined to attain a final, predetermined goal but an on-

going process of construction, consolidation, and even, from time to time, collapse. The state's external boundaries may well be fixed by international pressures and legal convention, but the state as an organization designed to fill the political space these territorial frontiers enclose is anything but frozen. Like class and ethnicity, the state is a contextual phenomenon.[58]

The proposition might not sound so bizarre if one considers specific cases. In Nigeria there have been major shifts in the contours of the playing arena since independence in 1960. Parliamentary rule and a three- and then four-state structure gave way to military rule and a twelve- and then nineteen-state structure. In 1979 the soldiers relinquished power to a civilian presidential and federal regime modeled on American lines. This state structure tried to prevent the ethnic tensions responsible for dissolving the polity of the First Republic from recurring. Political parties had to establish offices and a reasonably effective presence in thirteen of the nineteen federal states before the national government would recognize their constitutional legitimacy. Moreover, to be elected on the first ballot, a presidential candidate had to obtain the highest number of votes and "not less than one-quarter of the votes cast at the election in each of at least two-thirds of all the states in the Federation,"[59] a constitutional provision that became crucial in the summer of 1979 as Chief Awolowo unsuccessfully challenged the election of President Shagari on these grounds. Shagari served his first term and won reelection to a second in a bitterly contested election in 1983. But at the end of the year the army again intervened and terminated the second civilian republic.[60] This is not to argue these changes have necessarily been successful at reducing the ease of politicizing ethnicity,[61] but merely to suggest there have been substantial permutations in both rules of the game and shape of the arena.

In Zaire the state arena has also changed dramatically. Although at independence the new state inherited a highly centralized system of rule with a federal and parliamentary overlay, the rapid politicization of ethnicity induced a fragmentation in political and administrative structures. Six provinces became twenty-one as each major ethnic group sought to have its own political bailiwick. After Mobutu seized power he gradually rearranged the structure of the state. He reconsolidated the smaller provinces to eight and progressively depoliticized them by removing their legislatures and instituting state-party rule in 1967. In the 1970s the trend toward centralization continued in several policy areas as the state tried to increase its control throughout society. But by the early 1980s there were once again initiatives to decentralize certain aspects of administrative power.[62]

Depending on the situation, sections of the state acting with their own specific interests in view, members of the politico-commercial bourgeoisie, or the two forces acting in concert may effect such transformations. These changes aid some and hurt others, for they either open up or close off life and mobility chances depending on the shape of the state at any given time.[63] In this sense the state, like class and ethnicity, is a contextual variable, and the process of state formation is part of the triple helix. This triple helix is also the social field in which political actors elaborate and implement strategies of access and dominance.

Strategies of Access and Dominance

Access to, and dominance of, the state is absolutely crucial in much of sub-Saharan Africa, for, as already indicated, political power usually precedes economic power. Contrary to Marx's expectations, therefore, relations of power rather than production appear to determine class relations. Sklar has advanced this thesis in a compelling theoretical argument and stressed the importance of control over the means of consumption and compulsion.[64] Chazan's fine study of Ghana supports this position and notes that "Differences between the top and the bottom of the socioeconomic pyramid have been dictated primarily by access to state power and the control of economic exchange (as opposed to production)."[65] The importance of the state in achieving such control is evident.

Most contemporary African states are lineal descendants of the colonial conquest states imposed during European rule. The apparatus of the state thus evolved from the necessities of instituting and maintaining foreign control in a hostile environment. The colonial state was fashioned to maintain law and order; domination, not development, was the watchword of the day.[66] In addition to its role as gendarme, the colonial state (in conjunction with interested sections of metropolitan capital) shaped the contours of the colonial economy, determined access to resources, and thus had a direct say in deciding who would enjoy opportunities to develop wealth.[67] Because foreign interests controlled the most productive sectors of the local economies, in many cases the colonial state limited opportunities for indigenous capital accumulation and suppressed, or at least discouraged severely, competition from nascent African capitalists. When independence arrived, most economies remained firmly under control of external interests. In general, therefore, the only avenue open to Africans wishing to accumulate wealth and better their positions in life was through advancement in the state structure. Control of the state was a way to acquire substantial economic leverage.[68]

Access to the state remains crucial and its control provides the means to extract resources from the mass of the population—honestly, in the form of taxes, budgetary allocations, and pricing policies, and dishonestly, through corruption, graft, and extortion. Kitching's history of economic change in Kenya masterfully describes how local African elites flocked to Local Native Councils and used the resources of these state institutions to improve their own economic standing—a pattern that remains.[69] Similarly, and on the seamier side of the equation, a recent study of political graft and the spoils system in Zambia concludes the state is a resource in itself. Those with high-level access to the Zambian state receive not only their salaries, but also subsidized housing, medical allowances, and small loans for automobiles and refrigerators. In addition, larger loans are available for those seeking venture capital to enter business or farming. To be sure, the state extracted this wealth from the workers, peasants, and miners who produced it, and there is no reason to assume this transfer of resources was painless.[70] Certainly, as we shall see repeatedly, in Zaire the transfer of wealth from farmers and townspeople to the state is often vicious and oppressive.[71]

Dominance of the state is also important for it enables political leaders to renegotiate the terms of access to African resources granted to multinational corporations (MNC). Langdon's thoughtful study of the multinational corporation in Kenya's political economy discerns the emergence of a "comfortable symbiosis" between those who control the state and representatives of the MNC sector.[72]

> The benefits of symbiosis are shared: in the form of resources for the state, which helps the dominant African class which is dependent on the state for capital accumulation; in the form of direct resources for that class, through high salaries, directorships, shareholdings, partnerships, subcontracting opportunities and, the evidence suggests, some illicit favours; and in the form of bargaining advantages and market privileges for the multinations [sic], based on the informal political influence symbiosis generates. For the M.N.C. sector, the crucial reality is that symbiosis keeps it relatively unconstrained by government regulation.[73]

These observations concerning Kenya could be replicated almost verbatim and applied to many African countries. With only slight changes they would certainly hold true for Zaire. I wish to emphasize, however, that a facile application of crude dependency theory is usually unwarranted. Most states are certainly dependent, but nevertheless enjoy considerable latitude and room for maneuver within the broad structural constraints the international system imposes. The Mobutus and arap Mois are not puppets on a string; their position, and that of the states they represent, is more akin to one of dependent autonomy.[74] It is crucial to note the state provides the means to elaborate this "comfortable symbiosis," and the dominant politico-commercial bourgeoisie thus uses its control of the structures of the state to extract resources from the international system. But here, too, we should not assume this process is "neutral" or without costs. The costs to the state, depending on the particular context, might well be a form of indenture to international capital in the form of skyrocketing indebtedness, or the imposition of personnel from the International Monetary Fund (IMF) to set the state's finances aright, or a currency devaluation which, in most cases, burdens the poor most heavily. Zaire is an extreme example of a state whose leaders have mortgaged its economic future to continue their comfortable symbiosis with external sources of wealth.

The economic history of colonial rule and the subsequent emergence of a politico-commercial bourgeoisie firmly rooted in state power does not necessarily preclude the parallel development of an indigenous and economically productive bourgeoisie which owns and controls the means of production, but it does make this outcome more difficult to achieve and much less probable. Leys and Swainson now argue that such a bourgeoisie exists in Kenya—a position Langdon and Kaplinsky debate vigorously.[75]

The broad outlines of a similar debate are also taking shape over the nature of the bourgeoisie in Zaire. Janet MacGaffey has found there is, at least in parts of the country, a small number of substantial business owners who form a commercial middle class that is becoming a sector of the dominant class. These individuals do not hold political office and are relatively independent of political influence.[76] MacGaffey is doubtlessly correct concerning the rise of an independent class of entrepreneurs without significant attachment to, or contact with, the state—a phenomenon certainly not limited to Zaire.[77] Moreover, there may well be an inverse relationship between the health of the state and the existence of this class of independent businesspeople. As the state declines, independent entrepreneurial figures who operate beyond the state's reach (in what analysts now call the second or informal economy) emerge to fill the void. Although the aggregate economic weight of such informal networks can be considerable, their activities most often emphasize the provision of needed commodities and essential services, such as food and transportation, when the state can no longer furnish them. Second economies permit survival but do not usually stimulate creative and wealth-producing industrial investments. In any event, in both Kenya and Zaire this sort of bourgeoisie remains small and relatively unimportant politically. Furthermore, even should an economically productive bourgeoisie spring forth from the second economy, a close alliance with those who control the state is almost certainly in its long-term interests. For if this bourgeoisie fails to do so, the state may review licenses, quotas, taxes, and other regulatory measures to its detriment.[78] By way of example, in the 1970s one of Lisala's few relatively independent merchants was considering a political career and probably believed he would have fewer economic options without easy access to the state.[79] He was also perhaps aware the Zairian state's then-difficult period of decline could some day change. In short, given the inverse relationship between state and second economy, I strongly suspect if now-weak states such as Zaire are eventually revitalized, they will move to bring their burgeoning informal sectors under tight government control. I offer one word of caution, however. We should not necessarily assume a weak or declining state is a prerequisite for the existence of a second economy. Strong states, the Soviet Union for example, may well tolerate such informal networks if the governments are either unable or unwilling to provide certain economic services.

Ethnicity, like class, has to be considered in any attempt to treat complex strategies of access and domination. It has long been known that states may shape ethnicity. Southall convincingly demonstrates that Luhya ethnicity in Kenya emerged during the colonial period and was "closely linked to the colonial administrative framework, being in effect based upon and in part suggested by the administrative and territorial framework of North Kavirondo District."[80] In other words, colonial administrative imperatives coincided with the needs of people to coalesce around wider bases of identity to mobilize politically in a more efficacious quest for resources. This is an example of the formation of ethnic groups from the bottom up, based largely on administrative boundaries and using them as a convenience. States could also create ethnicity from the top down. Brett's seminal study of East Africa shows the British, guided by their policy of indirect rule, often fabricated ethnic groups so they could then delegate administrative authority to their newly named "chiefs." Furthermore, the colonial power had to maintain the resulting "traditionalism" because it was a major source of the regime's political and social control.[81] The colonial state, then, provided both an arena and an implement for the creation, consolidation, and politicization of ethnicity. This was especially true in Zaire where the colonial state forbade the formation of political parties but tolerated elitist cultural organizations constructed around ethnic identities.

Ethnicity may also arise in opposition to the state, especially when a group feels excluded from benefits the state has to offer and thus relatively disadvantaged. In Ethiopia the emperor's social policy dealt with the national (ethnic) question by subjecting most of the population to Amharization. Voluminous rhetoric not-withstanding, the state did little to provide those who rejected Amharization with social services or occasions to improve their lives. This association of the state with a single ethnic group, the Amhara, eventually provoked a reaction from the Oromo who succeeded in coalescing support from Oromo in all regions and so-cial classes in a cultural organization, *Mecha Tuloma*. The goal of this unit was to promote Oromo identity and to ameliorate their position in relation to the Am-hara, and Amharaized, who completely dominated the state. The Oromo move-ment successfully politicized ethnicity and precipitated an extended period of armed struggle pitting Oromo guerrillas against the Ethiopian state during the 1960s. Needless to say, other groups (Somalis, Tigreans, Eritreans) also felt ex-cluded from, and threatened by, an exclusively Amharaized state and reacted with equal violence.[82]

The Nande in Zaire had a different, and much less violent, reaction to exclusion. Prolonged and determined resistance to colonial rule coupled with poor education-al facilities in their area effectively excluded them from the lower levels of the colonial civil service. In consequence, when the Belgians departed rapidly in 1960, they were not strategically placed to move into powerful positions within the state. The Nande thus found themselves cut off from sources of both politi-cal and educational advancement under the First Republic. Their reaction has been to promote their own development through trade and agriculture—a feat per-formed with some success.[83] Nevertheless, their absence from the political hierar-chy is likely to have a deleterious effect on their long-term chances to accumulate capital.

For those who already control the state, maintenance of power often becomes a full-time task accomplished through several different, and not necessarily mutual-ly exclusive, strategies. These include, but are not limited to, a policy of alliance and co-optation of ethnic and regional leaders, repression and coercion, and ideological obfuscation.[84] Cameroon's Ahmadou Ahidjo was a master of ethnic co-optation. After the death of long-time opposition leader Ruben Um Nyobe, Ahidjo brought the Bassa into his conservative coalition by cleverly negotiating the co-optation of Mayi Matip. Once inside the regime's alliance, Ahidjo progres-sively isolated the erstwhile Bassa spokesman, thus neutering him politically. More generally, however, Ahidjo shrewdly associated the country's ethnic leaders with his regime, and these "barons" supervised life in their native communities on the president's behalf. Ambitious politicians also knew credibility as ethnic barons enhanced possibilities for success; some aspiring cabinet members actively created, or recreated, ethnicities to promote their own political advancement. The result, until the attempted coup of April 1984, was a regime of remarkable political durability.[85]

Mobutu is also a master of ethnic alliance and co-optation. The lengthy presence of Nguza Karl-i-Bond in the highest reaches of the polity assured Shabans that one of their own was close to the source of power. Similarly, even after Kamitatu-Massamba had written two books excoriating Mobutu, the president was willing and able to lure him back to Kinshasa with the offer of a ministry. Mobutu has always made sure former First Republic politicians like Kamitatu receive some of the Second Republic's plums.[86]

In these situations, then, the regime brings ethnic leaders such as Mayi Matip, or others whom it hopes will "represent" ethnic or regional sentiments, into the state to share its rewards. This argument does not preclude Sklar's hypothesis that ethnicity tends to result from the politicization of demands in the interests of the new men of power or aspirant bourgeoisies; it merely notes shrewd rulers will seek to ally the class interests of these potential ethnic mobilizers to their own by granting access to the state, thus decapitating and demobilizing potential ethnic trouble spots.[87] Markakis is therefore correct to argue "ethnicity is a factor whose weight serves, more often than not, to bulwark class and factional privilege, rather than comprehensive ethnic goals."[88] Had Haile Selassie pursued this strategy of co-optation and alliance, one wonders how historians would have written the story of Ethiopia's last fifteen years.

None of this excludes the possibility that, at times, those controlling the state will find it prudent to manipulate ethnicity in ways which affect both leaders and masses. Educational and occupational hiring quotas can be potent political tools when the state consciously deploys them. Excluded groups may come to identify themselves as disadvantaged ethnic minorities and perceive the state arena in ethnic rather than class terms. One result of this configuration would be ethnic resentment, and probably conflict, over access to the state and its rewards.

In Zaire most ordinary folk, and many educated individuals as well, believe an inner circle of rulers from Equateur dominates the state. Popular expressions such as "Nazareth," "Bethlehem," and "holy land" designate the *Mobutiste* Equateur heartland in daily conversation. Although this perception of a regime of, by, and for Equateurians is far too simplistic, people nevertheless think their lives are miserable and they have nothing because the state pours its resources into this one region.[89] The first quotation in epigraph speaks to this perception, as does another observation which would probably meet with unqualified agreement in most of Zaire.

And to top off everything, the gap being dug each day between the province of Equateur (Mobutu's region of origin, called Jerusalem) and the other provinces of Zaire is most poignant. The Province of Equateur, principally the modern city of Gbadolite, empties the others of their wealth. The others live with a penury of food (tons of meat, potatoes and other vegetables from Kivu are sent each week in military cargoes to Gbadolite). The Province of Equateur consists of the most beautiful cities in the Republic, roads freshly redone (without holes, like everywhere else in Zaire), factories (which work, unfortunately, at a loss), brand new hospitals, decent housing.[90]

Similarly, a Zairian academician from Kivu listened in nodding agreement to my tales of exploitation in the hinterland until I mentioned most of my findings came from the area around Lisala. At that moment he became so skeptical he could scarcely contain his incredulity. To be sure, this image of a flourishing, economically vibrant Equateur is, with the exception of Gbadolite, incorrect. But Zairians living in Kasai and Kivu need to know villagers in Equateur live in the same lamentable squalor they do—a squalor induced by politico-economic structures inherited from colonialism which rulers manipulate consciously to produce a desired result: wealth for the few at the expense of the many. Because of this widespread but erroneous image, opposition to the state could assume an ethnic and, given Zaire's culturally plural composition, necessarily fragmented visage.

Those who control the state can orchestrate ethnicity, but this does not mean that ethnicity lacks analytic independence as an explanatory variable. Although ethnic antagonism and conflict may come to the fore as part of an overall strategy of state dominance, as part of a strategy of upward mobility, or as a basis of intraclass competition for scarce resources, the distinct possibility nonetheless exists that things will fall apart. Politicized ethnicity might well be an ideology as Leys suggests,[91] but it is an ideology fraught with meaning and importance for most of us. If ethnic manipulations get out of hand or if those who dominate the state lose control, it is possible a violent ethnic tide will sweep away the state and its rulers. From this perspective, the task of statecraft is to keep ethnicity at bay.

Repression and state-induced violence is one way to insure that this does not happen, and many African leaders willingly unleash their armed forces on internal "enemies." In addition, most African states have political police apparatuses that provide information concerning trouble spots and troublemakers. Moreover, while the Amins, Bokassas, and Macias Nguemas will employ terror to remain in power, in one sense a resort to these methods indicates statecraft has already failed and the wool is being progressively lifted from peoples' eyes. Coercion of this sort seems to gain prominence as political legitimacy erodes. This is certainly true in Zaire, as chapters 3 and 4 will show.

State-induced repressive violence and fear are not the only means of channeling ethnic sentiments. In Cameroon, ethnicity pervades every aspect of social life. Nevertheless, Cameroon—like so many African states—has tried to drive ethnicity underground, and the only area of Cameroonian life where it finds overt expression is sports, most particularly soccer. Soccer teams are openly and proudly vaunted as "our sons" or the "sons of the soil." Most major ethnic groups have their own team whose backers passionately follow its fortunes, and violent altercations between partisans of rival teams occur periodically. When, in 1970, an administrative fiat of the minister of sports reduced the number of teams, the outcry was such that Ahidjo had to intervene personally to quash the measure. In this case, therefore, the state channeled overt ethnic sentiment into the safety valve of soccer. This, too, is a method of state control and manipulation of ethnic iden-tity.[92]

Yet another means of maintaining control of the state is through the propaga-tion of ideologies. Dominance is most easily achieved and most effectively im-plemented when people accept and internalize the state's ideological myths. Given the artificial and culturally plural nature of most African countries, it is not surpris-ing African leaders almost universally embrace ideologies of nationalism and na-tion-building. Briefly put, those who control the state incessantly preach the main task of all citizens is to build the nation. In addition, and as a corollary, nation-al leaders regard any subnational identity, including ethnicity, as a threat to na-tion-building and thus illegitimate. There is, then, an explicitly articulated hostility toward any subnational identification, even though much research has shown ordinary citizens perceive no conflict whatever between their national and ethnic identities. Chazan reports "Ghanaian youth see little or no conflict or con-tradiction between their local, ethnic or state identities"—a finding Kofele-Kale supports with respect to Cameroon.[93]

The Zairian state does not permit open discussion of ethnic identity and has outlawed ethnic associations. Other states have also banned the overt expression of ethnicity. As early as 1959, CAR passed a law prohibiting the use of ethnic terms; Sierra Leone has banned all mention of ethnic identities in official docu-ments since 1968; and, during the Acheampong regime, Ghanaian leaders banished the word "tribe" from government documents because they believed its use would detract from national unity. They also discouraged the use of ethnic group names as surnames and advocated an end to the practice of ethnically distinctive facial markings.[94] The Second Nigerian Republic's constitutional changes represented an effort to render overt ethnicity obsolete, or at least less than legitimate, thus institutionalizing the idea of "One Nigeria." Similarly, shortly after seizing power in 1969, Somalia's Siad Barre abolished clan identity by legislative ukase. But this subnational identity, like many others, proved particularly resistant to legalis-tic extirpation. Ingenious Somalis simply began referring to their "ex-clan" rather than to their clan. Furthermore, while Barre adeptly balances clans in distribut-ing offices, it remains an indictable offense to acknowledge this publicly.[95]

This is not to say the state is unaware of ethnicity—far from it; when the state desires to employ ethnicity for its own purposes through, for example, occupa-tional or educational quotas, it usually does so on a geographic or regional basis.[96] In this way it is possible to maintain the facade of "allegiance to the mystique of the national State."[97] There are thus times when, paradoxically, the state will wish to use ethnicity and suppress it simultaneously.

The appeal to nationalism and nation-building is merely one means of camouflaging the politico-commercial bourgeoisie's specific interests behind a broader and more widely accepted symbolic construct. While discussing educa-tion and its role in the process of class formation and reproduction in Tanzania, Samoff remarks that classes seek "to fashion the institutions of the state to reflect their interests. Day-to-day management is much simpler when these institutions themselves screen out challenges and cloak their decisions favouring the ruling class with the legitimacy of apparently universal norms."[98] Abner Cohen's study of the Creole state elite in Sierra Leone convincingly elaborates this interplay of particularistic interests and universal norms. Creoles, a small and particularistic elite, have legitimized their status by assuming universalistic tasks—in this case, by manning the institutions of the Sierra Leone state. Over the last generation Creoles have transformed themselves from an ethnic minority group into a state elite that guards "the authority structure of the State by upholding the independence of the judiciary, the neutrality of the civil service, free opposition, free expression, and free competition between rival political groups." Since Creoles dominate the judiciary and professional civil service, it is difficult to distinguish between their universally legitimate tasks as state officials and any private interests they may have. In upholding the sanctity and "neutrality" of the state, they are, in fact, furthering their own interests and insuring their continued dominance. Furthermore, aspects of Creole culture thoroughly pervade the national symbols which form the state as symbolic construct. Thus, should one attack, or merely question, certain symbols perpetuating Creole dominance of the state, one would also be attacking the idea of the Sierra Leone nation.[99]

Other ideological motifs legitimize, or at least make slightly more palatable, some nastier aspects of political life in Africa. One image which recurs in several locations is father of the family. As we shall see in chapter 5, President Mobutu enjoys casting himself as father of the large Zairian family. Since a family can have but one father and his word and decisions are supreme, by definition there is room for neither competition nor dissent. "Father" is not an elective office, and children do not question their father's wisdom for they know he has their best interests at heart whatever he decides. Mobutu and other members of the politico-commercial bourgeoisie have consciously adopted these metaphors. Hardly ~unique to Zaire, the same paternal imagery appears in other countries. In the wake of an abortive coup in 1964 the late Léon Mba once said, "I have been called the father of the Gabonese country, now this father is reflecting in order to define what he must do in favor of his family, in favor of his sons, certain of whom have gone astray. All that I can tell you is that he will decide as a father, with firmness, but with justice."[100] Political leaders can thus portray stern measures taken against segments of the population as paternal discipline rather than political repression.

The same images permeate political discourse elsewhere, most notably in Ivory Coast, Togo, and CAR. Houphouet, Eyadema, and Bokassa have also enjoyed the role of self-styled father of a large national family.[101] In Cameroon, Bayart reminds us, this type of paternal discourse has roots in both precolonial and colonial patterns of political dominance and subservience, but today masks a new political subjugation. In his words, "In the eyes of the social elite, Cameroonians are children and virtually fools"—children as long as they obey and, failing that, commit only small errors; fools when their "childishness" leads them to join the *maquis* or engage in violence against the regime of their "parents."[102]

Leys observed a related phenomenon in Kenya. While Kenyatta was alive he would receive delegations from districts and ethnic groups which would arrive with gifts and declarations of loyalty at the ready. This "court system" reemphasized the ethnic aspect of Kenyan politics, reinforced the president's distributional powers (or at least called attention to them), and enabled Kenyatta to assume the mantle of the father of the nation for all to see.[103] This type of court system goes hand in hand with the development of a paternal ideology and with the centralization and personalization of power—both widespread trends. In Cameroon, as in other regimes, the state has not only been centralized, but personalized and presidentialized as well.[104] In Zaire, no less than in Kenya, Cameroon, Ivory Coast, CAR, Togo, and Gabon, the power of the state flows from the presidency where the father of the national family holds court.[105]

Vansina reminds us one task of ideology is to maintain political quiescence by masking subordination, and presumably exploitation, to preclude revolt. In this regard, the lineage ideology of precolonial Equatorial Africa, based on kinship and thus perceived as "natural," was particularly effective.[106] As we shall see subsequently, this insight helps explain the broad appeal of the images of father and family as important elements of contemporary state ideology. A second task is to help erect and consolidate an economically privileged class. Before the colonial era, lineage ideology justified why some had more authority and wealth than others. Those at the bottom of the social hierarchy, the youth, believed they would one day become elders and therefore gain access to political authority and economic advantage. But many youths never scaled the social ladder, for elders changed genealogies as part of the struggle for power and dominance.[107] If those who control the state can successfully foster a belief in upward mobility, for one's children even if not for oneself, there are powerful psychological incentives for going along with the system. Although workers in Lubumbashi are aware of their exploitation, they nonetheless remain politically passive, hoping their children will some day be able to escape from their situation.[108] In Lisala, virtually all those interviewed, however lowly their station, had exactly the same extremely unrealistic hopes for their offspring.[109]

These ideologies, regardless of variant, preserve access to the state's rewards by maintaining some combination of political quiescence, social submissiveness, passive resignation, or popular acceptance of the prevailing political situation. As such, they are class actions and closure mechanisms to insure increased access to life and mobility chances for some, while systematically restricting them for others.[110]

Conclusion

This chapter argues we may understand the state in much of sub-Saharan Africa both as an organization particularly susceptible to domination by a social class and as a contextual phenomenon. In this latter sense the state, like social class and ethnicity, is a shifting, flexible, and intermittent phenomenon engaged in a continuous process of formation, consolidation, and—in more than one current case—dissolution or disintegration. Contemporary African social dynamics may be best explored by probing the triple-stranded helix of state, class, and ethnicity, and many specific sociopolitical outcomes result from interactions between these three contextual phenomena. In a chapter of this size one cannot cover all possible variations. Instead, by highlighting strategies of dominance and access to the state and its resources, I have indicated some possible directions such an analysis might take. Each strand of the triple helix contributes its part to the whole, and the overall picture should be familiar to students of politics in Africa. Simply put, the aim of most strategies of access and dominance is, first, to insure the politico-commercial bourgeoisie's continued dominance of the state and its considerable economic rewards through the maintenance of political quiescence; second, to prevent the emergence of unified, cohesive, and organized social classes at the bottom of the sociopolitical hierarchy; and, third, to preclude the mobilization of ethnic challenges either to the integrity of the state or to the power of its rulers.

We should probably view the triple helix of state, class, and ethnicity against the prevalent background conditions of insecurity and scarcity. Several observers believe ethnicity and insecurity vary directly. Leys, for example, notes ethnicity "consists in the fact that people identify other exploited people as the source of their insecurity and frustrations."[111] In addition, Mwabila finds workers in Lubumbashi seek refuge in their ethnic identities and contacts as a way to cope with the harsh realities of daily life.[112] On a more individual level, people often shift ethnic identities as a response to scarcity and insecurity as Obbo demonstrates in her examination of the Nubianization of Ugandan women.[113] In addition, ethnicity emerges as a salient reference point when conditions of insecurity and scarcity force members of the same social class to compete with each other for scarce resources. Lisala's bar owners thus mobilize ethnic support to obtain beer during periods of shortage.[114] MacGaffey found a similar pattern in Kisangani where businesspeople use their ethnic contacts to get access to goods in any quantity.[115]

In contradistinction, there is some reason to believe social class identity, particularly at lower levels of the hierarchy, varies inversely with insecurity and scarcity. Mwabila's Zairian workers, for example, do not cope with insecurity and scarcity by forging a working-class organization or seizing control of their union but, rather, by identifying with the fate of individual employers—with their firms.[116]

An important reason for pervasive scarcity in Zaire, and much of Africa, is the colonial heritage of extraverted monocrop and single-mineral economies coupled with their resulting dependence on the price of these commodities on the world market. But by no stretch of the imagination should recognition of these constraints imply that African states and their rulers are merely puppets reacting to conditions completely beyond their control. A good measure of the prevalent scarcity, particularly in the peasant sector, is the product of the dominant class organization, the state. Scarcity, furthermore, is often in the interests of the politico-commercial bourgeoisie and an aid to it in preserving its power. Many states, for example, have imposed agricultural pricing policies that drain resources from rural areas so their cities might eat.[117] Urban quiescence is often a sine qua non of continued rule for the politico-commercial bourgeoisie.

Insecurity is also a product of the state. The state's coercive arms leave uncertainty, fear, and occasionally terror in their wake as they perform their daily tasks in the countryside. Since much of the state's business in these locales is coercion, the next two chapters will examine some of the Zairian state's sinews of coercive power.

3

The State as Ear

Information, Coercion, and the Political Police

The protection of persons and their property is one of the essential tasks of the authorities of a nation. In this sector, despite the efforts furnished, much remains to be done, as has been repeated on several occasions by the authorized representatives of the public powers themselves. We note cases of kidnapping, arbitrary arrest, settling of scores and even torture, without speaking of thefts and other unpleasant occurrences.

—A. Kaseba, President of the Episcopal Conference of Zaire[1]

[I]f there is one thing working very well in Zaire it is the security police.

—Nguza Karl-i-Bond[2]

Bishop Kaseba attests eloquently and courageously to the insecurity of persons and property prevalent in contemporary Zaire. Behind this litany of abuse is the assumption that the state itself is largely responsible for such lamentable events. Since this book treats the state as a congeries of organized repositories of administrative, coercive, and ideological power and focuses on the behavior and appearance of the state at the local level, attention falls naturally on one of the state's main coercive arms, the political police. The Centre National de Documentation (CND),[3] Zaire's ubiquitous political police, compounds the insecurity ordinary people feel as they struggle to cope with the harsh and consistently deteriorating conditions of daily life.[4] If, as suggested earlier, Mobutu's quest for regime stability and political security contributes to pervasive personal insecurity among the citizenry, it becomes important to examine how the rulers of the *Mobutiste* state seek to reduce their own insecurity by strengthening the state's repressive arms and to explore any subsequent effects such actions might foster. But the CND does more than engage in the abuses cited in the first epigraph; it is also the state's ear and a key source of political, social, economic, and cultural information on life in the hinterland. Attention to the state's more general search for information thus becomes necessary and will lead us to consider the concept of surveillance. The second epigraph also furnishes food for thought since Nguza is not alone in believing the CND is perhaps the sole arm of the Zairian state that operates effectively. Is the CND truly an island of efficiency in an ocean of corruption, incompetence, and pervasive state decline? We shall see.

This chapter explores two sinews of the state. First, I shall discuss internal communications, for those who rule need timely and accurate political, social, and economic information. A short case study of the state's attempts to monitor and restrict the flow of weapons throughout the country will illustrate the problems involved. Gun control is an important and overlooked aspect of politics in Africa— especially since access to, and control of, the means of coercion is a significant factor in the dynamics of state power and social class formation. In Zaire it is all the more crucial since the state's leaders have no desire to relive the First Republic's political and military turbulence.

Second, I shall examine the CND's history and organization, as well as its various tasks. Although its violations of fundamental human rights receive much publicity and are increasingly well documented, its less notorious activities are of equal importance and pass almost unnoticed. Data on the CND's information-gathering activities will further illustrate the importance of processes of communications to the state. Because the CND is secretive and performs politically sensitive tasks, there are inevitable difficulties in obtaining documentation. In consequence, the picture sketched here will have to be both partial and tentative. I shall, however, place the CND in wider perspective by comparing it to similar organizations elsewhere.

Communications and Surveillance

In speculating on the origins of states, Giddens argues the storage of certain authoritative resources is usually of greater significance than the production of a surplus. States accomplish such storage through surveillance or activities involving "the collation of information relevant to state control of the conduct of its subject population, and the direct supervision of that conduct." This process is a vital element in the generation of state power.[5] Although such information-gathering activities occur in all contemporary states, Zaire's legacy of political turmoil has decisively conditioned these processes. We should view surveillance in Zaire both in Giddens's sense, as a means of gathering and storing information necessary to exert control and supervision, and as a means of constant reassurance to a psychologically insecure politico-commercial bourgeoisie.

The Zairian notion of vigilance subsumes both senses of surveillance. One learned disquisition, citing President Mobutu, defined vigilance as:

keen attention, sustained surveillance, exercised on all elements susceptible of making an attempt, from near or far, from the interior or exterior, on the life or survival of the State, its basic institutions, or its organs. Vigilance must lead the masses to unmask the enemies of the fatherland in their physiognomical changes and, in all their forms, to seek them out in their lair [*repère*], to master them and to smother their calling to destruction, anarchy, and trouble.[6]

The essay then distinguishes between passive vigilance exercised on oneself and active vigilance directed toward the environment and others.[7] Zairian political authorities repeatedly request active vigilance from all citizens. Thus, when a new subregional commissioner arrived in Mongala, he exhorted party militants to "denounce those citizens who will try, by subversive maneuvers, to cast doubt on the work executed by the authorities in the framework of the party."[8] But state officials are not content merely to encourage the population to greater levels of vigilance. Authorities, even at lower levels of the administrative hierarchy, seek to supplement active vigilance through various means. By way of example, Lisala's collectivity chief hired forty "militant informers" to unearth "irregularities" in the Cité.[9] Needless to say, the chief did not reveal the identities of these "militant informers" to the general public.

Surveillance activities occur not only when the regime is visibly threatened, as during Shaba I and II, but also when the *Mobutiste* state is secure and reasonably well entrenched. Even during these periods of state ascension, the legacy of regime insecurity inherited from the First Republic conditions the rulers of the Second. Internal reports, correspondence, and memoranda indicate Zairian leaders have generally perceived their hold on power as politically insecure. Mobutu, for example, has always been concerned with the peregrinations of politicians who made their mark in the era before his coup. Although many were initially co-opted into the structures of the new regime, their behavior was still a constant concern. The regional suzerain of Mongala Subregion had been Jean Bolikango, erstwhile leader of the Parti de l'Unité National. A politician known and loved in Lisala, Bolikango's frequent trips to this region were watched and reported—even while he was serving in the MPR Political Bureau. Rumors, invariably inaccurate, dealing with Bolikango's alleged actions on these visits, usually made their way back to the capital and caught the attention of central authorities who would then ask local territorial administrators to confirm their veracity. Although these tales were entirely without foundation, the regime feared that Bolikango, and presumably others like him, would seek to reassert their popularity and prestige in their ethnic bailiwicks and thus foment ethnic solidarity.[10]

The need for reassurance that all is well and the regime unthreatened surfaces clearly whenever the president is abroad. During these periods all territorial administrators must operate their radio, telex, and telegraph services around the clock. A demand that the party's youth wing, the Jeunesse du Mouvement Populaire de la Révolution (JMPR), patrol every night and maintain a high and constant level of vigilance usually accompanies this order.[11] Mobutu knows coups often occur when African heads of state are abroad, and prudence is thus the order of the day. This need for reassurance also asserts itself at other times. On taking control of the political affairs department in 1972,[12] the new state commissioner (minister) informed territorial administrators they would henceforth have to wire twice-daily reports on the general political, social, and economic situations in their administrative units, as well as indicate any criminal incidents. The state commissioner required such reports even if there were nothing noteworthy to remark.[13] But the state's insistence on surveillance is most visible when it attempts, at times franticly, to elicit information from the hinterland.

The impressive communications infrastructure the Belgians once erected to consolidate and centralize colonial rule has eroded substantially since independence.[14] Today Zaire's vast territory enjoys only the most rudimentary communications facilities. In consequence, authorities at all administrative levels often complain that subordinates do not forward requested information. This has been a serious problem since the early years of the Mobutu regime and local archives are littered with angry letters from administrative superiors demanding to know why subordinates have never furnished reports, data, and other documents. In February 1968 the vice minister of the interior expressed these concerns in a letter to regional commissioners: "The present case is but one example of a thousand for which I never receive an answer; I should also cite the case of the annual interior affairs reports, the census, and the budgetary estimates for your administrative units. All my letters addressed to you on these subjects have never been followed up despite numerous reminders."[15]

Most calls for information concern reports and dossiers bureaucrats are, in theory, supposed to file regularly. Although these routine matters date from the colonial period and territorial administrators draw them up according to long-established and well-known guidelines, there is usually much delay. In December 1970, for example, an official at the regional capital (Mbandaka) reminded all subregional and zone commissioners they would have to provide their annual reports for *both* 1969 and 1970 in the near future. Failing that, he wrote, there would be no vacations.[16] Appeals to the professional conscience of officials farther down the administrative hierarchy usually follow when such warnings fall on deaf ears. Thus, when the 1970 reports still had not appeared at Mbandaka by mid-January 1971, the same official reminded his subordinates "the nontransmission of your reports halts centralization and calls us to the attention of the central authorities. This message constitutes a last warning."[17] When such relatively mild calls fail to elicit the necessary documentation, the reminders take on an angry tone and threaten disciplinary action. "No delay will be tolerated and will result in disciplinary measures"; "I shall not hesitate to open a disciplinary action against laggards"; and "I shall unhappily envisage sanctions against authorities who fail," are common refrains.[18]

These same difficulties characterize the flow of communications in the MPR. In August 1974, Equateur's regional commissioner reminded his subregional commissioners they were supposed to send their reports on the party before the monthly meeting of the MPR regional committee.[19] Such delays exist throughout the hierarchy and are the rule rather than the exception. In June 1975, Mongala's subregional commissioner castigated the zone commissioner of Bumba because the latter's monthly MPR report was thirty-five days late.[20] But lags of merely one month are not unusual. The gap between the initial request for information, or a report, may often be longer than six months—even for supposedly routine documents. At the extreme, some officials may take more than a year to respond to a query, and threats of disciplinary action and criticism of "guilty inertia" do not speed up matters in the least.[21]

There are several explanations why even ordinary reports and information do not scale the administrative hierarchy expeditiously. First, there are the inadequacies of Zaire's communications network. On receiving a letter castigating him for failure to supply a report on time, Mongala's subregional commissioner claimed the delay occurred because "The Zone of Mobayi-Mbongo does not have easy contact with the subregion. Ordinary mail and telegraphic messages undergo a considerable delay. The telegraphic service hardly functions; the mail service is inexistent. These are the real difficulties that the administration of the interior knows—indicated many times—that we deplore."[22] Absence of, or deficiencies in, telephone and telegraph service is most acute for rural collectivities. Zone and subregional commissioners complain it is especially difficult to get information from these distant base units of local administration.[23] Second is the ever-present problem of transportation. Many bureaucrats who need to file reports are unable to obtain information from the countryside because they cannot get there. This was one of the most frequent complaints of Lisala's administrators: "Yes there was a service car but it was stolen. There was an accident and the garage boss told us that it was completely totaled. Now he uses it for his personal vehicle."[24] Questions of corruption aside, lack of vehicles and poor to nonexistent roads often make information-gathering expeditions impossible.

A third reason for delays in compiling and expediting reports concerns certain bureaucratic practices the national authorities have mandated. The Mobutu regime requires politico-administrative officials such as zone and subregional commissioners to serve outside their regions of origin and subjects them to frequent rotation. Inevitably, then, territorial officials arriving at a new post need some time to become familiar with the local situation. These frequent periods of readjustment and acclimation contribute to the lag in transmitting reports of all kinds.[25] Finally, there is the simple and universal problem of human failing. The case of an assistant zone commissioner in one of Mongala's outlying zones illustrates the point. Authorities reported the official's death and, inevitably and understandably, consternation ensued as those at higher levels tried to find out what had happened. After many messages, the subregional commissioner discovered this untimely demise had been the result of a careless telegraph operator who had transposed some words and dropped a sentence from a message. It took some time before the confusion cleared.[26]

A related but no less important problem results when these four factors—inadequate transportation, poor communications facilities, bureaucratic rotation, and incompetent officials—repeatedly confront insistent demands for reports, information, and data. Under such circumstances, especially when there are threats of disciplinary action, bureaucrats often resort to the fudge factor. A territorial official with wide-ranging experience at the collectivity level reasoned this way: "Suppose, for example, Mbandaka asks us to furnish, before the fifteenth of the month, the exact number of five year old children. We still send in a figure, but it is not real. Often enough the information is whimsical."[27]

In a general, diffuse way, the difficulties Zairian officials experience obtaining information from the hinterland heightens their insecurity because, if they cannot maintain surveillance, a threat to their continued dominance might arise. Some examples cited above do not speak specifically to questions of power and security. The quest for information is, after all, constant across social, political, economic, and demographic fields, and any regime needs knowledge of societal conditions if it is to govern. Nevertheless, the Zairian state's inability to provide even basic background information and timely routine reports almost surely helps create conditions in which the regime's legacy of political insecurity develops into a pervasive and permanent feature of the world view of Zaire's rulers. But, on certain issues, the regime's incessant demands for data may be directly and explicitly linked to its leaders' perceptions of power, control, and security.

Gun Control

The Mobutu regime's constant concern with unauthorized and unregistered firearms throughout the country is a dual legacy of the colonial and First Republic eras. Belgian rule made it all but impossible for ordinary Zairians to possess guns, for the colonial state obviously did not want to permit Zairians to own weapons they could turn on their masters. To be sure, Zairians in the colonial army, the Force Publique, bore arms, but even they may not have always had ammunition.[28] With regard to the First Republic, the memory of private armies and widespread rebellion is too fresh to forget. In 1968 the regime's leaders decided there were too many unauthorized weapons in the country, and, in consequence, they limited the right to bear arms to soldiers and police. Members of the political police, territorial administrators (zone commissioners), and prison guards would henceforth receive authorization to have weapons, only if the interior minister agreed arms were necessary for their jobs. All previous authorizations were declared invalid; only the interior minister could grant new ones.[29]

At about that time, therefore, the interior minister requested territorial administrators to begin a census of all firearms. The initial letter noted the "importance and particularly urgent character of the present instruction."[30] Despite the minister's desire for rapid results, these instructions were not sent to Equateur's zone and subregional commissioners for more than a month. When finally dispatched, the cover letter again stressed the importance of this task and provided the relevant forms.[31] Officials in the hinterland did not respond, and a reminder was sent out in September 1968.[32] A second reminder followed in February 1969, with a third the next month. The March letter emphasized that zone commissioners should include in the census even old hunting rifles (*fusils à piston*), owned by many in the region.[33] By May 1969 only six of twenty-three zones in the region had provided the necessary documents. Further memory fresheners, each worded more severely than the last, were sent out in June and August 1969.[34] Finally, in April 1970, almost two years to the day from the first request for a census of firearms in Equateur, the bureaucrat in charge of the matter finally threw up his hands. Less than half the region's zones had completed the firearms count, and six scathing bureaucratic reminders had failed to elicit the required information.[35]

Despite the regime's inability to achieve the registration of all firearms in this particular instance, the concern and desire have remained constant. In 1973 the state commissioner for political affairs issued a lengthy questionnaire covering most aspects of social and political life to guide territorial administrators on their inspection tours. The detailed attention devoted to firearms in the countryside is striking. There were fifteen questions on this subject: Where are the guns in this district? Who owns them? Who has ammunition? Do local administrative offices maintain a list of those possessing weapons of any kind?[36]

No evidence exists, however, indicating periodic administrative inspections successfully control weapons in the hinterland. The authorities probably realized this, for in July 1973 Equateur's regional commissioner launched a campaign to bring in all illegally held weapons. He instructed zone and subregional commissioners to hold educational chats and mass meetings with the people to explain the reasons for this requirement. If people did not surrender their arms by the end of the month, the army would take over the entire operation. The probably inevitable assumption was that the army would be far less gentle, and would conduct the campaign with far more enthusiasm, than territorial officials.[37] I remain unaware if the soldiers were unleashed or if they met with success, but I am inclined to doubt it, for in 1974 and 1975 stories circulated of people living on islands in the Zaire River who would open fire on any representative of the state foolhardy enough to venture forth in search of taxes.[38] Similarly, after an inspection tour Mongala's subregional commissioner reported being:

> scandalized by the proliferation of firearms . . . with which people would walk comfortably along the roads, even when they were seeking drink. That presents, certainly, a latent danger, as much for the security of men as for that of the State. . . . we must avoid as much as possible the dangers that the generalized possession of weapons causes, through the interdiction of the fabrication of arms and the carrying of firearms not legally authorized.[39]

Later in 1975 the political affairs department came up with yet another gun control scheme. This time the department would distribute numbered forms which would eventually replace all previous authorizations. As in the past, however, only the state commissioner for political affairs could authorize a citizen to own a weapon.[40] This particular regulation has remained in force and was reaffirmed in 1982 when the National Executive Council realized too many weapons were circulating and decided to annul all previously existing gun permits. The government proscribed all weapons of war and proclaimed it would permit firearms for hunting and self-defense only on the approval of the state commissioner and after collection of a fee ranging from Z 1,000 to Z 5,000, depending on the type of weapon.[41]

One additional remark on gun control. When, in January 1973, political leaders decided all collectivity chiefs would be subject to bureaucratic rotation, the regime quickly realized some chiefs were leaving with the hunting rifles Mobutu had distributed on various visits to their collectivities. In 1975 the political affairs department was concerned enough to insist the president had not made these gifts to the chiefs as individuals but, rather, as representatives of the populations of their collectivities. As a result, chiefs had to leave the rifles behind; to do otherwise would constitute illegal possession of firearms.[42]

Why, then, has the *Mobutiste* state been unable to implement stringent gun control measures? First, many Zairians use rifles for hunting and are simply not about to relinquish them. As Zaire's economic fortunes have declined and as its currency has been devalued, more and more people have become dependent on hunting for food. Confiscation of these firearms might thus constitute a threat to subsistence and could entail serious medical and political consequences.[43] Needless to say, if subsistence is at issue, the cost alone of a gun permit would place it well beyond reach. Second, the average citizen has no desire to seek authorization for holding a weapon from the state commissioner for political affairs. As two Zairian analysts put it, "Through fear of the bureaucratic world whose appearances are most often vexatious (police action, inquisition, diverse controls), illiterates organize things in such a way as to diminish to the maximum possible [extent] occasions of contact with the administration."[44] To apply for a gun permit would involve the citizen in a baffling, demeaning, and time-consuming bureaucratic morass—probably with little chance of success. Third, given Zaire's institutionalized corruption, it is entirely possible some territorial administrators use illegally held arms as yet another pretext to extract resources and thus have little interest in enforcing the measures. The state's inability to control and regulate these free-floating means of coercion probably contributes both to the generalized insecurity of the citizenry, as well as to its own psychological insecurity. Finally, the population's reluctance to abide by these gun control measures is also a means of resisting the state's pretensions of control. Such resistance is part of the struggle for space and an attempt to increase, however slightly, the range of autonomous action available within civil society.

Those who rule the Zairian state are obviously aware of the difficulties involved in assuring a rapid flow of accurate information from the hinterland to the capital. Officials in all administrative echelons are concerned about the failure of those below them to provide even normal and supposedly routine information. As mentioned previously, lower-level administrators often resort to the fudge factor and invent data when under pressure to produce a report or furnish information. This, coupled with normal administrative or organizational tendencies toward uncertainty absorption,[45] occasionally make high-ranking officials wonder about the accuracy of what they are reading. Most administrative officials, and not just those in Zaire, tend to minimize actual or potential areas of trouble in their reports and may, for example, describe a serious problem as a minor difficulty. National authorities are well aware of this and occasionally try to do something about it. In 1972 the state commissioner for political affairs criticized his regional commissioners for this tendency.

> In effect, during two sessions each day . . . our operators of the Okapi [radio] network communicate to the central station in the department these reports under the laconic form "situation calm." Now, at the same time, other information networks functioning in your regions describe political acts, criminal actions, and many other situations contrary to the economic, social, or cultural progress of the country.[46]

The CND is perhaps the most important of these "other information networks."

The CND

In institutional terms, the CND is the direct successor of the Belgian colonial Sûreté. For reasons most probably having to do with the fifty-year rule governing access to Belgian archives, our knowledge of the early organization and activities of the Sûreté has remained sketchy. We do know the Sûreté's first burst of development occurred because of the need to control the messianic movements which swept through portions of Zaire during the interwar years.[47] Certainly, in the 1940s the colonial state created camps such as Ekafera (used today to imprison dissidents) as Colonies Agricoles pour Relégués Dangereux to isolate members of these religious sects.[48] Nonetheless, the available evidence indicates the Sûreté's formal organization remained rudimentary for some time. When Emile Janssens, the last Belgian commander of the Force Publique, initially arrived in Zaire in 1939, one of his responsibilities was to take charge of the 2nd Bureau which, as he notes, did not really exist.[49] More specifically,

> There existed no coordinated legislation concerning the security of the State, any more than a security service, either civilian or military, for one could not call "security service" the rubber stamp which carried that name which was manipulated by a civilian functionary in charge of multiple other occupations in the governor general's cabinet.[50]

Janssens is uncharacteristically reticent on how he organized the security service and speaks neither of its specific tasks nor its accomplishments. But in the twenty years between Janssens's arrival and independence in 1960, the Sûreté grew enormously.

Prior to independence the Sûreté's mission was to guard the state's internal security by providing political intelligence and keeping track of the movement of persons. Then, as now, the political police did not employ many people but instead relied on a far-flung web of informers who were most probably paid on a "piecework" and occasional basis. There can be no doubt of the general information-gathering efficacy of the colonial political police, as Sûreté dossiers concerning political activities in the immediate preindependence period attest.[51]

In the turbulent years following independence, Zairian leaders consolidated and converted the Sûreté into a strong instrument of central rule. Although initially attached to the interior ministry, by mid-1961 the organization's director, Victor Nendaka, had been able to assert its autonomy, and the political police became directly responsible to the prime minister.[52] Knowing full well the value of such an instrument, perhaps because of his own alleged participation in it as an occasional informer for the Belgians,[53] Mobutu, after seizing power, brought the Sûreté rapidly under his sway and placed it in the hands of Colonel Singa, a close associate. It has remained under the president's immediate and secure political control ever since.

Although the organization's name was changed to the CND in 1969, the statute kept it under the president's direct authority and granted it administrative autonomy. Its tasks, in general terms, are to "watch over the internal and external security of the State"; more specifically, it has license to research and interpret political, social, economic, and cultural phenomena bearing on the state's security. To fulfill these responsibilities, the CND may maintain surveillance on individuals suspected of jeopardizing the security of the state. Furthermore, the organization has the duty to fingerprint Zairians for identification and is responsible for executing immigration laws and regulating the entry of foreigners. It is also the official link with Interpol.[54]

The CND enjoys an unusual degree of financial, judicial, and political autonomy. As is generally the case in Zaire, those branches of the state attached directly to the presidency often operate independently of any control. In financial terms, this means neither the prime minister nor the IMF scrutinize the CND's budgetary allocations, a point Nguza confirms. He relates that "the President himself would take care of it and the heads [*responsables*] of these [security] services would collect important sums, in any case regularly at least U.S. $20,000 per service, directly from the Central Bank."[55] When, in August 1983, dissident Zairian parliamentarians presented a memorandum to a visiting U.S. congressional delegation, they noted that, although agriculture is in theory the government's chief priority, the budget for this sector scarcely reflects this alleged importance when compared to the credits allocated to the security services.[56]

Although not mentioned in the enabling legislation, CND agents have wide authority to arrest, interrogate, and detain all those they consider a threat. Since these agents are attached directly to the presidency and may be prosecuted only with the consent of the head of the political police, their independence from the law and judiciary is assured. Moreover, until 1982 the CND was perhaps the only national institution of any importance not represented on MPR committees at all levels of the hierarchy—a source of concern for regional, subregional, and zone commissioners intent on exerting authority and control in their respective administrative areas.[57] But in the early 1970s authorities tried to find a way around this violation of the concept of centralized "unity of command" and created CND committees at various levels. These committees were presumably there to "oversee" the CND's activities that escaped control of the party, but they were probably unsuccessful at integrating the CND into the local-level command structure. As we shall see, the effective independence of CND agents in the countryside has remained a constant thorn in the side of territorial officials, and it is unlikely their integration into MPR committees will change this in the future.[58]   One might speculate, however, that the CND's continued independence reflects Mobutu's desire to maintain a distinct, autonomous channel of information, and he may not want CND representatives under local control, platitudes concerning unity of command notwithstanding.[59]

Although the organization and attributes of the CND have remained reasonably constant, in one area its character has changed significantly.[60]   During the First Republic, the state kept the ethnic composition of the Sûreté carefully mixed.[61] Mobutu has continued to apply this principle of ethnic mélange throughout the state structure to eliminate potential threats to his political dominance from the mobilization of ethnic sentiment by would-be ethno-regional suzerains. But he nevertheless appears to have exempted the political police from this procedure. While it is virtually impossible to obtain accurate information on the ethnic and regional origins of CND employees, the fragmentary evidence available indicates most members of the political police hail from the *Mobutiste* heartland, Equateur. Referring to Zaire's "strategic general staff of power" comprising all the state's security services, including the CND, dissident parliamentarians maintain that mere desire coupled with competence are insufficient to assure entry into these institutions. "Tribal origins and submission to the interests of the oligarchy and especially fidelity to the President-Founder are determinant."[62]   Reading between the lines, many Zairians suspect this means the CND employs, for the most part, either members of Mobutu's Ngbandi ethnic group or other loyal Equateurians.

This phenomenon is assuredly not limited to Zaire. In a fine study drawn mostly from non-African sources, Joseph Rothschild observes: "the area of recruitment of personnel into sensitive agencies of the state apparatus, for example, the armed forces and police forces, so as to assure these organs' institutional reliability . . . [can tend to supplement or occasionally replace] the impersonal criteria of functional competence with ethnic criteria in the recruitment and promotion of personnel."[63]   Rothschild's discussion underscores the long-term dangers of this strategy which are certainly applicable to Zaire.[64]   Zairians have come to view the political police not as a necessary and universal implement of state rule but, rather, as partisan players in an ethnic game. Two possibilities follow: first, there is a real danger ordinary Zairians will perceive the ultimate source of their oppression at the hands of the state in ethnic terms; in consequence, and second, in a post-Mobutu era residents of Equateur, themselves as much the victims of the CND as other Zairians, will be subjected to a violent and unjustified ethnic backlash. At this point, however, such observations must remain speculative. Nonetheless, the potential for abuse of the CND's substantial autonomy and extensive powers should be obvious.

Task 1: Coercion and Control

The first task the CND performs for the regime is to repress, coerce, and control the population through intimidation and fear. In testimony before the Subcommittee on Africa of the U.S. House of Representatives, former Prime Minister Nguza maintained the secret police exist to intimidate the population. "They would know exactly what time I left my house or what time I came back and so on. Instead of seeing whether there are foreign forces coming inside Zaire they would control the time of the Prime Minister, you see. So the people are intimidated."[65] Nguza is correct. The CND has fostered a reign of terror.[66] Perhaps ironically, Mobutu has also noted, and castigated, the excesses of the political police. In 1977 he called attention to this phenomenon in a public address.

> These abuses of power are ascertained almost everywhere: . . . agents abuse their titles and intimidate citizens by saying: "Attention I am with the CND; I am a soldier; I am a magistrate; I am the friend of the President." . . . Know that Zaire belongs to 25 million Zairian men and women. It does not belong to the friends of Mobutu, neither to a few privileged people, nor to their collaborators, nor to the soldiers, nor to the magistrates, nor to the agents of the CND.[67]

Three years later, in 1980, Mobutu again chastised the CND.

> My concern in creating it [the CND] was not to institute a kind of vexatious and underhanded police to antagonize the population. . . . Today, everyone claims to be CND, it suffices that one be seen to carry a Motorolla. They search houses, day and night; they proceed to unauthorized controls [*gardes-à-vous*]; in brief, they want to try to be smart. We are, moreover, one of the rare countries where everyone knows the operational agents of the information services, while everywhere else, these persons are unknown as such, see all, hear all, without being the subject of the least little suspicion.[68]

This self-criticism does not ring true. Zairians know Mobutu's empty verbiage rarely, if ever, provides sufficient motivation for those criticized to correct their behavior;[69] he intends it primarily for external audiences such as the U.S. Congress. While generally accurate, these presidential castigations seriously understate the case.

The CND frightens and intimidates people throughout Zaire. How could it be otherwise? If even Mobutu complains about the CND and laments its abuses, then what hope do ordinary citizens have when confronted with this powerful and awesome organization? High-ranking officials, even in a relatively remote location like Lisala, were afraid to say what they thought about most serious matters because of the CND's network of informers. Ordinary citizens felt the same constraints and were reluctant to discuss contemporary events in public places for fear of being overheard by an informer and jailed.[70] Such perceptions are by no means restricted to Lisala. People in Butembo often thought a Zairian researcher was an agent of the CND.[71] Similarly, a study of Kisangani revealed "An atmosphere of paranoid fear . . . people suspect others of being informers for the security police (CND) on very flimsy grounds and are sometimes fearful of divulging quite harmless information."[72]

One informant was especially afraid of the CND because of a previous encounter. Several years before I met him, this gentleman had been attending a training course for bureaucrats in Kinshasa. One morning he was called away from his studies at 8:00 when six or seven soldiers, all armed to the teeth, seized him. After identifying him they whisked him into a car and sped away. No one would tell him where they were going, or why. Eventually the car arrived at a subregional office where he was jailed. After about an hour, he was taken before the subregional commissioner who, using a familiar and contemptuous form of address, accused him of being a subversive element. Without being permitted to speak, he was again incarcerated. This process was repeated several times, but at no juncture was he allowed to defend himself or even discover why he was in prison. After a while he was transferred to the CND and subjected to their tender ministrations. Here, however, he got lucky. One of his jailers was an acquaintance who agreed to try to find out the charges. Unfortunately, these turned out to be theft and, more seriously, high treason.

The previous evening, bandits had broken into the post office and stolen some letters. Somewhat later, this same group tried to rob a store and, in the process, scattered the pilfered letters. My informant had written one of these to a boyhood friend. In it he complained about the misinterpretation of a new statute regulating the working hours of all state officials. Although bureaucrats would now have to work from 7:00 A.M. to 3:00 P.M. without a break, this, he wrote, was scarcely a normal schedule for a student following a prescribed course of study. He further expressed his hope that there would be a clarification and that the situation would return to normal. In conclusion, he wrote, "Tout passe, tout casse, tout lasse," or everything will pass in the end and things will soon get back to normal. The police, looking for a clue to the second robbery, had read this last phrase and construed it to mean the gentleman opposed President Mobutu.

After he had spent several harried and fearful hours explaining the phrase had nothing whatsoever to do with the president, police arrested a few of the thieves and brought them to the CND. None could identify my informant, so the robbery charge was dropped. After much discussion and textual analysis, the treason charge was also quashed, but the CND official in charge warned him sternly that in the future he must never criticize either the president or the regime. He was finally released roughly twelve hours after the episode had begun.[73]

This story is indicative of how people view the CND. Many Zairians could recount similar incidents, and most people know at least someone who has had a run-in with the political police. Unfortunately, not all such incidents end as innocuously, and when similar tales circulate they inevitably reinforce fear of the CND's network of informers and contribute to the climate of personal insecurity and political intimidation. But there is a deeper, and perhaps psychologically more subtle effect of such encounters with the CND. One remarkable commentary put it this way: "Each person convoked [by the CND] has the feeling of having, in one way or another, upset the order established by Mobutu himself, of having violated a 'taboo' and is, in consequence, very punishable."[74] The CND is, in short, one of the state's major "mechanisms of fear,"[75] and most Zairians are profoundly afraid.

One of the ways the CND performs its repressive task is through surveillance of those deemed subversive. Nguza's case has already been noted and needs no further elaboration. The CND also observes other officials whose loyalty to Mobutu may be suspect. It is customary, for example, for the CND to file regular reports on the activities of all members of the National Legislative Council (deputies) when they are in their constituencies during periods of parliamentary recess. These reports indicate not only where legislators are, but also what they are doing and whether they are behaving. Deputies notice this surveillance, and at least some resent it as both inhibiting and troubling. One even made so bold as to complain the CND harassed him by sabotaging a mass meeting he called to explain the meaning of Zairian authenticity.[76]

The CND does not restrict its surveillance to prime ministers and deputies. It also keeps tabs on students and other groups who have, from time to time, expressed displeasure with the course of events under the new regime. In the wake of serious student upheavals in 1969, the regime ordered many of the demonstrators back to their home villages. The CND carefully monitored their movements and made sure they were where they were supposed to be. Since those disturbances, Zairian campuses and schools have erupted in protest periodically and the CND has become one of the state's most important instruments for keeping them under control.[77] Thus, when Kisangani school teachers staged a wildcat strike in late 1983, the CND closely watched and, ultimately, repressed the strikers. Observers of the events in Kisangani described some of the strikers' problems.

> The teachers know themselves to be watched and spied upon and no longer know in whom they can have confidence. The schools are riddled with the Sûreté's informers, which does not make agreement between the teachers easier. The strikes are ending with threats and repression; they [the teachers] have to give way, unless they are heroes.[78]

Upheavals like this remain exceptional, however. The CND tries to forestall them by maintaining regular surveillance on all citizens. Regular pilfering of the postal service, common knowledge throughout Zaire, is one means of surveillance. When mailing letters, many Zairians omit return addresses from their envelopes for fear of attracting the CND's attention. Those fortunate enough to live near Zaire's borders often rent postal boxes in towns just across the frontier. This, too, is another way of trying to avoid the CND's long arm and is part of the struggle for space.[79]

Arbitrary arrest and imprisonment are two of the main devices the CND uses to exert control.[80] Although there are prescribed legal procedures for detaining those suspected of violating the security of the state, the political police rarely observe the niceties. They simply arrest and imprison suspects without recourse to appeal for as long as authorities desire. Furthermore, the CND seldom explains to the victims the reasons for these imprisonments. In 1975 a village in Mongala came under the influence of Jehovah's Witnesses, and children of the believers refused to sing the national anthem or chant the MPR's slogans and cheers. Local CND agents reacted immediately. They arrested two of the church's pastors and recommended their detention at Ekafera so this "scandalous subversion" would end.[81] In addition to the free exercise of religion, speaking one's mind too openly can also lead to arrest. In what must have been a moment of anger and despair, a man publicly proclaimed "the Ngwandi have become arrogant since their brother is at the head of the country; let these Ngwandi know that their reign will not be for a long time."[82] He was then charged officially with inciting ethnic hatred. It is worth noting one hears derogatory comments directed at Luba and other Kasaians much more frequently, yet those who utter them remain at liberty. But in this case the threat was directed against Mobutu, and that makes all the difference.

The CND also keeps close tabs on "dissidents" in universities and secondary schools. In December 1976, for example, two students from the Lubumbashi campus rashly complained about their meager student stipends. After printing and distributing leaflets stating their arguments, the JMPR's disciplinary brigade took them into custody and handed them over to the CND. The CND thought their actions imperiled the security of the state and held the students without trial for nineteen months.[83] We may reasonably speculate their detention was not pleasant. Furthermore, since both university professors and secondary school teachers have periodically gone out on strike for better wages, and such activities are illegal, the CND has become active in the repression of labor. In December 1977, the CND detained several professors from the Lubumbashi campus for a week when their colleagues struck for higher salaries.[84] The same thing occurred in Kisangani in late 1983 during the strike of secondary school teachers when the CND arrested several strikers.[85]

The last way the CND sows fear throughout the nation is through torture of political prisoners. Should one be unlucky enough to fall into the CND's clutches there is real reason to fear for one's life. Tortures of all kinds, ranging from crude beatings to more "scientific" applications of electric current, have become common. A few examples will suffice. In 1980 Amnesty International reported the central authorities left the CND posts and detention centers scattered throughout Zaire entirely unsupervised. Needless to say, this gave the officers in charge of them great latitude in treating those detained. Detainees were routinely deprived of food, held in such cramped conditions they could not lie down, and subjected to various forms of torture.[86] In March 1981 the CND arrested Professor Dikonda and abused him physically: they mechanically mangled his fingers and whipped him with an electric flex. Dikonda was released only after nine months of this treatment. Similarly, one of the leaders of a student strike on the Kinshasa campus was reported to have been beaten and given electric shocks during his interrogations for allegedly subversive activity.[87]

A participant in the 1983 teachers' strike in Kisangani has provided a harrowing description of how the CND operates. While walking along the street he was approached by two agents who showed him a summons to CND headquarters. On arriving at the CND center, an official questioned him and inquired why the teachers had decided to strike and were thus engaging in subversive activities. The CND official then offered him Z 1,500 if he would return to school and convince several of his colleagues to resume work. The teacher refused the generous offer and the official told him to reappear that afternoon. Later on, he was given a paper to sign without reading. When he proved reluctant, he was beaten but later released and told to return the next day. On the morrow, he was again told to sign the paper and when he declined, things got serious. Wire rings were placed on his fingers and he was given varying doses of electric shock. After a further refusal to sign, his captors applied a hot metal instrument to his genitalia.[88] Similar stories could be repeated, and an impressive body of documentation on these abuses is accumulating.[89] But those who live to tell their macabre tales are the lucky ones. Many others disappear without trace and reports of deaths in CND detention camps and centers have mounted.[90]

I offer one final word on this grisly subject. I have already noted central authorities often leave CND centers and camps entirely unsupervised. In addition, despite mounting evidence on conditions in these camps and on the scope of CND activities in them, agents of the political police continue to enjoy immunity from judicial inquiry and prosecution. Despite the prevalence of torture, the state has never prosecuted any CND official for these atrocities.[91] Such behavior is not a mere aberration; on the contrary, it is part of a deliberate policy of repression.

Task 2: Information Gathering

Another service the CND renders unto Caesar is the provision of fast and, in the Zairian context, relatively accurate information on political, social, cultural, and economic affairs. Although when measured against an absolute standard the quality of CND reports varies, it is nonetheless far superior to the efforts of other branches of the state. Moreover, the CND performs this second task, with but one exception I shall note later, with a minimum of uncertainty absorption.

Many reports provide detailed accounts of political life and of the population's reactions to national decrees. For example, when Zairians took over the plantation and commercial sectors of the economy in late 1973, the CND provided detailed commentary on the implementation of these measures in the hinterland: "From Businga we are advised that despite the decision of the National Executive Council concerning the restitution of the property of Citizen X to his Zairian wife, the acquirer has not agreed and still refuses to hand over the property to the *Zairoise.* . . . We are informed that the acquirer is supported by certain local authorities."[92] Another report from Gbadolite noted that Belgian missionaries in the schools were "very disobedient because they are responsible only to the Presidency" and their students had no knowledge of Mobutu's speech on the economy because the missionaries had never distributed it.[93] Still other communications indicate the local mood: one described people booing when a collectivity chief explained that all citizens, even infants, would have to buy an identity card; others note exactly who attends party rallies and who is conspicuously absent and thus considered indifferent. The CND reports any organizational initiative, even if not overtly political. When, for example, people in Bumba decided to form a cultural center, the CND furnished a detailed account of the creation of the new organization as well as a list of its leadership.[94]

Economic information is also a concern, and CND reports from Mongala meticulously note the economic climate: especially prices of specific goods and shortages of first necessity items. Competition, or lack of it, between merchants is also a matter of interest.[95] On one occasion a CND agent wrote to the sub-regional economic affairs officer indicating displeasure because highly placed individuals were selling beer at a higher price than the state allowed. He further noted this was causing much unfavorable comment in commercial circles and since the law was designed for all, it should be applied equitably without regard to social standing.[96] But such direct interventions in the process of policy implementation are rare, and CND agents usually confine themselves to reporting these matters to their superiors.

Throughout my stay in Mongala, I was often able to confirm the veracity of these communications. In general, they were far more detailed and probing than the reports of other arms of the state. The CND also seemed effective in tracking down rumors. In one instance, a CND agent visited a rural collectivity which had been the source of letters accusing the chief of exploiting and abusing the population. After investigation he noted that, although the chief usually takes the plight of ordinary citizens to heart by helping them financially, he occasionally required them to clear his fields and paid no more than a beer or two. In this instance, the letters denouncing the chief were correct.[97] In other cases, however, CND reports showed anonymous letters of denunciation were without foundation.[98]

As part of its information-gathering activities the CND occasionally becomes a silent ombudsman—ombudsman because the political police watch officials at all levels and report carefully on the coercive, oppressive, and exploitative actions so common in Zaire; silent because these reports are strictly confidential, few know they exist, such abuses are not detailed publicly, and little, if anything, is ever done to ameliorate the situation. The good CND agent is thus a faithful Boswell of oppression. The following excerpts are indicative:

> In the collectivity of Banda-Yowa, the present chief . . . practices a ferocious dictatorship; bodily torture outlawed ten years ago has been vigorously reinstated; a striking example is that of Citizen X to whom the chief gave a penalty of forty lashes. . . . In the collectivity of Monjamboli the prison director, with the complicity of the state agent, mistreats prisoners. . . . The prisoners do manual labor but the price of these labors is to the profit of the prison director. . . . He had them build three houses and sold them to teachers, the price of these houses was 48 zaires but we do not know where this money has gone.[99]

> The locality chief of Lokele-Mongala is practicing abusive behavior toward the population in his locality. In effect, the locality chief has invented judicial instructions, according to which he judges the villagers. He inflicts heavy fines without, however, issuing receipts; following which a good number of villagers have aban-

doned their homes to live on the islands in order to avoid the abuses of their chiefs. Fines without receipt of 5, 10, 12, 7, 10, 3, 2, 5 zaires.[100]

Contrary to the duty imposed on each agent of order, the urban police of the City of Bumba have made themselves the instruments of a swindle in the public market and in every corner of the City of Bumba. These elements of the police have resorted to arbitrary arrests and impose illegal fines of up to five zaires.[101]

Similar events occur all too frequently and the political police report them regularly.[102]

As one might readily imagine, because CND agents observe and report the abuses of other officials, they are not especially popular with their colleagues in territorial administration. In consequence, there is now, and has almost always been, a high level of tension between the CND and other arms of the state. Territorial commissioners usually phrase their complaint so as to note CND agents are not practicing "unity of command," a concept of Mobutu's favoring centralized control. By way of example, when Mongala's CND committee first met in 1970, the subregional commissioner rebuked and cautioned CND officials who wished to elude his authority. He also noted regional commissioners had to enlighten the president on affairs in their regions, and, in turn, subregional commissioners should inform regional commissioners on matters in the subregions. "We must," he said, "maintain unity of command and have to be subject to the hierarchy of authority."[103] CND officials who "brandish their attachment to the Presidency as veritable immunities, who place their arbitrary actions out of reach of all control by [regional] authorities" are the subjects of much invective.[104] But this is certainly a two-way street, for the CND invariably refutes such charges and, on the contrary, maintains territorial administrators are interfering in the business of the security of the state.[105] In any event, ombudsmen and watchdogs, · whether public or silent, are rarely popular with those whose abuses they uncover.

Task 3: Symbolic Reassurance

Along with information, the CND also provides symbolic reassurance to Zaire's politically and psychologically insecure leaders. It reassures central authorities that all is well in the hinterland and that they have nothing to worry about. In this sense some CND reports do display a curious kind of uncertainty absorption. For example:

During this ten-day period all remains calm across all the area of Mongala. All the people work in joy, doubling their energy thanks to the continuity of the new regime. The recent ministerial reshuffle accomplished by the Father of the Nation brought forth a great joy among the population which promises him a sincere attachment.[106]

And, "In conformity with the decision of the political bureau a joyous march of support for the President of the Republic took place at Bumba on 19 February 1972. Situation is calm."[107] The political puffery is blatant. One may legitimately doubt that people were working in joy or that their energy had doubled because of the new regime. We might also question how much happiness a ministerial reshuffle could elicit in the hinterland where many remain blissfully indifferent to such events. There is also little joy usually associated with marches of support since the state coerces many into participating. Nevertheless, both messages mention the calm prevalent in the area. The phrase "situation is calm" *(situation être calme)* appears in many CND telegraphic messages and reports and resembles a ritual incantation, a formula of symbolic reassurance. In other words, despite everything the reports may relate, no matter how disturbing, there is really nothing to cause serious concern.

Obvious internal contradictions in the following communications underline the point:

> You are informed that on 26 May 1974 the Zone Commissioner presented to the public thirty-six robbers who were sowing terror in the City of Bumba. These thieves are being kept in the central prison of Bumba which is not well maintained and their escape is to be feared. The operation continues. Situation is calm.[108]

One month later the same CND agent wired the following report to his superiors:

> Daily situation: Of the thirty-six robbers arrested at Bumba only twelve were brought to the prosecutor's office at Lisala. Twenty-four escaped from the prison at Bumba. Situation is calm.[109]

Similarly, when Mobutu returned from the People's Republic of China, he decreed, following the Maoist model, that all parents would have to register their preschool children (five year olds) in state-run nurseries. One CND report noted:

> Some parents do not want to register their children. A rumor is circulating that the President of Zaire wants to deprive them of the right to their children concerning the nurseries. Some say that their children will not even go to school. That is why the Zone Commissioner wants to tour the zone to explain the exact meaning of the decision made by the Political Bureau. Situation is calm.[110]

The situation was anything but calm. Porous prisons, escaped convicts, and parents afraid of losing their children do not bespeak a high degree of tranquility. Yet the ritual phrase "situation is calm" appears in each instance. Since this incantation bears little relation to reality, it becomes easier to see it as an attenuated form of uncertainty absorption calculated to reassure an insecure central leadership that, however serious the chaos reported, it still did not constitute a threat to the continuity of the *Mobutiste* state.

Conclusion

The dialectic of oppression created as conditions of insecurity and scarcity interact has contributed to the emergence of a psychologically insecure politico-commercial bourgeoisie which fears its political demise. This psychological insecurity, moreover, has become a permanent feature affecting the world view of Zaire's leaders. Ironically, this psychological condition has little to do with more objective measures of political control, stability, and continuity. Thus, even when by most standards the Zairian state is ascendant and in firm control, the insecurity of its leaders is never far from the surface. Memories of violence and swift political change have conditioned Zaire's rulers, and this chapter has indicated some of their reactions. Knowledge that other African regimes have fallen when the leader is abroad has led Mobutu to instruct the territorial administration to run its communications facilities twenty-four hours a day when he is overseas. The regime's surveillance of most politicians, especially those who once enjoyed a measure of personal popularity, also reflects its political insecurity. We have also observed the regime's concerted efforts to obtain a continuous supply of accurate and timely information on societal conditions. Assuredly, all states need information to govern; nonetheless, the absence of even routine and banal data on events up-country probably increases the insecurity of those who rule. The case study of gun control and the regime's inability to insure even minimal compliance speaks to this point.

One possible, though ultimately misguided, way of reducing this insecurity is to intimidate the population. The CND, or political police, is one of the main instruments the state uses to spread fear among the citizenry. Its violations of fundamental human rights diminish our common humanity and merit the strongest condemnation. But arbitrary arrest, imprisonment, and torture of political prisoners are not the only services this organization renders to the state. It also provides a wide range of information necessary to policymakers. Furthermore, it performs the role of silent ombudsman by informing authorities of the abuses the population suffers daily at the hands of the state. The important point here is that even if national political leaders do not know who has guns, or remain ignorant of precise demographic statistics, the CND does inform them, regularly and graphically, about the oppression of the population. The tragedy is they choose to do nothing about it. The CND's reports are a mechanism of control, intimidation, and, as we have seen, reassurance. The political police are creatures of the insecure politico-commercial bourgeoisie, and this element uses the CND to increase its own sense of political security. The problem, however, is the CND can only accomplish this task by provoking fear, intimidation, and personal insecurity among the citizenry.

Nguza's statement cited in epigraph indicates the political police are efficient. Much of the information presented here confirms this judgment. The CND gathers and relates information; it also intimidates the population effectively. In performing its tasks so well, it stands out as a beacon of relative efficiency in a sea of disorganization and mismanagement.[111] Let us underscore the word relative, however. The CND, like other Zairian institutions, operates in a society where corruption, dishonesty, and inhumanity have become all too common. To be sure, most CND reports I uncovered in Mongala were accurate, but this is not always the case. Callaghy notes CND reports in Kivu were not always reliable and were occasionally ploys in local political games.[112] By no stretch of the imagination are CND agents necessarily immune from the forces the dialectic of oppression sets loose. They, too, are subject to these wider societal pressures and know a fall from grace is always possible. They thus have the same incentives as other officials to profit from their positions while they can, and many CND agents use their offices to extract resources from ordinary citizens.[113] Undoubtedly, CND agents live well compared to other Zairians. In addition, they are certainly not insulated from the games of influence played at the polity's highest reaches. The intervention of high-ranking officials to quash CND dossiers on behalf of friends or relatives certainly occurs.[114] Similarly, certain agents have cooperated with enterprising individuals intent on manipulating the system who employ denunciation to the CND as a way to eliminate potential rivals in their quest to accumulate wealth.[115] Thus, there are unquestionably times when CND agents are drawn into the processes of social class formation, when they profit from their positions, and when they use their authority to oppress others gratuitously. At these moments, the CND's performance seems much more in line with that of other arms of the Zairian state.

In a slightly different though related vein, Giddens has argued that "there are no continuing relationships in any sphere of social life where the scope and effectiveness of the control which some actors have over others is complete." This is the basis for a dialectic of control which provides the weak "some capabilities of turning resources back against the strong."[116] Thus, although the CND deploys a formidable array of legal and extralegal tools to intimidate, repress, and coerce the population, in certain areas its control remains incomplete—areas of passive resistance.[117] Many, for example, seek to circumvent the CND's access to the postal service. Similarly, despite the network of informers throughout Zaire, many Zairians choose to opt out and exit, a subject discussed at greater length in chapter 7. We have also noted the CND often reports citizens who openly manifest displeasure with official announcements, or fail to participate in party rallies, or decline to march in support of the regime. Those who display such conspicuous indifference to the regime's "revolutionary imperatives" are surely aware the CND notes their absence and relates it to higher authorities. Yet they persist. Furthermore, despite the CND's relatively efficacious information network, despite the fear that the wrong set of ears will overhear a conversation, many Zairians still voice their discontent openly. People are afraid, but they do talk to each other about their situations after exercising a degree of caution. Only when such conversation is blatant, public, and obviously threatening will the CND act, as occurred in Mongala when a man had the temerity to criticize Mobutu and the Ngbandi. The CND does not appear to have the ability, or perhaps the desire, to eliminate these forms of passive resistance which are part of the dialectical struggle for space.

In dwelling on the CND at some length, my aim has been to treat, however incompletely, one of the state's important and rarely studied coercive arms. It has not been to imply that Zaire, or the CND, is unique.[118] After all, strong leaders wielded terror as an integral part of the precolonial state-building process in certain Central African societies.[119] The systematic practice of state-inspired terror knows limits in neither time nor space.

Observers of politics in Cameroon—a state that enjoys a much better image in Western media than Zaire—have called our attention to the omniscience and omnipresence of the political police, the abuse of powers of detention, the prevalence of fear and intimidation, and the presence of concentration camps and torture.[120] Other states also rely on networks of informers and security apparatuses, Ethiopia and Congo-Brazzaville come readily to mind.[121] But, in some regards, Uganda under Amin may provide the closest parallel to Zaire. The notorious State Research Bureau (SRB) was chillingly efficient at ferreting out internal threats to Amin's rule through the use of informers, intimidation, and terror. The SRB also enabled its agents to accumulate great personal wealth.[122] In these aspects the parallels between the CND and SRB are striking, although conditions are probably not yet as bad in Zaire as they were in Uganda. Also noteworthy in this comparison is that Uganda under Amin, like Zaire in recent years, was a polity in which other sinews of state authority were weakening. Is there perhaps an inverse relationship between state decline and and the role of the political police? Is it possible to see the emergence of a powerful, feared political police as a manifestation of a broader process of state erosion? While data from Zaire, Uganda, Guinea, and Iran tend to support this hypothesis, the evidence appears mixed.[123] Strong and ascending states (the Soviet Union, South Africa) do have active and prominent political police machines. We may also reasonably suggest the role, prominence, and visibility of the political police rises as the state's political legitimacy erodes. But we must temper such conjectures with the realization that evidence is sparse, for no political police organization welcomes the scrutiny of independent observers. All such ruminations must, therefore, remain tentative and exploratory.

But what are we to make of all this? I have argued that Zaire's psychologically insecure politico-commercial bourgeoisie has tried to increase its own sense of political security through a deliberate policy of repression and intimidation, led, in large measure, by the political police. This oppression has drastically reduced the personal security of the vast majority of Zairians and may ultimately contribute to undermining the continuity and security of the *Mobutiste* state which the CND is, in theory, supposed to safeguard. It would be incorrect, however, to assume that the CND is the sole arm of the state responsible for spreading fear and insecurity throughout society. Other sinews of the state—the army, gendarmerie, and party youth wing—are also involved.

4

The State as Bandit
Armed Forces, Coercive Force

From Bumba we are informed that . . . a com-
mando from Kotakoli [camp] disturbed the
reigning public tranquility by firing an
American bazooka, new model, into the ag-
glomerations of Bumba.

—Police Report[1]

Echoes coming from Bumba indicate a social
and political disorder created by soldiers
operating at night: they rape, they steal, they
pillage. . . . Gendarmes who have been there
[at Businga] a long time . . . commit acts of
banditry making use of their status as soldiers.
Acts of armed robbery and indiscipline are
often signalled. . . . Soldiers leave the camp,
invade villages, rape married women and girls,
permit themselves everything.

—Administrative Correspondence[2]

During the patrol I noticed that the mere
presence of gendarmes in certain corners made
people afraid.

—Administrative Correspondence[3]

When Zairians try to avoid the political police, they are often uncertain whether
a particular individual actually belongs to the CND. To be sure, most of Lisala's
residents knew the two local agents, but there was usually much doubt and specula-
tion about the identities of their informers. In large cities it is even more difficult
to identify CND agents accurately. There is no such doubt, however, concerning collectivity police,[4] members of the JMPR's disciplinary brigade, or gendarmes and soldiers in the FAZ. These members of the forces of order wear
uniforms and their status is clearly visible. This chapter examines these other

arms of the state's coercive power and focuses especially on the FAZ, the Gendarmerie Nationale (GDN),[5] and the party youth wing's disciplinary brigade.

It is not surprising state-sponsored coercion exists in Zaire. The very notion of coercion is built into the idea of the state, and all states, be they liberal democracies or more authoritarian regimes, rely to a greater or lesser degree on coercion to control their populations and maintain their territorial boundaries. Keegan makes the point nicely in his superb historical study of battles. "Coercion is a word to which the vocabulary of democracy gives grudging house room. The liberal state likes to believe that it works by consent and persuasion, that compulsion is a method of dealing with citizens to which only the lower forms of polity have resort."[6] Forces of organized coercion are among the basic links which connect state and society and are crucial to the state's efforts to maintain and increase its power and authority. Referring to the police, one scholar has called for a "theory of the state which is elaborated downwards."[7] Although doubtlessly a worthwhile goal, here I propose the reverse: to provide information and analysis on daily life in the countryside that will contribute toward a theory of the state which is elaborated upwards. Complex and abstract theories of the state are well and good, but do they further illuminate, or even resemble, the picture the state's coercive arms present as they go about their normal business and interact with people in far-flung corners of a country? What image of state-society relations emerges from these daily contacts?

As the epigraphs indicate, in Zaire these interactions are rarely pleasant, occasionally turbulent, often violent, and usually oppressive and extractive. Zairian military forces, as Young and Turner argue convincingly, earn their living through banditry and have become a scourge of society. Moreover, the state's use of coercion has become an ingrained habit in many parts of rural Zaire.[8] To understand better why this should be, I shall analyze the relations of these coercive organizations with the population in Lisala, its environs, and throughout Mongala. In addition, and through this analysis, the tasks of these coercive arms, in both theory and practice, will become apparent. My aim is *not* to present a close institutional study of these organizations—others have done that.[9] But to place this analysis of the state's coercive arms in perspective, a cursory overview of the institutional evolution of the FAZ and GDN is necessary. Since it is exceedingly difficult to separate these two organizations, and most Zairians find it difficult to distinguish between them, I shall, for most purposes, group them together and use the terms soldier and gendarme interchangeably.

Historical Overview

The Force Publique was formally established in 1888 during the era of Leopold II's Independent State and grew rapidly. The cost-conscious Belgians never sent metropolitan troops to the Congo to aid in the colonial conquest. Instead, they dispatched white officers and noncommissioned officers whom they entrusted with the task of running the colonial army and ensuring discipline among native recruits.

Moreover, the Force Publique always remained structurally distinct from the metropolitan Belgian army and thus differed sharply from both French and Portuguese practice. By 1897 it boasted a complement of 14,000, with only 2,000 Europeans in supervisory ranks. At its inception, the Force Publique's responsibilities were extremely broad: to occupy the colony, protect it from external aggression, maintain public order, and enforce the law. Thus, from its early years the colonial army performed tasks which are, in many places, the lot of domestic police. Its dual mission created an enduring tension within the Force Publique and its successors.[10]

During the army's early years, Belgian austerity resulted in an underofficered and overmanned force. In addition, unwilling recruits, poor pay, and the dispersal of troops throughout the territory (where they were often commanded by territorial administrators more concerned with civilian administration than military life) made discipline an acute problem, and several major mutinies occurred during the colonial period. Indiscipline, moreover, did not disappear at independence.[11]

The Force Publique gradually lost some of its wide-ranging responsibilities to other institutions. In 1926 the colonial state created a territorial (sometimes called provincial) police force and placed it under the command of the European territorial administrators. It maintained order, ran the prisons, guarded public buildings, and reinforced the chief's (later collectivity) police when necessary. After independence these territorial police devolved to provincial control and, in some cases, became private armies under the command of regional suzerains. The chief's police were primarily rural forces based in the collectivities. As the name would suggest, they served under the chief, who, with the advice of the Belgian territorial administrator, set terms of service, requirements for entry, and other matters pertaining to the operation of the force. The chief's police were thus decentralized units with no national, provincial, or territorial command structure. Like their counterparts in the territorial police, they wore uniforms and were responsible for maintaining order; unlike them, however, they did not bear arms and also had other duties such as court attendant, jailer, and messenger. These new organizations were independent of the Force Publique.

Another ordinance passed in 1926 confirmed a previously introduced distinction, internal to the colonial army, between *troupes campées* and *troupes en service territoriale*. The former were to defend against external enemies, the latter were to maintain internal order. But this dichotomy usually remained theoretical, for the colonial military sector often lost control of its *troupes campées* as civilian administrators increasingly asked them to act as police. In 1959 territorial troops became known as "gendarmes" and, although technically part of the Force Publique, came under the direct command of civilian administrators and performed as a rural constabulary. Never especially popular with ordinary citizens, most people knew these soldiers, gendarmes, and police were present to enforce the colonial political order. This lack of popularity also carried over into the postindependence era.[12]

There is no need to recount the long, sad story of the decline of order during the First Republic. In brief, none of the forces of order withstood the pressures which shred the sinews of the state. The army, gendarmes, and police dissolved, thus contributing to the state's decline. When fragments of these coercive institutions were not busily engaged in making war on each other, they made life miserable for ordinary Zairians. In 1961, for example, indisciplined soldiers rioted in the center of Lisala and engaged civilians in a two-day battle. The Force Publique's long legacy of indiscipline reappeared with a vengeance during these years.[13]

After Mobutu took control, he brought provincial police units under the Zairian army's supervisory control. This arrangement persisted until December 1966 when the state nationalized the police and created the Zairian National Police. The nationalization was part of Mobutu's plan to centralize power by depriving the provinces of their own military forces. Throughout this period the gendarmerie had remained a separate force in the countryside still, in theory, responsible for internal law and order. In 1972 Mobutu merged the primarily urban national police and the largely rural gendarmes into a unified force, the GDN. The state thus enlarged the gendarmerie substantially and made it an institutionally distinct component of the FAZ which also boasted a small navy and air force. In other words, only the collectivity police remained outside the FAZ's organizational umbrella.[14] The president directly commands both the FAZ and the GDN in his capacity as commander-in-chief of the armed forces. The preface to the legislation giving birth to the new military and police structure noted, "In creating the GDN, the Chief of State wanted to establish [*mettre sur pied*] a healthy, well-structured police force, with a proper hierarchy, belonging to the large family of the FAZ, but present everywhere, in all strata of the population and implanted in the most distant corners of the Republic."[15] The *Mobutiste* state has accomplished this, but at the expense of Zairian society.

Relations with the Population

In theory, the FAZ's main duty is to defend Zairian territory against external aggression and to preserve the state's sovereignty and territorial integrity. Also in theory, the GDN is supposed to maintain internal order and provide the usual range of police services. Reality is another matter entirely, however. The army's experiences in Angola in late 1975, and in Shaba in 1977 and 1978 indicate clearly the FAZ is usually less than successful when it must confront armed opponents. More often than not, however, Mobutu calls on both FAZ and GDN to deal expeditiously with any of their countrymen unwise enough to dissent from the present political order. Both services thus seem to receive most of their "combat" experience against essentially unarmed peasants, students, or schoolteachers. In this regard, their record is stellar.

Although an aim of the legislation unifying the national police and gendarmerie was to raise the caliber of the newly united service, the gendarmes assigned to Mongala have, by and large, remained a sorry and ragtag lot. In March 1968 there were 14 officers and 258 men distributed throughout the subregion, and the reports of the detachment's commander leave the impression that discipline and morale were in short supply. When the men "have no money, they very often arrive late to work. But on the contrary, when they do have money they get drunk in an inhuman manner so that they still come late to work, sleep during guard duty, and sometimes disappear from the job because of their drunkenness."[16] One report noted gendarmes rarely completed assigned tasks without an officer present, and most of the men simply did not have the qualities required of true agents of law and order. Too much drink, too much hemp, excessive familiarity with the local population, and disdain for officers from other regions or ethnic groups were characteristic traits. In addition, gendarmes themselves were often in jail for a variety of infractions including rape, theft, assault, extortion, manslaughter, and aiding convicts to escape.[17] Naturally, such behavior disadvantageously affects the local citizenry. On one occasion, for example, drunken soldiers dressed in mufti disturbed public order in Lisala by brawling with two collectivity policemen and then liberating the thieves whom the police were guarding.[18] One considerable problem, then, is the personnel's generally low quality. Zaire's forces of order are filled with refugees from the lumpenproletariat, often former members of the JMPR, who have little interest in performing their mandated duties.

Mongala's civilian administrators complain constantly about the soldiers' penchant for arbitrary arrest.[19] In 1973, Mobayi-Mbongo's local contingent of gendarmes lacked a camp of their own and were thus without housing in the area. As a result, they lived in homes usually reserved for civilian bureaucrats and were interspersed throughout their neighborhood. The civil servants were bitter over the behavior of the gendarmes, who would arrest their neighbors on the slightest pretext.[20] Although Lisala's military detachment was not as large as Mobayi-Mbongo's, soldiers nevertheless caused problems.

A letter to the relevant court captures what most Zairians suffer at the hands of their "protectors":

> I have the honor to bring to your attention the following case: During the night of 23–24 May 1970, toward midnight, I was forced to open my door at the Hotel Montagne, where I am lodged, to a soldier . . . under the pretext that he had been sent to make an inspection of the hotel.
> Having opened my room, these soldiers obliged me to go with them to the camp where I was put in jail all night without informing me why I had been arrested.
> The next day they required that I pay a fine of 20 Zaires (TWENTY ZAIRES) saying that they had found a woman in my room. Since I did not have that sum with me I remained until three o'clock; after paying this sum I was liberated, [but] they refused to give me even a receipt.
> . . . I ask you please, to the extent possible, to do whatever is possible to recover this amount . . .[21]

Gendarmes are unpopular for other reasons. Like other Zairians in positions of authority, those in uniform are caught in the dialectic of oppression and use their parcels of power to extract what they can from those in contextually inferior positions in the class hierarchy. One way they do this is to extort illegal fines from unlucky citizens who fall into their hands. At one juncture Lisala's tax collector claimed he was having difficulty because merchants were refusing to pay their taxes. The shopkeepers reasoned they had already given their taxes to the gendarmes who had been out collecting them—completely illegally. In consequence, they simply ignored the tax collector's demands for their annual settlement with the government.[22] When short of funds, soldiers and gendarmes also appear on the doorsteps of various establishments and invent infractions for which they claim merchants will have to pay a fine. To be sure, such violations are usually imaginary, but the traders know if they fail to comply they will face arrest and imprisonment until the gendarmes are satisfied. Needless to say, receipts are never offered in return for payment of these "fines."[23]

Lisala's experience with the forces of order reflects a larger, national, reality. By 1977 this situation had deteriorated so badly the government formally outlawed all the imaginary and ridiculous fines gendarmes, soldiers, members of the JMPR, and others in the territorial administrative service levied habitually.[24] As is usually the case, however, the culprits barely paused to catch their breath before resuming their customary practices. For several weeks in 1978, the GDN ran an announcement in the Kinshasa dailies informing the public, in both French and Lingala, that it was forbidden to pay fines to gendarmes. With the sole exception of a fee for a driver's license, all monies would have to go directly to an authorized government accountant. Furthermore, to pay a gendarme would expose the citizen to prosecution for corrupting an officer.[25]

Another serious problem, particularly up-country, is the tendency for soldiers to establish themselves as petty tyrants or local war lords and then inflict all manner of abuse on civilians in their vicinity. In one instance, the zone commissioner of Mobayi-Mbongo complained to the commandant of the FAZ detachment at Yakoma (in his zone) that certain military activities were causing severe problems. More specifically, he indicated the troops had arrested thirteen villagers and brought them to camp headquarters where they received corporal punishment and suffered bodily harm. Because of these events, the remaining villagers had become afraid and fled into the forest, where they remained. In addition, military authorities had never taken legal action, although during the previous year two citizens had been killed at the camp.[26]

Violence by the FAZ and GDN against their fellow citizens has become frequent and, from the perspective of the population, constitutes a major problem. Soldiers often encircle certain neighborhoods in towns and cities, and then pillage them systematically and enthusiastically. In June 1983, for example, the GDN undertook a vast sweep (*ratissage*) of the capital in hopes of ridding Kinshasa of bandits, unemployed, and others without valid papers. The intent was to arrest not only those targeted, but also those who sheltered them and others who failed to denounce them to the relevant authorities—probably a healthy percentage of the population. This operation also merits attention because of the explicit reversal of the presumption of innocence. One Kinshasa newspaper wrote "each citizen interpellated is presumed suspect until he justifies his respectability by the presentation of a citizen's identity card or an employment card."[27]

In Lisala such violence occurs often, and civilian authorities despair of bringing the soldiers under control. The soldiers' nocturnal excursions into the Cité would usually result in numerous complaints. One subregional commissioner wrote to the local FAZ commandant that he had many times noticed troops abusing the population during their patrols and had therefore decided to order the soldiers back to the barracks.[28] But this solution is usually temporary. Mobutu and his cronies believe the population has to see the implements of rule and coercive authority. As one Zairian general, speaking before the MPR's ideological institute, put it: "By its essential character as the holder of force, protector of institutions, and guarantor of public order, the Army incarnates Power."[29] Given, therefore, the necessity of keeping the army visible, each new team of commissioners in Mongala seems to have come up with the same, rather ineffectual, solution: a mixed patrol composed of the FAZ, GDN, and JMPR. In theory, the aim is to insure discipline through the mixed presence of different coercive arms; in practice, such mixtures rarely have any effect since members of all three services are interested in profiting from their nighttime duties.[30]

Although during my stay in Lisala there were numerous instances of gratuitous violence by local gendarmes, to the best of my knowledge, there were no cases of murder. Other regions, however, are not so fortunate. A careful inquiry into the Parti Révolutionnaire du Peuple (PRP) in eastern Zaire uncovered testimony about atrocities the FAZ had committed. An informant related the FAZ had executed all clan chiefs in one locality after forcing them to eat their own ears. Their pretext was the village sympathized with the PRP's revolutionary aims. Others reported a squad had wandered across eight passersby whom they robbed and massacred.[31]

Shaba Region has also suffered, perhaps more than most. In 1983, reports indicated the commandant of the GDN at Kipushi executed seventeen people. It would appear the victims were part of the commandant's own stolen car ring, and he feared their testimony would later compromise him. On an equally somber note, a military tribunal tried an army major for allegedly having tortured and killed a civilian. Before the verdict, however, the major received his lieutenant colonelcy and quickly left for new duties as a military attaché abroad.[32] During late 1984 and much of 1985 the FAZ conducted a series of violent reprisals on the citizenry of northeastern Shaba. The soldiers hit the areas of Moba and Kalemie especially hard because they believed the population had supported insurgents during their brief seizure of Moba in November 1984. Arbitrary arrest, torture, and extrajudicial execution became regular features of the FAZ's relationship with the local population.[33] Other examples of wanton violence, brutality, torture, and murder abound.

In early 1983 authorities arrested three workers at the Maluku steel mill after management complained they had stolen a small electric generator late the preceding year. The three suspects were tortured extensively and, under this less than gentle attention, one of them died. On learning this, their fellow workers rioted and torched the car of the mill's personnel chief. Further violence ensued as management summoned the GDN to restore order, and gendarmes arrested and imprisoned fourteen other workers. During the next two days troops encircled the town and entered homes in the small of the night, ostensibly looking for those without proper papers. Gendarmes released prisoners taken during this operation the next morning, after having first received substantial bribes. The sums extorted ranged from Z 300 to Z 1,000. In a letter concerning these events, the local curé wrote:

> In conclusion, I should like to express the wish that the authorities watch over peoples' dignity. In effect, it is a secret to no one at Maluku, that the practice of torture is done at the military inspectorate as well as at the local gendarmerie. It is always civilians who are the victims of it. We have seen the visible part of the "iceberg" [English in original]; the largest part being beneath the water. The pesterings and tortures [led to] . . . the . . . explosion during the events cited, but the ill is more profound.[34]

The ill certainly is more profound, and incidents like this have become common throughout Zaire. The FAZ and GDN regularly kill and torture their fellow citizens. Nguza has documented the executions of civilians which high-ranking members of the FAZ have ordered, and one former executioner has publicly confessed to having tortured prisoners for the *Mobutiste* regime.[35] Even Mobutu has occasionally castigated members of the state's coercive arms. In February 1980 he noted, "The Zairian has ceased to applaud the presence of the gendarme."[36] Notwithstanding the president's gift for understatement, it is more accurate to observe "the Zairian army today is synonymous with extortion, looting, murder, rape, and utter disregard for the protection of lives and property."[37] Why, then, do the forces of order consistently leave disorder, unrest, and abused citizens in their wake?

In addition to the legacy of indiscipline and the generally low quality of personnel in direct contact with the public, endemic corruption figures prominently, and there is ample evidence this factor significantly affects how the FAZ, GDN, and JMPR interact with Zairian citizens.[38] Any discussion of corruption should begin at the top of the polity, in this instance, the army. High-ranking soldiers and gendarmes are well aware of Mobutu's frequent rotations of officeholders to ensure none can build an autonomous base of power. They also realize Mobutu can grant an important position in the command structure today and revoke it tomorrow. Like their civilian counterparts, in other words, ranking FAZ officers are caught in the dialectic of oppression as scarcity and insecurity condition behavior. Soldiers are thus aware they should profit from their positions as quickly as possible, for the opportunities a military command presents will not be available indefinitely. In one of his periodic bouts of self-criticism Mobutu noted some of the more glaring effects of this social process. "But the truth is simply that all these cadres seem to have lost the rigor of military life and discipline in favor of all sorts of commodities: commerce, beautiful cars, beautiful villas, bourgeois life."[39]

The search for the good life consumes the lion's share of time and effort of many general officers. Military command can yield all sorts of material benefits;

all one needs is gumption and a flair for creative accounting. In south Kivu the FAZ has long tried to suppress the PRP rebellion. Over the years, command of Kivu's military district has become a lucrative plum for FAZ generals who usually establish a financially attractive arrangement with the PRP. By virtue of his command of the military district, the FAZ commander controls the major source of armaments in the area. The PRP obviously desires weaponry so it can continue its rebellion against the regime in Kinshasa. To obtain these arms, the PRP robs local gold mines and then exchanges its booty with the FAZ commander in return for the necessary munitions. In other words, everybody profits: the PRP receives weaponry, the FAZ commander gets the gold.[40]

Collusion with insurgents is not the only way a creative commander can benefit from his position. Foreign military assistance is often diverted from state coffers to private pockets. Zaire's military leaders appropriate U.S. trucks and C-130 aircraft and then use them for private businesses. They also divert other items— guns, gasoline, K-rations, Coca-Cola—from their originally intended purposes (that is, to supply Zairian troops) and sell them openly in markets. Enterprising generals pocket the proceeds of these sales so they contribute nothing to the national treasury. These practices continue even during national emergencies, and the diversion of $500,000 worth of American and other foreign military equipment during Shaba I was both immediate and blatant.[41]

Ranking FAZ commanders engage in primitive accumulation in other ways as well. A key military position is a token of the president's good will. Under Mobutu's system of rule, "good will" usually means the officer has a place in line for presidential largesse, and these magnanimous gifts can constitute an important source of revenue. In addition, military commanders usually receive "psychological action funds" to aid them in smoothing over any difficulties which might arise in the normal and legitimate conduct of the state's military business. These monies appear on no budget I am aware of, but they are nevertheless substantial. In theory, to provide a commander with some budgetary latitude in case of emergency is probably a good idea. In practice, however, commanders regularly pocket these funds and put them to work supporting mistresses, buying villas, or running commercial enterprises. Ordinary funds earmarked for normal operating expenses are diverted in similar ways, as are the salaries of the soldiers under one's command. It also appears the FAZ has removed military salaries from the centralized computer listings so individual commanders can have more control over funds ostensibly destined to pay their men. As we shall see presently, this practice, perhaps more than any other, has a direct and deleterious effect on the civilian population who come into contact with local garrisons.[42]

High-ranking officers do other things that adversely affect both the smooth running of the state and how civil society perceives the armed forces. Not all these activities concern accumulating funds. Equally often military officers create problems by interfering with civilian administration. A case in point is the late General Bobozo, who long held an active interest in his region of origin, northern Equateur. Bobozo entered the Force Publique in 1933 and eventually became a sergeant, the highest rank a Zairian could obtain under Belgian rule. He was Mobutu's sergeant during the 1950s, and there was some family tie between the two men. Although never trained for command, Bobozo—like other noncommissioned officers of his generation—became an officer after independence. Mobutu named him commander of the FAZ in 1965 either because of their family attachment and personal loyalty, or because Bobozo was too incompetent to pose a threat to Mobutu's continued rule, or both.[43]

Bobozo hailed from the collectivity of Abumobazi in the Zone of Mobayi-Mbongo and always maintained a close interest in the affairs of his home. He intervened frequently in the life of this collectivity, and territorial administrators stationed there usually took a dim view of his machinations. In 1969, for example, an assistant subregional commissioner went to Abumobazi to install a new collectivity chief. The general did not like the commissioner's choice, one of the local notables, so he ordered soldiers based nearby to intervene directly. They incarcerated the commissioner and deposed his choice for the position. The soldiers then installed Bobozo's preferred candidate, his brother, and eventually released the commissioner.[44]

General Bobozo again intervened in local matters several years later when he instructed his brother, now firmly ensconced as collectivity chief, to eliminate the collection of the *contribution personnelle minimum* (CPM), the annual head tax. Bobozo made this magnanimous gesture because villagers had already performed numerous road-building labors on behalf of the collectivity, and he felt the government should reward them by eliminating the tax. This caused problems for territorial officials since the collectivities depend on this tax to pay their employees and the zone commissioner of Mobayi-Mbongo was thus forced to fire some personnel. The following year, 1973, saw the good general back to his old tricks. He again unilaterally abolished the CPM in Abumobazi and, this time, successfully arranged the intervention of the minister of finance, who ratified and legalized the decision. Moreover, as a reward for all their services to the state (and the general), Bobozo nominated all of Abumobazi's locality chiefs for membership in the National Order of the Leopard, a national honorary society. This episode is indicative of the problems he caused in the area. All ordinary citizens in this part of Zaire had to participate in various road-maintenance schemes, and the state exempted no one else from paying the CPM—a fact which undoubtedly rankled people in other locales. The territorial administrators were also less than pleased by this attention from one of the highest-ranking generals in the army, for it only complicated their lives.[45]

One other serious problem arises when Bobozo and other military barons intervene in local affairs. Put simply, when local garrison commanders see their generals intervene with impunity in political and administrative processes to realize all sorts of ridiculous whims, the sentiment grows that they, too, are immune from the normal rules and laws of the state and have license to conduct their affairs however they choose. This certainly contributes to the tendency of many local commanders to behave as independent war lords. During the years (1972–

73) General Bobozo was toying with Abumobazi's tax structure, Mobayi-Mbongo's zone commissioner often complained about the behavior of these soldiers. He directed one such complaint to the district's military commander:

> In effect, several reports are often addressed concerning these soldiers cited to higher authorities [and] no exemplary punishment has been given to them.
> I have arrived at the end of my strength. These soldiers are so indisciplined during the exercise of their functions. All they do is mistreat the population, make away with their goods, tax them with illegal fines, and I don't know what else.
> In conclusion, I ask, purely and simply, their immediate transfer.
> In the contrary case, I will see myself forced to decline responsibility to the competent authorities. This is not the first time complaints have been made about the savage dealings of these soldiers.[46]

Clearly at his wit's end, the zone commissioner could do nothing. Local garrison commanders know they are not ultimately responsible to territorial officials. They also know as long as they have the support of their military chiefs, men like Bobozo, zone commissioners can never bring them to heel. In other words, those at the top of the command hierarchy, the generals, set the tone and provide the example for those beneath them in the attitudes and procedures to follow when dealing with both local politico-administrative officials and the people themselves. Generals usually pass corrupt practices down the chain of command.

The most usual form this takes is when superior officers appropriate salaries destined for their troops. Soldiers generally know the funds they are supposed to receive will not be forthcoming and therefore use their positions to extract resources from the citizenry. Monies, goats, chickens, and all worldly goods are fair game for gendarmes on a rampage. The troops have other ways to increase their incomes, and the obvious fact they bear arms is of great importance. Members of the FAZ will occasionally rent themselves out as private guns and enforcers-for-hire in local disputes. People involved in conflicts with fellow citizens will approach off-duty soldiers who, in return for payment, will make life miserable for an opponent. The services provided vary according to the situation. At times they might do no more than rough up someone; in other instances they have set villages aflame. What matters is the contracting party's ability to pay. In situations like these, soldiers are not acting on behalf of local courts but, rather, as independent entrepreneurs and hired vigilantes.[47]

Although all these activities are reprehensible, it would be wrong to characterize them as corruption for the sake of corruption, or even corruption induced by cupidity. They are often the actions of men with families who must make ends meet at the end of the month. There is thus a major qualitative difference between corrupt practices at the higher and lower ends of the military hierarchy. I offer this observation not to excuse the brutality of enlisted men, but to point out their motives may have more to do with survival than accumulation. Corruption, in other words, has different meanings and motivations depending on where one stands in the social class hierarchy. For the general, corruption may mean Mercedes and mistresses; for the corporal, a full larder; for the peasant, an empty belly and undernourished children. Unfortunately, such fine distinctions offer little solace to the peasant or city dweller victimized by rampaging gendarmes.

The state rarely punishes soldiers guilty of abuses against the population. Although they usually escape punishment for their misdeeds, the president and his military advisors occasionally feel the need to set a few examples. In almost every case of "exemplary punishment," however, those who are sanctioned with loss of position, fines, or imprisonment are either lower-ranking officers or ordinary soldiers.[48] The state seldom touches those most responsible. Furthermore, these "clean up" campaigns generally occur when Mobutu would like to refurbish Zaire's image because of international pressure, such as a new round of negotiations with the IMF or an important juncture in the U.S. congressional appropriations cycle.

Gendarmes are also able to abuse the population with impunity because of the structure of Zaire's legal system. All officers, noncommissioned officers, and enlisted men in the GDN are judicial police officers (*officiers de la police judiciaire*, OPJ) who have the right and responsibility to seek out legal infractions and arrest those responsible. In theory, their responsibilities as OPJs end at the territorial boundaries of their station. Thus, a gendarme assigned to the Zone of Lisala can make arrests within the zone's territorial limits, but not outside them.[49] This power of arrest enables them to jail citizens for alleged offenses and to use the threat of arrest to extort payments in cash and kind.

Ultimately, however, the problem of control arises because civilian magistrates and OPJs cannot effectively enforce the law on errant members of the FAZ. When gendarmes violate the law, the task of bringing them to justice rests with their officers. But in isolated areas, sergeants and corporals command many local garrisons. Officers appear infrequently, if at all. Who, then, in the local context, is going to make the arrest? According to the code of military justice, civilian authorities may arrest soldiers for wrongdoing, but military authorities can restrict their access to military camps and personnel if military secrets are involved.[50] Under these circumstances even the lowliest sergeant will soon discover his camp has crucial military secrets which simply cannot be exposed to prying civilian eyes. But such subtle legal subterfuge is almost never necessary because gendarmes have substantial firepower, whereas civilian magistrates and judicial inspectors do not. Even should an officer be present and the appropriate papers filed and sent up the chain of command, there is no guarantee military authorities will act. In numerous cases civilian authorities have lodged complaints and opened judicial dossiers which the military's legal machinery then simply ignores.

As some of the correspondence cited previously indicates, there are territorial commissioners and magistrates who would like to prosecute soldiers and gendarmes who abuse their positions. Thus far they have been unsuccessful. One magistrate explained, "It is not possible to control them. The sergeant majors are officers of the judicial police. The sergeant majors obey only their military chiefs. They are more obedient to the lieutenant than they are to us. They take refuge before the military authorities. They are not afraid of civilian authorities. Civilian justice cannot touch them; they are regulated by military justice."[51]

All this places civilian territorial authorities in an ambiguous position. On the one hand, they need the gendarmes and other forces of order handy to suppress banditry and attempts at revolt. They know the power of the state must be shown to be appreciated. Lisala's archives contain numerous requests from various commissioners requesting additional gendarmes because, as political authorities, they feared they would be the first and most visible targets of the "bandits."[52] Yet, on the other hand, they know gendarmes, when present, will be both uncontrollable and a source of constant irritation because of their tendency to live off the backs of the population and intervene in local political affairs.

The FAZ and the GDN are not the only groups who badger the population. There is also the JMPR, whose disciplinary brigade requires separate treatment because it is a specialized arm with distinctive tasks. The JMPR is also, strictly speaking, one of the few Zairian institutions clearly recognizable as an arm of the party rather than the government. In theory, its major tasks are vigilance, the protection of youth, prevention of "incidents," and the provision of information.[53] But in performing these tasks, members of the disciplinary brigade often abuse their responsibilities in much the same way gendarmes do, and there is little doubt the vast majority of Lisala's population see them as coercive and extractive representatives of the *Mobutiste* state. Legally, the directors of the JMPR are OPJs who have the power of arrest in judicial matters punishable by a maximum of five years of penal servitude. Brigade members do not have this authority but can, in case of flagrant violation, and in the absence of proper legal authority, pursue and arrest wrongdoers.[54]

The problem, however, is that, like soldiers and gendarmes, brigade members are often incompetent, seldom controlled adequately, and tend to act as a free-floating source of oppression. When the brigade participates in nocturnal patrols throughout the Cité of Lisala, for example, there are usually complaints of theft, arbitrary arrest, and extortion.[55] An annual report assessing the brigade's overall performance in Mongala put the matter starkly:

> Our elements of Mongala's Disciplinary Brigade do not conduct themselves as they should. The majority of them are indisciplined and incorrigible. . . . The program that we have traced them is not always followed and respected.
>
> During the course of the year, three quarters of them were the objects of arrests, summonses to the prosecutor's office, to the police tribunal, to the gendarmerie, etc.; despite that, these brigade members do not want to change their behavior. . . .
>
> As far as vigilance is concerned, we have always indicated to you that our elements of the Disciplinary Brigade work with much loyalty and fidelity.[56]

This document candidly pinpoints the difficulties. Although supposedly agents of order, brigade members are usually less than popular with their fellow citizens. Even when not involved in making arbitrary arrests or imposing illegal fines, people still treat them with suspicion because they know the brigade is also watching them and reporting their activities.

The JMPR's disciplinary brigade can also be a source of annoyance for politico-administrative officials. From time to time, "overzealous" brigade members will take it on themselves to uncover and report financial irregularities to higher authorities.[57] This certainly does not endear them to local officials, and, when it occurs, those whom they denounce try to transfer the brigade members in question. In this regard, then, these brigade members—like CND agents—maintain an antagonistic relationship with territorial officials.

The disciplinary brigade is a source of oppression which, like the FAZ and GDN, increases the misery of the population. Furthermore, ample evidence indicates politico-administrative officials and even JMPR directors often have great difficulty controlling the brigade. The reasons for this indiscipline are not hard to find. Most brigade members are unemployed youth without much education who tend to be drawn from the lumpenproletariat; in consequence, the dividing line between the brigade and overtly criminal elements is extremely thin. One of Lisala's schoolteachers cogently expressed the population's view of the disciplinary brigade by noting President Mobutu had performed a valuable service in giving the brigade uniforms, for people now knew who the thieves were and could identify them from afar.

In late 1981 party officials in Kinshasa decided they would have to do something about the disciplinary brigade. Because it was so compromised in the eyes of the public, they determined it would be best to eliminate it entirely. The procedure followed was typically *Mobutiste*; authorities abolished the brigade and then immediately resurrected it under a new name, the Corps des Activistes pour la Défense de la Révolution. This ostensibly new branch of the JMPR was to assure revolutionary discipline and vigilance without, however, either repeating old errors or reverting to the practices of the unlamented disciplinary brigade.[58] But, as is so often the case, the new name was merely cosmetic and has not changed the relationship between the JMPR and the Zairian people.[59]

To this point I have discussed these coercive arms of the state as homogeneous ethnic wholes, as though their patterns of recruitment are irrelevant. But recruitment and access to the highest positions in these organizations are critical because these questions often influence how the citizenry perceives the state. In evaluating the significance of the ethnic factor, it is important to realize Zaire has never had an ethnically balanced or representative army. The Belgians believed certain "martial" races were more suitable for military service than others. In consequence, the Force Publique recruited disproportionately among favored ethnic groups like the Bangala, Tetela, Zande, and Luba-Kasai. Recent research, however, has noted that actual recruitment within these groups usually focused on people at the "physical, social, and educational margins of traditional societies," on those who were anything but warlike.[60] But the colonial army was still overwhelmingly drawn from Equateur and the northern, Lingala-speaking part of Haut-Zaire. Furthermore, since the Force Publique was a Lingala-speaking institution, other Zairians easily came to identify this coercive arm of the state with the country's northwestern quadrant.[61]

Mobutu has an obvious interest in maintaining the loyalty of the state's coercive arms, and, if anything, he has consciously accelerated and intensified the army's long-standing pattern of ethnic recruitment. Perhaps more than others,

Mobutu knows a coup d'état represents the most direct threat to the continuity of his rule. An exiled Zairian believes, "One master idea inspires the Zairian army's system of organization and promotion: the obsession of a coup d'état."[62] Mobutu has translated this fear into a system of advancement which insures generals remain loyal, compliant, and completely dependent. Competence is rarely, if ever, a factor since one of the things he fears most is an effective military establishment. One of the easiest ways of establishing loyalty is to limit access to the military's top positions to ethnic brothers and others from Equateur. The regime has imposed these limitations more stringently in recent years, and it is safe to say natives of the president's home region thoroughly dominate the upper reaches of the FAZ and GDN.[63] The more Mobutu's political and psychological insecurity has grown, the more he has relied on ethnic quotas in the military, and the narrower and more restrictive these have become. The dissident parliamentarians who met with a visiting U.S. congressional delegation in 1983 indicated the FAZ had, in effect, ceased being a national institution. Citizens from most of Zaire's regions had simply been purged from the armed forces, and the range of acceptable recruits was being further narrowed to exclude even those from two of Equateur's southern subregions: Mongala and Equateur. As a result, recruitment focused increasingly on the northwest corner of Equateur, especially the subregions of northern and southern Ubangi (Gbadolite and Gemena). The parliamentarians further noted ethnically homogeneous elements from Ubangi now compose the presidential brigade.[64]

The likely consequences of this progressively narrowing base of recruitment are immediately dangerous and, in the longer perspective, potentially devastating. Some of these considerations appeared in relation to the CND and do not bear lengthy recapitulation. Nevertheless, it is again worth citing Rothschild on one crucial point:

> [W]hen such ethnically skewed military, police, or administrative agencies are deployed by the central government to help it cope with a serious domestic interethnic conflict (or, indeed, any kind of domestic crisis), they will not be accepted by the contending dominant and subordinate groups as the neutral instruments of some supraethnic *raison d'état* but will be perceived as ethnic participants, reflecting prevailing ethnopolitical stratification, with an ethnic stake of their own in the mode and shape of the conflict's prosecution and resolution. . . . In other words . . . the overethnicization of important, and in theory neutral, institutions of the state may compromise their legitimacy and discredit their acceptability as supposedly impartial executors of the society's transcendent regulative rules and values.[65]

It is thus significant that the dissident parliamentarians, who hail mostly from Kasai and Shaba, included the following passage in their memorandum to visiting U.S. congressmen: "Once definitively realized, will not this tribalization of the Army result [*déboucher*] one day in a genocide conceived as an efficacious means for subduing all the other regions politically and economically and thus reducing them to a state of slavery?"[66] Such fears are by no stretch of the imagination restricted to the polity's upper reaches, however dissident. Callaghy's work on local politics in Kivu and Bas-Zaire clearly indicates many others share precisely the same worry. One village chief recounted that soldiers from Haut-Zaire had told him they would do everything in their power to provoke the local population and, if successful, would try to exterminate them.[67] Is it any wonder, then, most Zairians actively despise and fear these coercive arms of the state?

Conclusion

Observers of the Mobutu regime agree the forces of order are less than popular with their compatriots. Few would disagree with Nguza's statement: "To intimidate the population and mistreat it, there are the only actions that soldiers appreciate."[68] Certainly, this would be part of the prevailing perception of the state's coercive arms in the Zairian countryside. But most ordinary folk, if they were willing to talk at all about the subject, would probably add other observations to an overall appreciation of these armed forces in their own lives. Speculating on the relative absence of radicalism in the rural areas, one Zairian social scientist noted that risk is a factor worth considering.

> [D]espite the increasing weakness of the state, the harassment of the rural population by the local party cadres and the soldiers is always present. Although the peasants view these local party structures as weak and corruptible, they have no doubt in their mind about the capacity of the state for repression. . . . people have come to change their perception about the reality of the state. But there is no doubt in the mind of the people that the state is always strong.[69]

While I generally agree with this judgment, one small nuance must be highlighted. Would it not be more accurate to say the state, or at least its coercive arms, is *relatively* strong? The reason is simple. Soldiers and gendarmes have weapons and the will to use them; peasants and town dwellers do not. A journalistic account of the Tanzanian invasion of Uganda and the subsequent overthrow of Idi Amin highlights the FAZ's relative strength. Tanzanian troops in hot pursuit of Amin's forces often crossed into eastern Zaire and discovered border posts were rarely manned. They thought the central government had forgotten its soldiers so far from the capital. The Tanzanians found Zairian troops more interested in obtaining their good boots than in anything else. The local population befriended the visiting Tanzanians and told them to come back and liberate Zaire when they were finished with Uganda.[70] The state was obviously weak, but people felt it was still too strong to overthrow without significant outside assistance.

That this was the attitude of Zairian citizens when confronted with foreign soldiers on their territory indicates, as perhaps nothing else could, the low regard people have for the FAZ and GDN. It is difficult to quibble with the understated judgment of the thirteen parliamentarians: "the ditch between the army and the population grows larger each day. Their reciprocal relations are made of mistrust rather than collaboration and mutual esteem."[71] But how can trust and esteem develop when soldiers wantonly fire bazookas into population centers; when they rape mothers, wives, and daughters; when they steal livestock, crops, and money? The problem, ultimately, is that both citizens and soldiers know the latter are not present in the countryside to protect lives, property, or the state's territorial integrity.

What, then, are the operative tasks of the Zairian state's coercive arms? First, as already suggested, the FAZ, GDN, and JMPR are present to intimidate and control the population. Nighttime patrols, *ratissages*, and raids on villages all play their role. Second, and obviously related, the forces of order are responsible for violently repressing revolts, strikes, rebellions, and any other regime-threatening manifestations of unhappiness with the *Mobutiste* social, economic, and political order.

Despite its importance, I have deliberately chosen not to deal with this task at greater length because the subject has been adequately covered elsewhere, and examples abound of FAZ and GDN actions against both urban- and rural-based dissidence. We already know much concerning the state's repression of the population in Shaba in the wake of Shaba II in 1978; the massacres in Idiofa, Bandundu, after the Kasongo affair in 1978; the massacres at Katekelayi and Luamuela, Kasai Oriental, in 1979; and the FAZ's reign of terror in Moba and Kalemie in 1984 and 1985.[72] On each occasion the state unleashed its power on a part of the population which local representatives of the *Mobutiste* order deemed subversive. Each of these series of events also underlines a point made earlier. The power of the state is relative and depends on the perspective from which one views it. Shaba II demonstrated the FAZ was incapable of meeting a military challenge from armed and organized rebels without exhibiting a completely demoralizing dependence on Mobutu's Western allies. But the aftermath also demonstrated the FAZ, despite its shortcomings against opponents able to return fire, could still make short shrift of unarmed and unorganized Zairian peasants.[73]

Earlier we saw how the coercive arms dealt with labor unrest at Maluku. Similarly, in chapter 3 we mentioned the violent suppression of the schoolteachers' strike in Kisangani. Such tasks are also an important part of the Zairian army's operative mandate. In all these actions against the population the forces of order are clearly interested in enforcing and representing the power of the state. This is the third major task of the Zairian state's coercive arms. It matters little to Mobutu if his armed forces are able to repel an invasion. He knows if his regime should face serious difficulty he can always call on his friends in the West for succor. Shaba I and Shaba II demonstrated that. Nor does Mobutu care if his military and police forces are corrupt and inefficient. Corruption and inefficiency are, after all, watchwords of his regime. But it is crucial these same corrupt and inefficient forces maintain a certain degree of strength relative to the population. They must be able both to represent the power of the state and to occupy available political space. The state, when viewed from abroad, may well be weak according to certain evaluative criteria analysts choose. But, from the vantage point of the villages and towns, even a ragtag, underpaid, poorly disciplined, and utterly corrupt platoon of Zairian soldiers represents a truly awesome power.

Their often-chaotic presence and occasionally anarchistic behavior constitutes a latent threat to Zaire's people—a threat, moreover, they understand only too well. What of the question posed at the beginning of this chapter? How closely do the state's coercive arms, when viewed from the hinterland, resemble the theoretical images of the state the "architects of abstraction" have so painstakingly constructed?[74] Frankly, not closely at all. Most who write about the state and focus on its component coercive organizations usually assume, correctly, the essence of the state is somehow connected to centralized control maintained over the arms of coercion. State-building is thus usually perceived as a struggle waged by a growing and increasingly powerful state with a vocation to dominate and subjugate various forces and groups in society. The difficulty occurs when analysts assume centralization rather than demonstrating it.[75]

It has, for example, become commonplace in the literature on Zaire to note Mobutu's first initiative after seizing power was to set in motion a process of centralizing power in his own hands. He reduced the number of provinces, created a single party, and brought police and military forces under centralized command. True enough. But one of the striking phenomena to emerge from this study of how Zaire's coercive arms interact with the population is the great extent to which the state leaves military and police commanders in the field on their own. On paper the FAZ, GDN, and JMPR are centralized organizations. Mobutu is commander-in-chief of the FAZ and GDN, and he names the head of the JMPR. What exists on paper, however, does not necessarily exist in the countryside. As we have seen, sergeants or corporals command many garrisons. Remote military and police outposts are inspected rarely, if at all. Communications within the military chain of command, moreover, are doubtlessly just as chaotic and irregular as they are within the civilian administration. In addition, the transportation network is no better for the FAZ and GDN than for politico-administrative officials and magistrates.

In a general essay on the police in Africa, Marenin observes police tend to be dispersed "and are under local control or none at all, at least in their daily activities."[76] The organization charts, in other words, may look centralized, but local posts usually have enormous latitude. Thus, ostensible centralization is coupled with effective lack of control, particularly over daily and routine tasks. Although the powers in Kinshasa are perfectly aware of the "ordered anarchy" which the forces of order regularly induce in the countryside (they have reports from the CND), they extend little or no effort to exert disciplined control over local FAZ and GDN commandants. Ironically, a good measure of decentralization thus exists under the umbrella of the ostensibly centralized state. One great paradox is that, for the most part, the citizenry assumes the soldiers and gendarmes who regularly oppress them are, in fact, acting at the behest of the centralized power. The state is thus a complex entity—singularly monolithic in the mind of both theorists and citizens, but actually a complicated congeries of only imperfectly controlled organizations and institutions, each motivated by different imperatives.

Throughout this chapter, I have alluded to politico-administrative officials and magistrates who wish to control the state's coercive arms in their respective bailiwicks. They complain frequently, and probably sincerely, to the national government that FAZ and GDN contingents are beyond their reach and out of control. They thus face an anomalous situation in which the tools of the state's coercive power do not truly operate at the behest of the state's most important local representatives. Neither commissioners nor magistrates are able to control sergeants and corporals. They fail because those in power in Kinshasa are either unwilling or unable to do anything about the situation. The result is a constant and free-floating source of insecurity in the countryside. Villagers know a squad of gendarmes might appear and install a reign of terror; commissioners know they can never count on either the gendarmes' presence if needed, or their sobriety if present. Military and police detachments in isolated up-country areas are often left to their own devices, and, in effect, this means the local contingent can generally do as it pleases. Coercive power without significant control increases insecurity among both rulers and ruled.

5

The State as Family, Mobutu as Father
Political Imagery

> The MPR presents itself as a large family to
> which all Zairians without exception belong.
> All Zairians are born equal members of the
> MPR. . . . In the large family of the MPR the
> occidental notion of majority and minority is
> out of place for the children of a single family
> are not divided into majority and minority
> clans. . . . This characteristic of familial or-
> ganization distinguishes the MPR from classic
> political parties.
>
> —Engulu Baangampongo[1]

> Citizen Mobutu Sese Seko, in his capacity as
> father of the large Zairian family, profoundly
> touched by the fatal accident provoked by a
> falling tree in the enclosure of the *Ecole of-
> ficielle de la Gare* which resulted in the death
> of one pupil with three seriously wounded, has
> just sympathized with the misfortune of the
> stricken families by giving them Z 2,250.
>
> —*Elima*[2]

> A good chief is a father of a family. As a
> father, he must punish his children but first he
> gives advice and directives. But if the
> children do not obey, they will be punished,
> but that is not his fault, obviously.
>
> —A lower-level clerk[3]

The political police and the state's other coercive arms are not alone responsible
for the continuity of the *Mobutiste* state. No state can long exist on mere coercion; leaders must persuade people to accept, willingly or with resignation, the
reigning political order. Although regimes may arrive in power and initially main-

tain themselves through force, they most often achieve stability and continuity by encouraging citizens to accept valid symbols and metaphors of authority. As in most states, Zaire's rulers have inherited a complex, multifaceted ideological and symbolic superstructure which they revise and recreate every day. This superstructure aids immeasurably in maintaining political quiescence and in assuring that more than naked force supports the regime.

Zairian leaders often justify political directives and policies on the grounds they will be good for the larger national family. As the citations above indicate, images of father and family pervade all levels of political thought and discourse. The state presents the MPR as a large family; President Mobutu casts himself in the role of father of the Zairian family or as father of the Zairian nation; and, finally, many of Lisala's bureaucrats believed an ideal administrative chief, or superior, was someone who would treat subordinates in much the same way a father would behave toward his children.

These idealizations of father and family are both part of and, in turn, contribute to a widespread pattern of political authority in contemporary Zaire. The notion of authority patterns derives largely from Eckstein and Gurr, who define it as "a set of asymmetric relations among hierarchically ordered members of a social unit that involves the direction of that unit," and their definition provides a useful starting point.[4] Elaborated as part of a larger project on congruence theory, Eckstein posits that, in general, political stability, high levels of governmental performance, and—I would add—legitimacy will result where patterns of authority in social institutions such as families, schools, and private enterprises are congruent with (that is, resemble in broad outline) patterns of authority in the formal political arena.[5] The concept of authority patterns thus directs attention to specific points of comparison between families, schools, state agencies, churches, and other private organizations. To what extent do relations between parent and child resemble those between teacher and pupil? Between principal and teacher? Between administrative superior and subordinate? Between president and citizen?

Eckstein has applied his ideas to politics in Norway, while others have studied patterns of political authority in different contemporary social settings.[6] Equally germane is the work of historians on early modern Europe. One scholar has noted, in reference to France under the *ancien régime*:

> To make a clear-cut distinction between private and public life . . . is of limited relevance to the analysis of old-style monarchical societies. In the latter case, the family as an institution had many of the characteristics of a public institution, and the relations of kinship served as a model for social and political relations. The authority of a king over his subjects and that of a father over his children were of the same nature—neither based on contract, both considered "natural," accountable only to God.[7]

But neither the family, nor the patterns of political and social authority it engendered, were in any way immutable givens. Ariès traces the evolution of the European family and the concept of childhood across centuries and notes the family became the building block of the state and the basis of the monarchy only after considerable time.[8] Callaghy has explicitly compared the similarities in social formation between Mobutu's Zaire and France in the age of absolutism. Parts of his analysis feature, though do not emphasize, the presence of familial imagery in both states.[9]

The concept of authority patterns is also useful because it forces us to penetrate the state's ideological and symbolic facade to see where these images originate, how the powerful manipulate them, and, importantly, whose interests they serve. Although still valid, the observation of Marx and Engels that "the ideas of the ruling class are in every epoch the ruling ideas" has become banal.[10] Rather, as Giddens suggests, the key is to demonstrate how "structures of signification are mobilised to legitimate the sectional interests of dominant groups, i.e., to legitimate *exploitative domination.*"[11]

This chapter, therefore, will not examine directly any of Zaire's explicitly propagated formal ideologies—Zairian nationalism, authenticity, and *Mobutisme.*[12] Instead, it will probe the more deeply-rooted ideological and symbolic moral matrix undergirding both Zairian state and society. What is the significance of this pattern of political authority and symbolic moral matrix? What does it mean? Why has the Zairian population accepted it so readily? To answer these questions, I shall first explore certain aspects of these pervasive paternal and familial metaphors. In doing so, the ideological cement of the *Mobutiste* state, in other words, the imagery, metaphors, and symbols which provide a basis for continued rule, should become clear. Although the state itself is intimately involved in creating symbols and images, organizations within the realm of civil society also participate actively. Churches, schools, and media all play an important role.[13] I shall then detail how and why this imagery evolved. What, in other words, are its precolonial, colonial, and postindependence origins? Finally, it will be worth considering how this ideological cement affects public policy, how those in power abuse and manipulate these images, and the meaning and importance of the state's dominance over ideological discourse.

Pervasive Metaphors

Research conducted in Lisala included interviews with a wide range of administrative, political, and educational personnel at the level of the subregion, zone, and collectivity. During these formal and structured encounters, respondents answered the following questions: "In your opinion, how should a good administrative chief behave? How should he act? What must he do?" Although the bureaucrats occupied different positions within the state apparatus, their responses displayed a remarkable, and surprising, uniformity. The twenty-three subregional administrative service chiefs, fourteen lower-level clerks at the zone and collectivity, ten politico-administrative commissioners, five MPR officials, and five school officials all had strikingly similar responses to queries concerning their ideal chief or administrative superior.[14] Administrative position, age, ethnicity, or level of education did not appear to affect the basic themes contained in the responses.

Moreover, as should become clear from the answers themselves, the characteristics arbitrarily extracted from the data below are not mutually exclusive.

The first salient theme or characteristic to emerge is that of teacher. Many respondents believed a good administrative superior should instruct his subordinates and provide examples of good work habits and procedures. "A good chief should set an example for his subordinates. He should always be present and give a good work example." And, "Normally, a good chief must, before anything, respect subalterns, so that you, yourself, will be more respected. Be dynamic. A chief should not always punish, but should also correct."[15]

Morality is closely related to the notion of the chief as pedagogue. Lisala's bureaucrats believed their chiefs should also be repositories of moral virtue and set a good example for their subordinates. In their words, "A good chief is respected on the moral plane. He must know the difference between good and bad"; "He should be just. No sentimental judgments. He must control his outbursts. He must behave as an authority. He must be reserved where women are concerned"; and, "He should be just to everyone. And then [lead] a moral, healthy, and exemplary life. And then love of work. Worry about others concerning their problems."[16]

Sociability was also mentioned frequently. Many believed an ideal administrative superior should be open, friendly, hospitable, and receptive toward subordinates. A good chief "must be easy [to get along with] and should have relationships with his agents. He must be decisive. Intelligent. There should be social relationships with the agents. One chats with agents after working hours. One drinks together sometimes." Similarly, "We are approached by people who have a different upbringing than we do. One has to avoid an authoritarian attitude. Before everything, sociability"; and "A good chief must be sociable because in being sociable there will not be any information which escapes him."[17]

Competence is yet another theme present. Although not mentioned with the frequency of some other characteristics, many bureaucrats nonetheless said one quality they thought important in a bureaucratic superior was ability. They did not define competence narrowly, however; many subsumed notions of goodness, understanding, dignity, politeness, fairness, and concern for subordinates under the broader rubric of technical ability. As one respondent put it: "A good chief is he who really knows how to execute or give the plan of work to his collaborators. A competent chief thinks, above all, about his collaborators and subordinates. He is nasty toward those who do not obey, but he is not wicked. He really knows how to lead his personnel. He is wise and competent."[18]

Authority and decisiveness also appeared regularly in the catalogue of ideal qualities. More specifically, "He should be punctual and dynamic and authoritative. He must assert himself"; "To have an authoritative air"; and "A good chief should be severe but not nasty."[19]

Most traits these bureaucrats enumerated are clearly those they see as paternal, and paternal authority is an idealized model for exemplary bureaucratic behavior in Zaire. A father is a teacher—he instructs; he is a repository of moral virtue; he is sociable, listens to opinions, and cares for those under his control; he is competent, decisive, dynamic, and authoritative. Many bureaucrats made explicit the analogy between father and administrative superior. In their opinion, a good administrative superior ought to behave as a *"bon père de famille,"* as a good father of a family.[20] In addition, "A chief has to educate his personnel as a father educates his children"; "He gives examples to his children. . . . He cannot punish his children all the time"; and, "A good chief must . . . [not] hurt those he administers. Not be rude, but authoritative, . . . firm. A chief has to know how to decide. But a chief must be a father, supple."[21] Other responses did not directly invoke the analogy, but their tenor was broadly paternal.[22]

This notion of administrator as an idealized father is common in Zaire and appears throughout the state's hierarchy. It is found not only in the responses of bureaucrats to specific questions, but also in formal written directives from national and regional authorities. One set of instructions for regional administrators reads as follows:

> We must also recognize that a Command-level Functionary has human duties to fulfill toward his personnel. It is not because an accountant . . . commits a blunder or an error that one must automatically open a disciplinary action against him, or remove him. A Chief is also a Father and an educator. It is therefore suitable to analyze well the censured action of the subordinate agent. . . . Perhaps it is only a simple error of ignorance on his part? In that case, it is better to educate, correct, warn to enable him to feel his errors and give him the opportunity to correct them.[23]

Similarly, one regional commissioner told subordinates to remain dignified; open to dialogue with those administered; and receptive to advice and counsel from administrative collaborators and subordinates.[24] Although these instructions do not specifically invoke the paternal analogy, they nonetheless stress these same fatherly qualities. A political commissioner's address to a special committee on administrative reform contains identical themes.

> The Chief knows his subordinates will discover all his defects as quickly as his qualities. The Chief must be . . . of even temperament . . . objective. He will make himself feared and will observe continuously. He will respect his collaborators and reason with the guilty. He will take his responsibilities come what may. . . . He must, however, know how to make others work . . . be frank and direct . . . courageous. He must know how to obey before making himself obeyed. In the absence of these qualities, there is no true Chief.[25]

In his study of the influence of society and culture on Zairian administration, Mpinga-Kasenda discusses the Zairian notion of chief and argues this cultural preconception affects both administrative procedures and the relationship between citizens and state. Mpinga feels Zairian administrators often act in light of their cultural preconceptions of how a chief should behave, rather than according to impersonal Weberian bureaucratic norms. They thus devote substantial time to chatting with people, listening to their problems, and deciding each case on its particular merits rather than according to official rules. The cultural expectation is that a *"bon père de famille"* will decide, not a letter-of-the-law bureaucrat.[26]

Mpinga's argument is convincing. Lisala's archives are filled with letters, both from bureaucratic subordinates and ordinary citizens, requesting intervention by understanding and sympathetic fathers rather than bureaucratic officials. One bureaucrat, requesting money for the maintenance and reconstruction of his territory, wrote: "I have the honor to ask you to please examine the case of the Center of Lisala with the attitude of a Chief of a family for there are no rules without exceptions."[27] Similarly, when Air Zaire's local representative requested three hectares of land to construct housing and other facilities for its personnel, his letter to the subregional commissioner closed with the phrase, "Knowing your spirit of *bon père de famille* . . ."[28] In both cases, the supplicants couched their requests for administrative action in language comparing the decision-maker to the father of a family and thus invoked his sense of paternal solicitude.

It is but a short leap from father to family. Zairian officials often mention that they and their particular offices are merely part of a larger family. One of Lisala's JMPR directors reasoned this way: "You know, it is as in a family. The child is there to safeguard the father. The child aids the father of the family. The JMPR is a branch of the MPR. The vigilance it does is for the MPR. The MPR is the father."[29] Others frequently resort to the same imagery. At a meeting of subregional administrative service chiefs to discuss the next year's budget there were numerous references to the *bankoko*, the Lingala word for ancestors. In addition, the budget officer emphasized repeatedly that he was the eldest person present and that "We all form a family."[30] In retrospect, the chairman probably perceived himself as the father of a family. This would explain both the references to his relatively advanced age and to the presence of the ancestors. In many African societies, ancestors are an integral part of the family and there is usually respect, if not deference, for older members, both because of their wisdom and because they are a living link to the deceased.

The comparison between family and administration, or family and political party, or family and nation is striking. While Lisala's bureaucrats might possibly have used the images of father and family to illuminate certain things to a foreigner because these metaphors were easy to grasp, the regime's highest-ranking policymakers nevertheless explicitly employ such imagery as well. The citation in epigraph from Engulu, longtime member of the MPR Political Bureau and the president's crony, is a case in point. Bokanga's study of Zairian cultural policy is also germane. He writes, "The basis of Zairian cultural policy is Mobutism, the doctrine of the People's Revolutionary Movement, that vast family which brings all the citizens of Zaire together under its roof."[31] Ranking officials thus consciously present the MPR and the Zairian nation as one large family; a family unified under the leadership of its "father." President Mobutu actively portrays himself, and is painted by the mass media, as father-chief of the national family.

Zairian mass media are state controlled, follow explicitly the line that ruling authorities trace in such matters, and portray nation and party as an all-inclusive family. Examples from one of Kinshasa's daily newspapers demonstrates the point. Referring to the place of the child in the MPR, *Salongo* maintained, "The MPR, like an attentive parent attached to his progeny, constitutes a framework where each child—boy or girl—feels loved and surrounded by affection. . . . the Zairian child has the right, in the bosom of the large family of the MPR, to an intellectual education, to better nutrition, to health care, and to a moral development."[32] The press also uses the familial metaphor in speaking of the handicapped. "Having realized that a family better merits this name only when it succeeds in gathering to its bosom all its daughters and all its sons, . . . the MPR has assigned itself the difficult task of taking particular care of these militants."[33]

The image of the father also appears frequently in the written press. The teacher is "a father for his pupils"; the territorial administrator is "the father and the great animator of the party before those he administers."[34] But newspapers usually reserve this image for the president and describe his every action in glowing paternal terms. For example, when Mobutu met with students at Kinshasa's university campus in 1979, the press laconically described a rather turbulent session this way: "During the course of this meeting which brought the father and his children face to face, the students received from the Guide the promise that their complaints will be the object of an attentive and diligent examination."[35]

More generally, the press treats virtually all Mobutu does as actions of an enlightened and benevolent father figure. These extracts merely sample this voluminous outpouring.

> The good father of the family is he who consecrates his life entirely to his children. He knows neither fatigue nor respite. For his daily worry is the salvation of his own. This is the case of the Guide Mobutu. . . . Wherever he passes and wherever he will pass it is this image of Mobutu Sese Seko, father of the family, whose constant worry remains the promotion of the material and moral conditions of his children.[36]

> And as a good father of the family, clairvoyant, considerate, attentive, and affectionate, the Guide Mobutu Sese Seko has, one more time, traced the route to follow and indicated the principal moral rules . . . [Zairians] are expected to respect.[37]

> In all times, the President-Founder of the MPR has always preoccupied himself with the well- and better-being of the Zairian people. Of which he is, moreover, the well-loved and generous father.[38]

The press reinforces the image of Mobutu as father by constantly cataloging the Guide's magnanimous gestures. Whenever a new development project is completed—be it a renovated building, a new construction, road, or hospital—the press presents the new or rebuilt facility as a gift from the President-Founder to his children, the Zairian population. An electric generator in Kivu; a new supply of drugs, blankets, and sheets for a hospital near Tshikapa; the sum of Z 180,000 for the renovation of Bukavu; Z 8,000 for the construction of a new administrative building in Limete; and even a hearse for the city of Mbuji-Mayi are all "gifts" from "The Father" that demonstrate his paternal love and solicitude.[39]

Since Mobutu is their father, it is only fitting Zairians have a mother. This role is usually divided between the president's spouse and the memory of his mother, Mama Yemo. For example, the late Mama Mobutu's annual reception for the wives and children of the accredited diplomatic corps always provided an occasion for the press to laud her maternal solicitude and present her as the mother of all Zairians.[40] Moreover, when she died in 1977 she was described "for each one of us" as an "affectionate, attentive, considerate, irreplaceable mother."[41] The anniversary of the death of Mobutu's mother usually calls forth press coverage referring to her as "our mother."[42] Maternal schizophrenia reached new heights in 1980 when, on the eve of a papal visit, the president married his consort of long standing, Mama Bobi Ladawa. Mobutu then announced his new wife would not be so pretentious as to try to do more than the late Mama Mobutu but would devotedly "aid me to support the heavy burden of my responsibilities of chief of State, conductor of men and father of the family, educator."[43] At the time of the wedding the press clearly downplayed the role of Mobutu's new spouse. Nevertheless, within a relatively short time articles appeared extolling her maternal qualities in much the same terms once reserved for the late Mama Mobutu. A lengthy piece about one of her farms noted the dispensary benefits from her "maternal solicitude" and that it was open both to her workers and their families and to neighboring villagers. In one worker's words, "Each time she comes to the farm . . . it is first toward us that the Citizen Presidente goes to inquire about our situation and our problems. And it is with the heart of a mother that she listens to us."[44] Similarly, the press began using her birthday as an occasion to describe her maternal gifts to the sick, needy, and destitute. By 1983 "her name had become a veritable sesame in the milieus of the poor and disinherited . . . [She had become] the mother of 30 million Zairian men and women."[45]

Like most potent symbols, the father image is ambiguous. At times, the idea of father is conflated with the notion of chief which, we shall later see, also has paternal overtones in some Zairian cultures. Never was this more pronounced than on Mobutu's fiftieth birthday in 1980. To celebrate properly this signal event, itself a yearly national holiday feting the nation's youth, Mobutu traveled to Lisala. For three festive days, Mobutu was installed as the grand customary chief of the Bangala. During the coronation, participants recited the usual litany of Mobutu's virtues and named him Mobutu Moyi, literally Mobutu the Sun or Mobutu the Light. Furthermore, the presiding chief declared the ceremony's true meaning was that Mobutu was now the greatest Bangala chief and "above him, there is only God."[46] Although Mobutu thus became a latter day Sun King, the event's historical and cultural legitimacy was somewhat suspect. In the first place, Bangala ethnicity was an artificial creation of the colonial period which later acquired political significance immediately before independence.[47] Second, the man who crowned Mobutu had absolutely no historical standing; he was merely a long-serving collectivity chief and thus an appointed politico-administrative official. These ironies notwithstanding, the ceremony deliberately presented Mobutu as a precolonial chief, harkening back to a time when, in some cultures, the chief was perceived as a father figure.

On one level all this is part of a consciously orchestrated personality cult in which all Zairian media actively glorify the president. Moreover, local authorities force the population to participate in *animation* (political cheerleading, dancing, singing praise songs) and marches of support.[48] In all these activities, Mobutu is always the father of the nation and his current spouse, or the memory of Mama Yemo, serves as the national mother figure.

The media attribute all material progress and infrastructural development directly to the president's magnanimous paternal solicitude. These are "gifts" from the "father" to his "children." In a one sense, then, all flows from Mobutu, the ultimate source of bounty, and citizens must show frequent gratitude to their national father. For example, to close a regional conference on coffee-growing at Isiro, the regional commissioner thanked the president on behalf of the region's coffee farmers. After all, the Guide's "incessant concern to develop agriculture harmoniously and rapidly" was surely why the conference took place.[49] In a related vein, while exhorting his troops to even greater efforts on behalf of the Zairian revolution, the Captain-General of the FAZ asserted the army was the personal creation of the father of the revolution.[50]

This notion of "gift" from, and the consequent "debt" toward, the father of the nation merits comment, for in Mobutu's system of rule it serves several important purposes. First, it underlines the ostensibly centralized nature of the Zairian state. To read the local press, one would never think a national budget existed. Instead, one would receive the impression that all expenditures, even for routine matters such as the construction of new administrative buildings or the replenishment of a hospital's supply of pharmaceutical products were a consequence of presidential magnanimity. Even though the national budget is a misleading document and the presidency directly controls the lion's share of resources, it is still fatuous to assume that *all* could possibly come from his hands. Nevertheless, that is precisely how the media portray these things. In brief, this procedure emphasizes Mobutu's total control since all resources pass through his hands. He is, therefore, the ultimate distributor. V. S. Naipaul captures succinctly this aspect of Zairian reality. "The President issued a statement, just to let everybody know that what the Big Man gives the Big Man can take away. . . . He gives and he takes back."[51] The lesson is obvious. People had better toe the approved line or else Mobutu will "take back."

Second, and perhaps less obvious, these presidential "gifts" create bonds of dependence between leader and follower and contribute to the leader's ability to maintain his power and control. Anthropologists have long been aware of this aspect of gift-giving, and Barth's classic analysis of Swat Pathans remains relevant.

> Gift-giving and hospitality are potent means of controlling others, not because of the debts they create, but because of the recipient's dependence on their continuation. A continuous flow of gifts creates needs and fosters dependence, and the threat of being cut off becomes a powerful disciplinary device. In contrast to the giving of salaries and bribes, which places responsibility on the chief who pays, gifts and hospitality give a chief political control over followers without saddling him with responsibility for their actions.[52]

In the last chapter we saw that high-ranking FAZ officers often receive presidential largesse, which may be a considerable source of supplementary income. These gifts, however, make the military men (and civilian officials, too) more dependent on the president for the continuation of these considerations. As their dependence grows, their loyalty to the source of this bounty increases apace. The "gifts" from Mobutu to his people may be seen, in part, as an attempt to extend, at least symbolically, this general principle to the entire population.

Dependence is not the only result of giving gifts. Another is "debt." Sahlins reminds us societies dominated by, and committed to, kinship relations usually manifest a moral commitment to generosity. But generosity in such circumstances is a two-edged blade. The generous chief is a model for his kinsmen; but, at the same time, his generosity is a substantial constraint. More specifically, "Because kinship is a social relation of *reciprocity*, of *mutual* aid; hence, generosity is a manifest imposition of debt, putting the recipient in a circumspect and responsive relation to the donor during all that period the gift is unrequited. The economic relation of giver-receiver is the political relation of leader-follower."[53] There is, however, both a significant ideological element and a catch here, for, as Sahlins again indicates:

> [I]n strictly material terms the relation cannot be both "reciprocal" and "generous," the exchange at once equivalent and more so. "Ideology," then, because "chiefly liberality" must ignore the contrary flow of goods from people to chief—perhaps by categorizing this as the chief's due—on pain of canceling out the generosity; or else, or in addition, the relation conceals a material unbalance—perhaps rationalized by other kinds of compensation—on pain of negating the reciprocity. . . . [M]aterial unbalances in fact exist; depending on the system, they are borne by one side or the other side, headman or people.[54]

In other words, when Mobutu assumes the role of generous father-chief he speaks directly to a broad cultural and historical understanding of generosity, reciprocity, and obligation among kinsmen. Vansina, for example, argues that Mobutu's style of rule derives from the precolonial big man "who tied clients to himself by favors and expectations of favors, and dropped them whenever their stature or their power bases acquired features that seemed to give them some independence of maneuver."[55] In a fundamental sense, many precolonial Zairian polities resembled the "Big Man" model of governance. In these systems, moreover, generosity was often incumbent on those wishing to rise in the social hierarchy.[56] Personal rule, based on the power and authority of an individual, was crucial and did not depend on formal political office. In some regards, this system closely resembles what Price, in an excellent analysis of Ghana, calls the "Big-Man Small-Boy" syndrome. Big man and small boy encapsulate a pattern of normal behavior between people of unequal status, wealth, and power, which, although paternal, may contain highly authoritarian elements. The big man looks after the welfare of his social inferiors, retainers, and dependents; he makes decisions; and he gives orders. He is conspicuous both in his generous distribution of largesse and in his exercise of power and authority. On the other side of this equation, the small boy demonstrates an equally conspicuous gratitude for the bounty the big man showers on him and behaves toward the big man in a way

that is fulsome in its manifestation of respect and deference. The context of social relations is crucial in determining these roles. It is entirely possible that a
big man in one context (say, in relation to his own children) might well be a small
boy in another (for example, in regard to a bureaucratic superior).[57] The big man
model of politics illuminates certain aspects of Zairian political behavior and is
obviously related to the metaphors of father and family.

In addition, Mobutu's gifts subtly remind people of their moral obligation to
reciprocate his fatherly generosity. This is the third purpose of the paternal imagery prevalent in Zaire. Mobutu distributes largesse to the population and thus
creates an implicit moral and material debt. The billions of dollars he extracts
from the Zairian people is therefore only his due. The father bestows gifts on his
children and what he receives in return is merely repayment of an outstanding and
never-ending obligation. Through clever manipulation of the image of a generous
father, Mobutu has created a system in which all he receives is but the demonstra-
tion of a culturally embedded concept of mutual exchange: no theft, no corruption, no exploitation; only grateful "children" repaying their generous "father."

The mass media are not alone in proffering these symbols to the Zairian people.
Mobutu also spreads the images of father and family throughout the collective
consciousness and often explicitly invokes the paternal metaphor in his speeches.
Many of his public pronouncements contain phrases such as these: "As a good
father of the family, we have traced the method to follow"; and "the most elemen-
tary prudence commands a government, like a family chief, not to spend above
its revenues."[58] In addition, Mobutu also likes to consider himself a chief. By
way of illustration, "The last word must return to the chief. I am the chief";
"The respect due to the chief is obligatory and sacred. When a chief decides,
then he decides, period, that's all"; and "Doesn't it come to mind that in our
African tradition, there are never two chiefs? . . . can anyone tell me if he has
ever known an African village with two chiefs?"[59] Similarly, in discussing his
relationship with Nguza and his role in advancing Nguza's career, Mobutu also
played the chief: "Good. I receive Nguza. He kneels before me. I am for authenticity and in Zaire [*chez nous*] if you kneel before the chief, all is absolved.
Everything is washed away."[60]

All Mobutu's close collaborators know the president requires public allegiance
and spread the preferred vision whenever possible. While permanent secretary of
the MPR's political bureau, Nguza addressed the Belgian Royal Institute of International Relations in these terms:

> Since then [Mobutu's seizure of power], all the ideas, all the concerns, all the preoc-
> cupations of the entire people and of each Zairian individually converged toward the
> President of the Republic and toward him alone, becoming thus the nucleus of na-
> tional opinion. Thus was born a direct democracy such as existed in our tradition-
> al society where all the interests, all the palavers, all the problems found their solution
> near the patriarch who was at the same time *father and chief* of everybody.[61]

Here Nguza was certainly trying to flatter the president before a distinguished,
and perhaps skeptical, Belgian audience. But the true power of the images of

father and family is usually better reflected when diplomatic considerations are not involved. In addressing the regime's luminaries at the MPR's ideological institute, a FAZ general said, "The moral education of the soldier will also concern itself with the respect and maintenance of his weapon. The soldier will learn to treat the tool placed under his guard as a good father of a family" (perhaps thus evoking a peculiarly Belgian sense of bourgeois thrift in the management of the family's wealth).[62] When schoolteachers went out on strike in several locations in late 1983, students supported them by organizing demonstrations. In Likasi the territorial commissioner met with students and the transcript of their dialogue shows again the paternal imagery's power and pervasiveness. They addressed the commissioner in these terms: "You, Commissioner, you are our father [*papa*]. We, your children, have a problem [and] we want you to give us the solution."[63] Moreover, when grousing about his low salary, one of Lisala's bureaucrats phrased his complaint in terms of the paternal metaphor. "We have to have confidence in our president who has always thought of his children."[64] A general who believes a soldier should treat his weapon as carefully as a father would manage his family's resources; demonstrating students who address the central authority's local representative as "father"; and a bureaucrat unhappy about his salary who hopes the president will think of his children all demonstrate how these images and symbols have permeated society at large. More importantly, perhaps, such examples indicate the population has accepted and incorporated the imagery into its own perceptions and political discourse.

Although Mobutu and his collaborators propagate these images, the state is not solely responsible for their hold on society. In Kivu's substantial informal economy people often apply an idiom of kinship to business apprenticeships. Groups of young shopkeepers, or credit seekers, just starting out and hoping to establish themselves and their enterprises generally approach an older, wealthier merchant. The beginners are "sons"; the older man becomes their "father." The sons work for the father for a period and help him accumulate more wealth. In return, the father sets up the sons in businesses of their own and introduces them to the wider local trading network. Although this relationship between old and young has nothing to do with family, its participants explicitly refer to it in paternal and familial terms.[65] I wish to emphasize that this way of conceiving the relationship occurs in a milieu where the state is held in disrepute; where businessmen operate either at the margins of, or beyond, the state's long reach. There is thus no reason to assume the contemporary state is entirely responsible for spreading the symbols of father and family, and it becomes important to trace the origins of this political imagery.

Origins of the Imagery

Precolonial Political Heritage

A product of colonial conquest like most African states, Zaire is an artificial entity encompassing a diversity of indigenous ethnic groups. Although Vansina has correctly noted the fundamental unity of Zairian cultures, we must still exercise extreme caution when generalizing about precolonial politics and society.[66] Moreover, delineating the influence of precolonial politics and society on the images of father and family is highly complex because "family," at least as we commonly understand the term in the West, is a category that had little precise meaning in precolonial Africa.[67] Among Bakongo in Bas-Zaire, for example, the family has never been a well-defined entity and there is no precise word for it in Kikongo. People have spouses and children parents, "but the domestic functions we associate with families are mostly carried out by other groups than nuclear families."[68] Another difficulty arises because throughout this region lineage structures provided a basic ideological charter which changed over time. The prevailing ideology of kinship was so pervasive that even slaves were incorporated into it.[69]

Vansina's historical and anthropological work emphasizes that lineage, long the basic building block of anthropology in Africa, is not an immutable aspect of African social structure but a flexible, changing, and complex ideological construct which was consciously manipulated in the struggle for power and wealth. Like all ideological concepts, notions of lineage and family legitimized political rule, justified inequality and exploitation, and generally provided societies with a moral charter. Lineage, then, was a political ideology which ultimately justified and "explained" why some had more power, influence, and wealth than others.[70]

In most Zairian societies, however, structures and terminologies of politics and family were so closely interwoven that distinctions between the two realms become almost purely analytical. People regularly used the idiom of kinship both in the politics of small-scale societies in the forest and in the Lunda empire in the southern savanna. In this latter case, people extended notions of kinship to refer to fixed political relationships between positions in the Lunda state so that the holder of a hierarchically superior office became, in effect, a "father" in relation to his "sons," who held subordinate positions. These relationships were not between individuals but, rather, between the offices themselves.[71] It was, in other words, common to find a near congruence between familial and political terminologies and roles throughout the area that now forms Zaire.[72]

In almost all Zairian cultures, the role of father was certainly serious and important, and, from the child's perspective, the father's position at the head of the nuclear family made him the first concrete representation of authority. This initial presence of paternal authority is important even among matrilineal peoples, such as the Yansi, where eventually the maternal uncle comes to play a dominant role in the child's life and fortunes.[73] For the matrilineal Basakata, the most crucial relations within the basic family are those between father and children. Compared to the maternal uncle, the Musakata father incarnates understanding, tenderness, and comprehension.[74] The cash economy and spread of capitalist values and mode of production has accentuated the fundamental importance and influence of the father. Those matrilineal Bakongo laborers in Mayombe, Bas-Zaire, employed regularly on plantations are neither "target" nor migrant workers because their substantial occupational stability is reproduced and transmitted across generations. The effects on both family structure and the role of the father have been significant, for the more the father is integrated into this rural working class, the greater the son's chances for later social mobility. Moreover, this change in the local economy has meant the father's influence now predominates over the maternal uncle's.[75]

There is thus little doubt the father plays a singularly important role in the life of his children in most Zairian cultures. A study of the image of the father among Tetela boys expresses one aspect of this extremely well.

> The Tetela consider the father as the living symbol of the survival and unity of the group. He possesses a divine authority which is transmitted from father to son. . . .
> The father thus occupies a privileged place. He possesses an authority which he holds from the ancestors. He has the duty to guard and to perpetuate the customs . . . . The ancestors manifest themselves through the father, making him speak and act. The father represents more than his own person. This reference to the ancestors of the clan confers on him considerable authority, prestige, and power. The father thus always remains an inaccessible and sacred personage for his children.[76]

Obviously, few fathers live up to this glorified image, and when children realize their fathers are human, and therefore flawed, psychological tension usually results.[77] Nonetheless, most Zairian children, especially boys, are close to their fathers, for they usually initiate the child into the society's social relations.[78]

In many precolonial Zairian cultures the role of chief was closely associated with the overarching family structure. Membership in a certain lineage, usually a senior one, was often crucial in determining who became chief, or even had the opportunity to become one. Here, too, political life and family structure intermingled closely. But chiefs had different roles in different cultures. Some Zairian societies, like the Kuba, had hereditary rulers in charge of established, ongoing administrative hierarchies; in others, such as the Bapoto, the chief was at best a first among equals with limited power.[79] The Mongo had a constitutional monarchy which circumscribed the chief's power. In this society, as in many others, people thought the chief was "The Father" of the group and his authority was paternal.[80] A word of caution, however. Among the Mangbetu, and presumably others, many chiefs and would-be chiefs used the ideology of fatherhood either to reinforce their political power and legitimacy or as a claim on chiefly office. The image of the father was thus also an ideological weapon in the struggle for power and perquisites, and the mere existence of the imagery and its association with a certain chief, or pretender, did not necessarily indicate great power. Leaders and followers were usually engaged in a constant process of renegotiating the terms of political authority and the paternal imagery and its concomitant ideology was but one arrow in the political quiver.[81]

The Colonial Era

The colonial state also diffused a certain paternal imagery, and those who manned the outposts of empire "often extended overseas a system of rule . . . patterned after the relationship of authority which existed in the metropole between parent and child and school and child."[82] Even the most liberal and sincerely motivated colonizer displayed a deep-seated paternalism. In this regard the Belgians were probably no different than the British or French. The Belgian system differed, however, in the degree to which paternalism and paternal roles became deliberate aspects of colonial policy.

In neither British nor French colonies was there such a concerted attempt to create the ideological concept of the *indigène* [native]. This notion established the boundary line between white European and black African worlds and also indicated, in broad outline, policies for dealing with Congolese. In most policy areas, the aim was to provide a tutelary and educational authority while, at the same time, insuring Africans complied with the exigencies of the European capitalist system. This also entailed preventing or constraining any spontaneous or creative reactions to the penetration of capitalist values and ideas. The aim was total control: political, physical, intellectual, ideological, and cultural. The creation of various types of *politique indigène,* as well as the concept of an undifferentiated, homogenized, and culturally uniform native, alienated ordinary people from their cultural roots to a far greater extent than in either British or French colonies.[83]

The Ministry of the Colonies made sure territorial administrators received detailed instructions on how to behave in virtually all situations. The paternal and ideological vision of Belgium's colonial enterprise invariably permeated these guidelines.

> In their relations with the natives, agents will never forget that their capacity as educators creates for them the imperious obligation to everywhere and always give a good example. . . .
> *The maintenance of the authority of the government must, before everything, be the constant object of the preoccupations of our functionaries. . . .*
> The populations can be developed and the Colony progress only in order and under the aegis of a solidly established authority. . . .
> . . . The native must be convinced that the authority intends to make itself obeyed and that all serious disobedience, as soon as known, will be punished without an excess of severity, but also without weakness.[84]

In other words, the colonial administrator was to teach by setting a good example; be forceful and give paramount concern to the maintenance of established authority and order so essential to progress; and immediately correct disobedience, firmly but without severity. These and similar instructions, contained in a lengthy volume that was required reading for the entire administrative establishment, certainly had a profound effect on ruler and ruled in terms of both the imagery and the role models they helped create and diffuse.

The Catholic church and its missionaries were an integral part of the colonial establishment and worked intimately with the administration. Catholic influence was considerable, for the colonial state all but abdicated its educational policy to the various religious orders, and missionaries controlled most schools in colonial

Zaire. (There were also a much smaller number of Protestant schools and, after the mid-1950s, a nascent network of secular institutions.) Furthermore, because of the Catholic church's near monopoly over education, it was certainly the colonial state's premier ideological apparatus.[85]

Louis Franck, one of the major colonial ministers, argued "only the Catholic Christian religion, based on authority, can be capable of changing native mentality, of giving our Blacks a clear and intimate awareness of their duty, of inspiring in them respect for authority and a spirit of loyalty towards Belgium."[86] Two major assumptions are implicit: first, one task of religion is to inculcate respect for authority; second, blacks had a specific mentality. These assumptions were closely related in practice, and I shall discuss them together because missionaries believed Africans were children who needed to be taught respect for authority.

The Scheutist Fathers, primarily responsible for evangelization in the area of Lisala, fully shared this view of their flock. To be sure, they felt blacks had certain positive characteristics such as ingeniousness, the remarkable ability to carry things on their heads, and great physical agility. But the negative character traits they discovered more than counterbalanced these "positive" features. These were: intellectual idiocy, the psychological level of large children, and moral poverty.[87] These harsh judgments were not unusual for the time and place, and most other missionary groups agreed that blacks were little more than overgrown children. The corollary was that they therefore needed the European missionary's firm, guiding, and paternal hand.[88] Mazrui has cogently analyzed one result of this perspective:

> The ritualistic language of Christianity in terms of "children of God," and the whole symbolism of fatherhood in the organizational structure of the Catholic Church all the way from the concept of "Pope" to the rank of "Father" among some priests, took on additional significance in African conditions. The metaphor of fatherhood within the Catholic hierarchy reinforced filial tendencies among African converts. Again the repercussions went beyond the particular members of that denomination, and reinforced the dependency complex in the society as a whole.[89]

There is more at issue here than a diffuse, imprecise mind set or world view. Administrative circulars and instructions on education destined for missionaries and teachers deliberately reinforced the notion that Africans were children, and some of the standard injunctions are eloquent on this point. The *Receuil d'instructions aux missionnaires* noted that when dealing with natives, "A deliberately given order must always be executed. The native belittles a chief who does not make himself obeyed . . . the voice of authority has something sacred, even in the eyes of the primitive and the proffered word must be inviolable."[90] Children, even "primitive" ones, respect strength and firmly established authority.

Instructions sent to primary school teachers repeatedly emphasized that Africans had yet to attain the stage of logic and thus had to be addressed in simple, well-ordered sentences "like they are ordered in Europe when one speaks to children aged seven to eight years."[91] If the preferred educational method was simple childlike sentences, then the major vehicle for them was the "general chat" (*causerie générale*). These chats were considered the most important part of the colony's educational program, and missionaries and teachers usually used them to inculcate respect for authority.[92] Unfortunately, these chats deemphasized the students' ability to reason while stressing both dogmatic methods and an appeal to ultimate religious authority. Respect for authority was a constant theme of circulars, instructions, and, presumably, general chats throughout the era.[93] Even as late as 1958 the diocese of Lisala's quarterly bulletin for schoolteachers affirmed that "Civic education will comprise, in the first place, discipline and the respect of superiors."[94]

Thus far we have been discussing both a general view of authority and the specific perception missionary educators had of their students. These were certainly important, but colonial schools went even further and diffused a role model laden with explicitly paternal imagery. The formation of African primary school teachers emphasized both father and family. One student related that when his mother died she told him that, although he would never see her again, she was leaving him a new mother and father—the school.[95] Though doubtlessly an exaggeration, there is nevertheless some truth to the assertion that colonial schools operated as surrogate parents. This was especially true of boarding schools where missionaries tried to isolate their charges from society's "pernicious" and "sinful" elements. For example, one account of education for women noted:

> Inasmuch as the girls enter when they are five or six years old and stay until they are married there is always a wide range of ages in the group. Therefore for the sake of discipline and home training, the entire group is divided into families. The older girls are the heads of the various homes and each house has a family of six ranging in age from five upward. . . . The matron is the mother of all these various families and her word is law, just as the chief is respected in all African villages.[96]

The Belgians deliberately tried to instill in their African primary school teachers the belief that they were paternal figures and should therefore act accordingly. One set of instructions for teacher-training schools maintained the qualities necessary to become a good primary school teacher were "the virtues necessary to a good father of a family, a citizen, a good Christian, qualities and virtues that they must make their students acquire."[97] Similarly, a manual for primary school teachers noted "the school's environment is neither a barracks, nor a prison, but a family where the teacher is a father and the pupils, his children."[98] Throughout this particular manual, the comparison between family, on the one hand, and school, on the other, is overt. Thus, "at school, as in the family, the child must feel at home. . . . In a family, daily work is organized. Each has his work under the direction of the father of the family. The school must also be organized."[99]

The manual's chapter on authority is particularly noteworthy and continues the analogy between family and school. In the family the parents exercise authority, but, while in school, the teacher exercises authority over the pupils. The teacher's authority is absolute: "all authority comes from God who delegates it to legitimate superiors. These superiors pass it on to the teacher, whom the pupils are obliged to obey as God."[100] Given this background, it becomes easy to understand why colonial schools were not hotbeds of critical political thought. Teachers with broad political interests were unlikely to flourish in this environment."[101] Furthermore, the manual enjoins teachers to exercise authority with simplicity and dignity; to provide an example of good morality; and warns against abusing authority to exploit or tyrannize pupils. The teacher must respect his pupils and be self-respecting as well. Finally, the teacher has to be firm. Such firmness, however, must be paternal, lest too great a severity rob pupils of initiative.[102] Other qualities and traits the primary school teacher should have include looking much, listening everywhere, and speaking little; not being too friendly with the pupils, being dignified and reserved; and speaking in a serious voice and not shouting too often.[103] Extraordinary in all these injunctions to primary school teachers is their congruence with the images of authority held by administrators in Lisala. If one were to change only slightly a few basic terms, they would be near identical. Catholic missionaries had educated many of those interviewed, and, for better or worse, certain lessons have endured and an imprint of idealized paternal authority remains.[104]

Although state and school were primarily responsible for creating and diffusing these images during the colonial period, corporate and industrial giants fully shared this general perspective, and an all-embracing paternalism governed life in mining and agricultural compounds. Perhaps the classic example was the Union Minière du Haut-Katanga (UMHK), which deliberately instituted a pervasive cradle-to-grave paternalism that resembled a totalitarian subculture.[105] The company's view of its workers was fully consistent with those of missionaries and colonial administrators. A 1946 policy memorandum stated this perception most clearly.

> . . . [E]ach one in his sphere of action must be a moral as well as technical educator for the Blacks whom the Company entrusts to him.
>
> The colonizer must never lose sight of the fact that the Negroes have the souls of children, souls which mold themselves to the methods of the educator; they watch, listen, feel and imitate. Under all circumstances, the European must show himself to be a calm and balanced chief, good without weakness, benevolent without familiarity, active in method and, above all, just in punishment of misbehavior, as in the reward of good behavior.[106]

The Independence Period

Another factor partially accountable for the pervasiveness of the images of father and family is Zaire's history of postindependence political instability. The early dissolution of the sinews of the state resulted in the emergence of regionally based patriarchs. Willame argues Zairian politics during this period was patrimonial. "Modern patrimonialism appeals to the masses by presenting the ruler as the 'father of his people' [and] . . . the ruler legitimizes his authority by looking after his subjects' welfare."[107] On a more psychological and speculative level, we might also say Zaire's unending strife under both postindependence republics has produced widespread sentiments of insecurity.[108] It is thus possible the dialectic of oppression has engendered a situation in which people unconsciously search for a protector, a father, to shield them from these seemingly unpredictable and uncontrollable outside forces and events.

Since we have already discussed the pervasiveness of the images of father and family under Mobutu, there is no need to reiterate the argument that leaders of the Second Republic have made deliberate use of these paternal and familial metaphors. This is also a contemporary source of the imagery of father and family. But why have these images found so fertile a terrain in present-day Zaire? Why have they anchored themselves in the collective consciousness? What messages does this imagery convey?

Moral Matrix

The images of father and family are so pervasive because they strike a resonant and deeply embedded cultural chord. In other words, they form part of a culturally valid and largely implicit comprehension of the limits of political legitimacy based on a complex and largely unarticulated moral matrix of legitimate governance derived from an idealized vision of patterns of authority and behavior within the family. I shall present the main aspects of this moral matrix only in broad outline, for much is still unknown.

The imagery of father and family and the moral matrix on which it is based provide, first of all, an implicit promise of nurturance and paternal care. One study of adolescents in eastern Zaire noted: "In our epoch, . . . the father remains the principal authority in the eyes of the majority of the adolescents questioned. The great majority express considerable confidence and positive feelings toward him. There are multiple reasons. Two seem essential: the father is considered as the one who 'gives life' and who procures the necessary material benefits for the children."[109] Fathers in Zaire are providers. Recall the commentary of one of Lisala's bureaucrats who felt his salary was insufficient but hoped the president would think of his "children." There is thus, within the imagery and symbols, a promise of paternal care.[110]

Meillassoux's model of the domestic community in Africa divides society into elders, youth, and women. In this context, "father" does not necessarily mean biological sire but, rather, he who nourishes and protects. The eldest man in the productive cycle usually plays this role and provides younger men with the subsistence goods necessary to continue economic reproduction. In addition, he also furnishes the women necessary for marriage and the continuation of social reproduction. The "father" thus "feeds" and "marries." Notions of kinship are used both to support an ideology of power and to legitimize dominance. Even if political domination is imposed from outside the community, it tends to be expressed in ordinary kinship terms. "The sovereign is assimilated to an elder . . . or to the father. He is entitled to 'eat' his subjects as his own children, i.e. to receive part of their labour or the product of their labour. Conversely he is expected to protect them."[111] If we accept the paternal premise of nurturance, then people have a right both to be cared for and, importantly, to have individual relations with the powerful father figure so they may negotiate the conditions of nurture. As Sennett points out, this right is assumed and exercised on a face-to-face basis in many non-Western societies and is a crucial premise of the moral matrix.[112] Implicit, therefore, are the promises of protection, provision, and security. Implicit, also, is the assumption that the "father" must provide these benefits or else lose support and legitimacy. In one indictment of Mobutu's regime, a Zairian academician argues "the 'Father' of the Zairian people has failed to satisfy the basic needs of his 'children' for food, shelter, and clothing."[113] Although this critic places the familial metaphors in inverted commas, the moral matrix itself remains valid; the problem rests with neither matrix nor metaphor but with the father who has failed to fulfill his culturally defined responsibilities.

The imagery is attractive to many because, first, it speaks to a universal psychological need for an assurance of security.[114] Second, the metaphors create an intimacy between rulers and ruled and thus succeed in representing complex political realities in a simplified form.[115] In one sense, this is the task of any ideology, and Vansina notes that lineage ideology in the precolonial forest area "reduced a complex reality to an elegant blueprint."[116] Third, the images are "natural," and, as Gellner observes, "That which is inscribed into the nature of things and is perennial, is consequently not personally, individually offensive, nor psychologically intolerable."[117] Furthermore, such symbols and imagery mask an exploitatively unequal flow of resources with authoritarian overtones, aspects mentioned earlier in the context of paternal "generosity" and the resultant "debt." Because people widely perceive the symbols shrouding such unequal exchanges as natural, exploitation appears that much more palatable. Similarly, because the "father's" authority is "natural," people may have greater tolerance for paternally based authoritarian rule than we might expect.

Symbols and imagery of this kind are ambiguous. Moreover, the more they are ambiguous, the more they are flexible and the more they are powerful.[118] Abner Cohen puts it this way:

> Kinship relationships provide primary, affective moral links with other men, and are thus instrumental in the creation of selfhood. At the same time these relationships may be instrumental in articulating organizational functions, such as the definition of the boundaries of the group, or the provision of channels for the communication of group messages. This "bivocality" is the very basis of the mystery in symbolism. Often a man performing a ritual or participating in a ceremonial is simply unclear, mystified as to whether his symbolic activities express and cater to his own inner needs or the organizational needs of the group to which he belongs. At times he may be inclined this way, at others that. And it is this ambiguity in their meaning that makes symbols powerful instruments in the hands of leaders and elite groups for mystifying people for particularistic or universalistic purposes, or both.[119]

Mobutu can thus invoke the symbolism of father and family to evoke simultaneously several powerful, though partially contradictory, images. In the first instance, and on a corporate level, he is the father of the all-inclusive national family to which all Zairians belong from birth. Second, and on a more personal level, he is the father of each Zairian. This imagery permits him to establish an intimate, individual relationship, at least in symbolic terms, with every citizen. This ambiguity in the level of the imagery and the relationship enables Mobutu to play off one symbolic level against the other. For example, since all he does is, by definition, for the benefit of the corporate family, he can assert his actions always place the good of the whole uppermost. But political actions and policies obviously aid some while hurting others. Any sacrifices resulting from these policies then become necessary for the good of the national family and a vital part of nation-building. If, then, an unlucky or disadvantaged citizen should invoke his personal relationship with the father and request or expect nurture, Mobutu can claim he has acted for the good of the entire clan. Similarly, there is a sense in which gifts and other manifestations of presidential largesse may be portrayed merely as the father taking care of his children. Here the personal level of the symbolism dominates, and gifts to cronies, collaborators, and kinsmen can be rationalized as the fulfillment of the promise of nurture implicit in the moral matrix. Others may well complain about this, but they also realize that Mobutu is acting out the culturally legitimate role of the generous father.

These symbols have another ambiguity. The president and the media may present any attempts to question the *Mobutiste* political order as efforts by ungrateful children to usurp the role of their father who, after all, has their best interests at heart. In this sense the imagery of father and family is so powerful and immediate, I would guess even those who reject the present political order probably do so with considerably mixed emotions. While many of us rebel against our fathers as a normal part of growing up, few of us are able to do so without significant feelings of guilt and personal insecurity.

Images of father and family enjoy a cultural legitimacy in Zaire, but politicians may still manipulate valid symbols in illegitimate ways. As we shall see, some uses Mobutu finds for these symbols have a distinctly seamy side. Vansina persuasively argues precolonial lineages had marked ideological components, and that under the guise of the legitimacy of family, gross disparities of wealth, income, and status existed.[120] Certainly, many contemporary uses of paternal imagery are cynical manipulations of a "natural" phenomenon designed both to enrich the politically powerful and to legitimate harsher aspects of their authoritarian rule. They thus present those with enough temerity to protest, or even revolt, against the present sociopolitical order as misguided children. Similarly, the metaphors enable Mobutu and those in power to portray political repression as firm "parental" discipline for prodigal "children" in need of a political spanking for their own good.

Mobutu and others who currently employ the imagery of father and family have sought to freeze it. Ajami makes the point cogently in relation to Sadat's Egypt.

Sadat's symbols—the community of love, the country as family, himself as the "eldest of the Egyptian family"—serve the same narcotic purpose: escape, a fake har-

mony of interests, a curious avoidance of politics. The myth of the family serves
to freeze the society. . . . Sadat does not seem to be able to move the society—the
best he can do is to stay on top, more like royalty than an active executive. He is
beyond politics, beyond criticism.[121]

Meillassoux's model implicitly assumes that one day the juniors, the youth, will
become elders and thus enjoy more fully the fruits of society. Along these lines,
Kenyatta's classic anthropological study observed that prior to the colonial occupation a well-understood Gikuyu convention dictated one generation should hold
political power only for thirty to forty years. At the end of this time a special
ceremony formally transferred power to the rising generation.[122] Meillassoux and
Kenyatta notwithstanding, Vansina's study of the Central African forest peoples
indicates this did not always occur, and the youth more than occasionally remained
in socially inferior positions.[123] In a related vein, Sennett observes that in these
kinds of societies illegitimate authority "would be precisely the attempt to freeze
the conditions of authority into a single mold. Illegitimate authority . . . would
be identified with permanence."[124] A sense of movement and political rotation
is thus central to a cultural understanding of the topic. In other words, "elders"
have to permit "children" to "grow up," and the "father" must not seek life-long
power. This is the second crucial premise of the moral matrix of legitimate governance.

A political leader's tenure in office is a particularly sensitive question in most
African states. Although there have been numerous examples of peaceful and constitutional transfer of power, few reigning heads of state willingly relinquish their
power and authority. In the generation since most of Africa achieved independence, there are only the examples of certain soldiers who have returned to
the barracks voluntarily, and Senegal's Léopold Senghor. Cameroon's Ahmadou
Ahidjo, Siaka Stevens of Sierra Leone, and Tanzania's Julius Nyerere are at best
partial examples: Ahidjo because his alleged involvement in a subsequent plot
against his chosen successor, Paul Biya, questions the sincerity of his initial action; Nyerere and Stevens because they have retained control of state-parties. This
sorry record notwithstanding, many African leaders do understand the implicit
strictures and limitations the moral matrix of legitimate governance places on their
tenure. Why else do most military leaders who seize power invariably proclaim
that after their job is done, after they have put things right, after they have cleansed
the polity of its ills, they will willingly return to the barracks and hand over power
to a civilian government? In practice, however, things work differently, and the
return to the regiment often occurs only symbolically when they exchange khaki
for mufti. Civilian leaders have no better a record. Even if they achieve power
through reasonably democratic means, they often subvert the processes which
brought them to office and thus eliminate the possibility that others could benefit
from the same procedures.

When Mobutu and the military high command seized power on 24 November
1965, the original proclamation declaring military rule was silent on how long the
soldiers would govern. The next morning, however, Mobutu announced he was

assuming power for five years, and he reiterated the pledge several weeks later.[125] Most Zairians approved of the military coup. The previous regime was thoroughly discredited and politically bankrupt, and during the first five years of his rule few could gainsay Mobutu's popularity and legitimacy. In the early 1970s, however, things started to unravel. The precise date of the slide is impossible to determine accurately, but certainly by late 1970 and early 1971 cracks were beginning to appear in the edifice and the regime's political support began to erode.[126] While this must remain purely speculative, I would argue one reason for this was a popular perception that the "father" was beginning to "eat" too much and seemed to be enjoying his power too much to contemplate honoring his promise to relinquish it.

To weight precisely the exact importance of each aspect of the moral matrix is impossible. These are cultural predispositions and implicit understandings rather than precise numerical variables. It is thus impossible to determine whether, say, a father who nurtures but remains in power too long will have more legitimacy than one who fails to nurture but speedily departs at the expiration of his mandate. The only answer I can now offer is that it depends on a host of other factors which analysts of politics in Africa usually study: economic conditions, degree of corruption, ethnic tensions, divisions within the ruling elite or ruling class, and the extent of exploitation, to name but a few. The culturally defined moral matrix is thus a background framework, not a major explanatory factor. Its overwhelming importance, however, is that without a proper comprehension of these cultural understandings, we will increasingly fall victim to vitiated and erroneous analyses of the other variables analysts commonly employ.

Conclusion

The imagery of father and family constitutes a symbolic representation of an implicit, culturally enracinated moral matrix of legitimate governance which derives largely from an idealized vision of patterns of authority within the family. The distant origin of these symbols may be found in both precolonial patterns of governance and in the kinship ideology which justified significant inequalities in status, wealth, and political power. We may discern more proximate origins in the diffusion of state and school during the colonial period, as well as in the explicitly paternal role models both colonial administrators and missionaries propagated. The precolonial heritage and the legacies of more than fifty years of Belgian colonial paternalism provided a fertile field on which Zairian politicians could sow, yet again, these paternal and familial metaphors. Mobutu and his collaborators have consciously manipulated these images with the result that they now permeate both state and society. But the presence of these metaphors, and the confusion of political and familial sectors which it produces, is far more than a footnote to contemporary Zairian affairs. These symbols furnish the regime with a tough and durable ideological cement that not only renders some brutal aspects of *Mobutiste* rule more acceptable by presenting them with a smiling face, but also affects significantly the conduct of governance and the implementation of public policy.

Political leaders can, and do, abuse these images. Engulu's remark, cited in epigraph, that the children of one family do not divide themselves into majority and minority clans both obfuscates and denigrates fundamental principles of democratic rule. In 1974 the regime promulgated a new constitution and an official publication subsequently detailed the changes. It noted, "the CHIEF has the plenitude of the exercise of power," and "In Zaire the Chief is the incarnation of the MPR family; it is therefore by virtue of this that he exercises the plenitude of power."[127] In everyday language plenitude of power has one meaning: Mobutu decides. In this conception there is room for neither debate nor dialogue, a point Kamitatu-Massamba raises explicitly. Kamitatu argues cogently that precolonial rules of Zairian political discourse (known as *palabre*) require the chief and his council to hear both sides of any dispute in public. All present have the right to participate in the debate, and chief and council retire to render judgment only after all interested parties and spectators have spoken. Once they reach a consensual decision, the chief is responsible for its execution. Only at this point is the chief's decision no longer open to question.[128] Nguza argues a related point and notes the Lunda emperor not only discusses questions openly with his counselors, but also permits the existence of a "loyal opposition" figure who can, when necessary, even go so far as to insult the emperor and remind him of his fallibility. This loyal opposition speaks in his own name, in the name of his peers, and, perhaps most importantly, in the name of the people who dare not speak so harshly to the emperor themselves.[129]

The use of the image of the father-chief to rationalize the centralization of power in Mobutu's hands has contributed to a paralysis of decision-making at all but the highest levels of the state. When asked what decisions they could make at their level, most of Lisala's bureaucrats replied they had no authority to decide anything. "The chief of state makes decisions. . . . Work here is always restrained because one cannot make decisions."[130] Others concurred: "One may not make decisions at the subordinate level"; "I do not like to make decisions since all decisions are made at Kinshasa or Mbandaka"; "Decisions always come from the central government. . . . We only make propositions and submit them to the superior authorities. I cannot make decisions"; and, finally, "Here we simply execute."[131]

This implementation mentality is rife throughout the bureaucracy and results, at least in part, from the ostensible centralization of the Zairian state. Lower-level officials refuse to exercise responsibility for fear they will anger their superiors should something go wrong. Nevertheless, we may also attribute a portion of this bureaucratic inertia to the image of a single chief, one father, who decides issues of state for the good of the larger Zairian family. At the opening session of the MPR's Second Ordinary Congress in 1977, Mobutu frankly criticized this tendency to pass the buck up the administrative hierarchy. "Without doubt in the Zaire of our ancestors, it is inconceivable to have two Chiefs at the head of the State. But, this does not mean that subordinate cadres, holders of popular power by delegation, should cease holding themselves responsible and act irresponsibly in the sectors which are defined to them in the Constitution and the laws of the country."[132] The president then chastised a minister of lands who personally distributed lots, and a vice-rector of the university who personally supervised food in the dormitories.

The incessant refrain that there can be but one chief, one father, as well as the tendency toward the centralization of power it rationalizes, legitimizes, and reinforces, is replicated at each lower level of the state hierarchy. Every little father-chief wants to act as a small-scale model of the president, as one who ostensibly encourages subordinates to make decisions and demonstrate initiative, but who by subtle gesture and attitude actually discourages it. Mobutu may castigate ministers for their reluctance to act independently, but one suspects he is actually pleased. An examination of Ethiopia before the revolution notes Haile Selassie had no interest in having competent ministers because he wished his own abilities to shine in comparison.

> How could he show himself favorably if he were surrounded by good ministers? The people would be disoriented. Where would they look for help? On whose wisdom and kindness would they depend? . . . Instead of one sun, fifty would be shining, and everyone would pay homage to a privately chosen planet. . . . There can be only one sun. Such is the order of nature, and anything else is a heresy. But you can be sure that His Majesty shined by contrast.[133]

Mobutu Moyi (the light, the sun), supreme chief of the Bangala and father of the large Zairian family has absolutely no intention of letting other sources of light and competence compete for popular allegiance.

I noted earlier the media's role in the well-orchestrated personality cult which daily sings Mobutu's praises in glowing paternal terms. The "gifts" from the president to his people underscore and perpetuate the vision of a fatherly political figure whose only and constant care is for the welfare of his children. Unfortunately, those in power also use this imagery both to justify questionable actions, and to eliminate justifiable criticism. When questioned about rumors that the president controlled some 30 percent of the state's budget and diverted much of it for private purposes, one of Lisala's bureaucrats, himself an occasionally strong private critic of the regime, remarked sincerely that "the Chief does not have to justify that to his subordinates."[134]

There is still another way Zairian leaders abuse the imagery of father and family. Since flexible symbols permit political leaders to portray those who rebel as wayward children, political repression against them becomes parental discipline. When thirteen dissident members of the national legislature wrote a lengthy, critical open letter to the president in November 1980, and then had the further audacity to circulate it clandestinely, Mobutu seized all copies and ordered the arrest of those who had signed it. Tried before a disciplinary committee of the MPR's central committee, the dissidents were initially sentenced to death, but then subsequently exiled internally. The "thirteen," as they were soon called, rapidly became the focus of much activity by the regime's opponents. Events proceeded apace and by 1982 the thirteen had formed an opposition political party, the Union pour la Démocratie et le Progrès Social (UDPS). At several junctures Mobutu reiterated his unwillingness to tolerate an opposition party, or even a minority current within the MPR, and the state harassed the thirteen at every turn.

Throughout this period of political repression, Mobutu presented his case to the Zairian people in the usual paternal and familial terms. Speaking before an audience composed of chiefs from Kasai Oriental, the home region of many of the dissident parliamentarians, the president declared "I am the chief of State, [and] as such I cannot be vindictive toward those fellow citizens who insult me. In effect, even among my own children there are those who are docile and others stubborn. One must not therefore believe that Tshishekedi, Makanda, Ngalula and associates are my enemies." Mobutu further explained that if citizens commit grave errors, he acts as a father of the family who, when a child behaves badly, will punish him severely until he repents, but will then reintegrate the offender into the family's affections so that the newly reformed child can continue to work for the progress of the entire household. The president concluded by hoping these stray sons had now understood their errors.[135] When Mobutu addressed the legislature shortly afterward, he reaffirmed that the thirteen were "militants to be reformed and capable later . . . of retaking their place in the bosom of the large family of the MPR, once proof has been established that they have come to their senses. I am the father of the large Zairian family and if I know how to love, I must equally know how to punish."[136] Or, in other words, the velvet glove of paternalism hides an authoritarian iron fist.

This imagery has an obvious hold on President Mobutu; what is equally obvious is that he manipulates it for his own political purposes. Less obvious is that these powerful symbols grip the collective consciousness. In part, this was evident in the responses of Lisala's clerks. It is also apparent in that even those who oppose the *Mobutiste* regime now use these metaphors widely. Moreover, the way in which these symbols reappear in the writings of the opposition underscores the pervasive hold of the moral matrix and the extent to which Mobutu's appropriation of some of its significant language and expressive metaphors works to his political advantage and enables him to dominate political discourse.

Nguza's following statement is indicative: "Yes, I accuse Mr. Mobutu of having committed an economic crime. This crime is all the more cruel that it is perpetrated by the one who even passes himself off as the Father and the Protector of the nation."[137] So, too, is the phraseology of Kanyonga Mobateli, who refers to "the personality of the father of the Zairian dictatorship."[138] The argument, especially in Nguza's case, is not that Mobutu is wrong to adopt these paternal and familial symbols but, rather, that in doing so he has failed to live up to some unstated norm of behavior or, in the terms of this analysis, the implicit strictures of the moral matrix of legitimate governance. The problem, then, from the opposition's perspective, is that their choice of language subtly reinforces the myth of the father they wish to topple.

Mobutu and his representatives have been quick to seize this advantage and invariably argue their case to skeptics in the same familiar paternal and familial terms. For example, in 1982 Sakombi Inongo, then temporarily out of favor and power, responded to Nguza's accusations in an open letter. Speaking directly to Nguza, Sakombi wrote:

> It is thus that . . . you have not yet understood why you were amnestied, nor why the Chief gratified you with so spectacular a promotion, despite the fact that the Regime's high dignitaries reminded him constantly, at the time, that amnesty was not amnesia. The explanation . . . is however that the President of the Republic has risen very high on the ladder of wisdom, that he knew how to remain a Father, in the full sense of the term.[139]

Moreover, in a later passage, Sakombi criticized certain men, presumably those like Nguza, for having adapted badly to sociocultural changes. These people, "when the occasion permits it, always cool their heels . . . in the halls of the residence of the Chief of State, looking for a foster Father. . . Who, furthermore, never hesitates to extend his generous hand."[140] One last example follows. In late 1983, U.S. Protestant missionaries gathered in Washington, D.C., to reassess the role of their church in Mobutu's Zaire. One Zairian delegate, himself a member of the MPR central committee, responded to tales of exploitation, torture, and massacre in these terms: "A true African cannot oppose his father." The rejoinder from a Zairian opposed to the regime was simple and eloquent, "Mobutu is not my father."[141]

Nevertheless, the images of Mobutu as father and of the state as family are constantly reinforced through the mass media and in Zairian schools. A well written, regime-approved civics text argues the president is "Chief of the large Zairian family, [and] the father of the Nation," while continually driving home the point that "respect for the public authority" is a civic obligation.[142] Even if students are critical of what is occurring in their country, and many are, the notions of father and family will probably continue to exert a powerful hold on both the collective consciousness and, perhaps, subconsciousness, thus making the state's ideological cement stronger still.

Although Mobutu and those around him have abused the symbols of father and family, it would be shortsighted to view these cynical manipulations merely as the ideological ploys of a corrupt and rapacious class intent on maintaining power. There are strong elements of that, to be sure. But even so, we still must ask why they have chosen the images of father and family for ideological presentation rather than other images? The reason is that such imagery is culturally relevant and strikes a responsive chord not only in Zaire, but, as we saw in chapter 2, elsewhere in Africa; that legitimate governance in Zaire, and in much of Africa, is based on the tacit normative idea that government stands in the same relationship to its citizens that a father does to his children. There is a substratum of belief which views paternal authority as legitimate as long as the implicit understanding of rights and duties contained in the moral matrix of legitimate governance is not violated. When African political leaders behave as responsible fathers; when they care for, nurture, and provide security; when they do not seek eternal power and they respect the normal rotation of generations; legitimacy, and thus stability, are maintained. But when they violate the implied cultural norms and unarticulated promises of political "fatherhood," legitimacy erodes, tensions mount, and instability, repression, or both, ensue.

Zairian leaders would be well advised to keep their promises, implicit or otherwise. For, as Scott reminds us,

> The most common form of class struggle arises from the failure of a dominant ideology to live up to the implicit promises it necessarily makes. The dominant ideology can be turned against its privileged beneficiaries not only because the subordinate groups develop their own interpretations, understandings, and readings of its ambiguous terms, but also because of the promises that the dominant classes must make to propagate it in the first place.[143]

The long-term problem in Zaire is not that these images are present but, rather, that leaders have ignored the cultural norms and understandings they imply. The consequences of this failure for the *Mobutiste* state could be devastating; they have already proved catastrophic for the Zairian people.

6
The Insecure State, I
Resistance Within—The Magistrature

> It is inadmissible that a foreigner or a Zairian
> citizen, who sees the shadow of the magistrate
> or gendarme come into view, feels terrorized
> rather than secure.
> —Mobutu Sese Seko[1]

> The judicial apparatus is quasi inexistent. It is
> Mr. Mobutu who makes the law; he cynically
> organizes trials and decides in advance the sen-
> tences to pronounce on defendants. Judges are
> coerced into forgetting national and internation-
> al law to conform scrupulously, on pain of
> very severe sanctions, to the directives of Mr.
> Mobutu and his single party, the MPR. Cor-
> ruption in this sector has reached its height.
> —Nguza Karl-i-Bond[2]

The magistrature, like other branches of the state, has grown enormously since
independence.[3] This chapter views Zaire's professional magistrature as a pocket
of resistance internal to the state and focuses on the upper-level judicial hierarchy
and judicial affairs in and around Lisala, rather than on the workings of the chiefs,
notables, and local-level courts. The judiciary's position is curious because in
their implementation and manipulation of the law, magistrates are simultaneously a source of state power and an obstruction to those who would wield it at will,
especially the territorial commissioners, the president's direct representatives in
the countryside. Justice's proper and desirable role in the Zairian Revolution
under the Second Republic's self-proclaimed revolutionary regime is thus a major
theme. What is the role of the courts and judicial power in relation to the more
overtly political sectors? How should the Mobutu regime integrate magistrates
and the judicial system into its political orientations? These queries preoccupy
magistrates throughout the republic, for at issue, ultimately, is the overarching
philosophical, legal, and political question of judicial independence. Why has the

magistrature been both able and willing to resist some of the regime's political dictates?

To understand better the role of the judiciary some background information is necessary, and here students of the Zairian magistrature face a difficult task. With the impetus of the behavioral revolution in political science, the study of institutional settings fell out of favor. As a result, several generations of scholars of comparative politics have either ignored the courts or treated them as afterthoughts. If anything, political scientists saw them as secondary factors in nation-building. The courts and the politics of the legal order have thus largely remained terra incognita to political scientists who have studied Zaire and other African societies. Young's magisterial study of politics in the First Republic, for example, contains little on this subject, while Young and Turner's equally comprehensive successor volume on the *Mobutiste* state ignores the courts entirely. This omission is all the more surprising since they include a legal system as one of the state's essential attributes or defining characteristics. Callaghy's work, moreover, provides but a brief account of the lower-level courts.[4] Only recently have students of comparative politics, especially neo-Marxists concerned with the state, rediscovered the importance of the state's legal apparatus.[5] Although legal scholars, judges, and attorneys have produced a voluminous literature on Zairian law, it is of uneven quality and distinctly limited utility. Nonetheless, occasional reference to it will be inevitable.

Historical Overview

Zairian law at both upper and lower levels of the state's hierarchy is the direct result of Belgian overrule. The colonial experience, as Wyatt MacGaffey cogently argues, created a plural society, but there was no encounter between the forces and institutions of "modernity" and "tradition." "The 'customary' sector was a political artifact of colonial rule, endowed with an ideology of 'tradition' in which Belgians believed and to which BaKongo gave lip service when it suited them to do so."[6] Although in theory handed down from the ancestors and grounded in local precolonial history, in reality contemporary colonial forces fabricated and shaped unwritten "customary" law at the grass roots. There was nothing "traditional" about it.[7] MacGaffey's insight holds for both other parts of Zaire and, as Chanock indicates, much of Africa as well.[8]

At the state's upper reaches, the Belgians constructed the Zairian legal system in the image of their own, but without its democratic provisions. In this regard, they were no different from the French or British. The colonizers introduced European written law into Zaire during the era of the Leopoldian Independent State, when royal decree, promulgated as need arose, was the tool for enacting basic legislation. As time passed, these royal decrees, based generally on metropolitan precedent, eventually became a considerable body of written law known simply as the "Codes."[9] In Zaire, as in Belgium, the *procureurs* (public prosecutors) are magistrates (*debout*/standing) responsible for seeking out infrac-

tions, preparing, and then prosecuting cases before the sitting (*assis*) justices. Although the two branches of the magistrature are administratively distinct, individual judges often move back and forth between them, and here the term
"magistrate" covers both categories.

   In general, there was an important ambiguity in the role and position of standing magistrates. On the one hand, they were judges, part of the judicial power,
and the Colonial Charter guaranteed their independence from the executive. The
state could suspend this independence only in times of emergency when there was
a threat to public safety.[10] In this context they were completely independent and
free to follow their legal and professional conscience. On the other hand, they
were also part of the executive power and subject to the hierarchical commands
and directives of the attorney general, the governor of the colony, and the minister of the colonies. This executive aspect of their position came to the fore when
implementing legislation, regulatory dispositions, and the judgments of the courts
pertaining to the maintenance of public order.[11]

   Nevertheless, magistrates took their judicial independence seriously throughout
the colonial period and clung to it tenaciously whenever the executive tried to
encroach. Speaking before the Belgian Royal Colonial Institute in 1932, one of
the great colonial proconsuls, Pierre Ryckmans, declared, "Good feeling is not
the rule between administrative and judicial authorities and shocks are frequent."[12]
In 1931, for example, the revolt of the Bapende in Kwilu resulted in a purge of
the territorial administration. After the revolt, an independent-minded magistrate
reported in detail on the abuses of the state and private companies in the area.
Although an integral part of the power of the state, the magistrature often sang a
discordant and critical note in the usually harmonious chorus of state, company,
and church. In general, both the colonial administration and the companies considered the judiciary far too independent and thus, from their perspective, prone
to meddle in affairs which did not concern it.[13] Paradoxically, therefore, although
judicial organs have always been a manifestation of the central state's sovereignty,
the magistrature maintained positions of internal independence which often con-
flicted with other arms of state power. This pattern of structural conflict within
the state continued after 1960 and has remained a constant difficulty for both territorial administrators and magistrates under the Mobutu regime.

   Like its colonial progenitor, the Zairian judiciary is now a well-entrenched arm
of state power. This was not always the case, however, for the judiciary was one
of the branches of the Zairian state the decolonization affected most severely. The
Belgian magistrates who ran the system departed virtually en masse after independence, and Zaire was set adrift without qualified judges. While waiting for
Zairian universities to begin producing the requisite personnel, non-Belgian expatriates and acting judges temporarily promoted from the ranks of the more competent court clerks filled the interim. Despite severe disruptions, several factors
mitigated against complete collapse. In the first place, expatriates and court clerks
did, in many cases, render herculean service to the state. Second, the sudden
departure of experienced Belgian magistrates affected the system more at the top
than at the bottom because local courts at the collectivities and zones handled the

vast majority of civil and criminal cases. Collectivity chiefs and notables continued to hear cases, while zone commissioners still presided at their level. In other words, only the upper levels of the judicial hierarchy, from the subregion up, were disrupted notably. Finally, the judiciary was usually able to remain aloof from regionalization and the politicization of ethnicity which plagued other branches of the state; thus, it retained at least the appearance of ostensible judicial independence and political neutrality inherited from the Belgians.[14]

Courts and Commissioners: Judicial Independence

Since the advent of the Second Republic, relations between magistrates and territorial commissioners have been strained and generally hostile. After a tour of Equateur in early 1970, the then regional commissioner noted a "total lack of understanding between the different services functioning in the interior and especially at the headquarters of the District [subregion]. This situation is much more marked between other administrative services and the *Parquets* [prosecutor's office]." The commissioner felt this "lack of understanding" denoted insufficient interaction between the parties, and he therefore ordered weekly meetings to review areas of contention.[15] But while lack of regular meetings and absence of personal contact might explain part of the problem, there are other more serious and basic reasons for tension between the judiciary and the territorial service.

For one thing, there is the larger question of judicial independence. This prickly issue has resurfaced persistently since Mobutu seized power and is a perennial source of tension between magistrates and commissioners. Conflict over the incomplete integration of the magistrature into the state's administrative hierarchy is a constant irritant. Subregional commissioners exercise a political mandate, hold presidential appointments, and represent Mobutu in their administrative circumscriptions. In theory, the Zairian administration practices "unity of command" which, in practice, means that all correspondence to higher levels of the state structure must pass through the subregional commissioner's office. Failing that, the commissioner is at least entitled to receive copies of reports from administrative services at the subregion. Nevertheless, despite the often-emphasized "unity of command" ethic, magistrates rarely, if ever, send the subregional commissioner copies of reports or judgments. When asked specifically about professional relations between themselves and the subregional commissioner, one magistrate replied, "There aren't any. . . . We do not ask their opinions before doing something. We deal directly with Mbandaka. In the subregional committee of the party there is collaboration. No, I don't send him any letters."[16] Another maintained, "There is no professional relationship. We are completely independent. No, we send our letters directly to Mbandaka or Kinshasa."[17] In other words, magistrates generally work outside the established administrative hierarchy, and this causes tension between themselves and politico-administrative officials. In this regard, their relationship is similar to the one between commissioners and the political police.

A second reason for this tension also stems directly from the concept of judicial independence. Stated simply, judges are the only officials in Zaire who have the right to say "no" to politico-administrative officers such as the subregional and zone commissioners. The commissioners are all OPJs who can arrest law breakers. After making an arrest, a commissioner can compile a judicial dossier and then forward it to the *parquet* for prosecution. But magistrates must see the process conforms to prescribed procedure; should they determine either that there has been no infraction, or that the commissioner has exceeded his legal authority, they may quash the dossier and order the prisoner's release.[18] One prosecutor elaborated:

> If the Zone Commissioner arrests someone arbitrarily, I report to liberate him. In this case there is no conflict, I must do it. It's my duty. . . . They must be liberated. I am the superior authority when dealing with arrests. . . . Certain authorities believe that people have to be afraid so they can be respected. Thus people are arrested arbitrarily. I liberate them.[19]

This magistrate also indicated he had not often done this because only one zone commissioner in Mongala ever made arbitrary arrests. It was, he claimed, no longer a problem. But in a slightly different context and in response to a different query, the same judge indicated zone commissioners often exceeded their legal competence in inflicting excessively severe fines or overlong prison sentences.[20]

Documentary evidence also belied the magistrate's optimistic assessment. In early 1974, the minister of political affairs wrote to regional commissioners deploring the daily plethora of arbitrary arrests which, coupled with illegal detention, had become common. Vehemently condemning these practices, he described a "climate of terror in the interior" and warned commissioners not to usurp the courts in punishing wrongdoers. Similarly, in legal affairs in which they were personally involved, the minister admonished commissioners not to crush others by taking the law into their own hands.[21] As we saw in chapters 3 and 4, arbitrary arrest was then, and has since remained, a widespread problem. In 1978 the political affairs minister visited Bas-Zaire and publicly castigated territorial officials who regularly sought out legal infractions. That, after all, was a job for the gendarmes.[22] Unarticulated but certainly implied in the minister's remarks was an awareness that many commissioners use their legal powers to extract resources from the citizenry. A commissioner in need of funds can arrest someone on a trumped up charge and then, for a small "consideration," forget the matter. The enterprising politico-administrative official can substantially supplement his monthly income this way, and such manipulations occur frequently. Illegal arrests thus induced conflict between commissioners and courts. The realization that magistrates could, and would, intervene to free those illegally detained must have been particularly galling to commissioners proud of being the president's men and, in theory therefore, the unquestioned and untouchable local power. It must have also troubled those who felt the judges' independence posed a threat to a significant source of personal revenue.

Equally annoying, at least from the perspective of various commissioners, was the penchant of the magistrature for enforcing the law even to the point of arresting and prosecuting politico-administrative officials. In Kivu and Bas-Zaire, Callaghy found poor relations between territorial administrative officials and judicial authorities. The latter, moreover, harassed and arrested territorial agents.[23] The same phenomenon also occurred in Haut-Zaire, where the attorney general had to instruct magistrates to act with "the greatest circumscription and after ripe reflection" in such matters, even though the prosecutor's office was "in no way bound by the opinions of the political or administrative authorities."[24] Similar events occurred in Mongala and caused much tension between commissioners and judicial authorities. An official at Lisala's *parquet* described the situation. "Zairian justice has problems with other political authorities who sometimes are ignorant of the role of justice. You have, for example, in a subregion a subregional commissioner, or a zone commissioner, who tries to make himself superior to a judicial authority." He also wryly observed that, "very often it is these grudges which create problems enough between justice and the political men."[25] Or, judicial independence and constitutional law aside, prestige, power, and turf are at stake.

Presidential ukase finally resolved the contentious issue of judicial authorities arresting politico-administrative officials. Ordinance-Law No. 74–255 of 6 November 1974 gave the president of the republic the unique right to authorize the prosecution of territorial officials holding presidential mandates (regional, subregional, and zone commissioners). Similarly, magistrates could not prosecute collectivity chiefs, who held mandates from the minister of political affairs, without the latter's formal consent. An administrative circular clarified these points and emphasized that only the gravest matters should be brought to the attention of either the president or the minister, given their already heavy work load. In less serious cases, authorities would have to take administrative rather than legal steps. The circular further instructed commissioners to convey these new dispositions to the population so that they would stop writing letters and otherwise complaining to the relevant judicial authorities.[26] The new law clearly weakened the magistrates' position in their dealings with political officials and effectively rendered commissioners immune from prosecution. In commenting on the 1974 law one judicial official noted it would play a large role because commissioners and chiefs "permit themselves anything and make fun of justice which cannot arrest them. We can only put our hands on them after the agreement of the authorities."[27]

The *parquet*'s judicial review of decisions of lower-level courts at the collectivity is a third and, at least in Mongala, less obvious source of tension between magistrates and territorial authorities. When queried, magistrates invariably declared they overturned judgments of the local courts after review. As one judge put it, "These judges do not even speak French and we very often annul their decisions."[28] Although in theory magistrates were supposed to inspect all collectivity courts monthly, this actually proved impossible. Vehicles were almost never available, and the judges were thus physically restricted to Lisala. Inspection of the lower courts, although mandated and probably desirable, rarely happened;

judicial review seldom occurred.[29] This is why no one mentioned the *parquet*'s powers of judicial review as a source of conflict between magistrates, and commissioners and chiefs. But should the magistrates ever become more mobile, this now latent source of structural conflict and opposition stemming from the magistrature's quasi-independent position within the state will undoubtedly surface.

The discussion of these specific causes of conflict between political officials and members of the judiciary has emphasized the magistrates' administrative independence, disputes over powers of arrest and detention, and the task of judicial review—all areas of judicial power contained in the Belgian legacy which conformed to that society's notions of an independent judiciary's appropriate role. But these areas of contention also derive from different contemporary visions of the Zairian judiciary's proper and desirable role. How is the magistrature to be inserted into the *Mobutiste* order and what powers should it have?

During the First Republic, legal scholars such as Antoine Rubbens believed Zairian authorities had successfully guaranteed magistrates the independence their judicial mission required. His commentary on the 1964 constitution noted the independence granted career judges compared favorably to the situation of their colonial predecessors. "Never had colonial magistrates known as many juridical guarantees, and their merit is precisely to have created, or more exactly to have transplanted to the Congo, the traditions of science, dignity and of integrity in honor of the Belgian magistrature."[30] Even during Mobutu's early years scholarly opinion on judicial independence remained constant. In 1970 Rubbens confidently maintained, "The *parquet* is totally independent with regard to the different organic political entities and public services of the Republic."[31]

But as Mobutu gradually consolidated power, political authorities increasingly attacked the magistrature in general, and the notion of judicial independence in particular. In 1972 Bayona-Ba-Meya, a judge later to serve in several high judicial positions, affirmed the magistrature's independence but noted it "is both more and other than the absence of political pressures. The independence of the prosecutor's office exists especially at the level of its conscience. . . . But the independence of the prosecutor's office is rather relative because of its hierarchical subordination."[32] In a similar manner, the then attorney general and later prime minister, Kengo wa Dondo, argued that the emergence of the MPR as the nation's supreme institution had simplified both the task of the magistrate and the entire question of judicial independence. More specifically,

[I]n the MPR, justice has become an organ of the Party; the magistrate is free, because he serves a cause, an ideal, a nation; he is free because, within the limits of the laws of his country, he can exercise . . . in all independence his functions of investigation, issuing summonses, or rendering judgment, in brief his jurisdictional mission. . . . But this independence is conceived and exercised only within the limits traced by the laws conceived and inspired by the MPR.[33]

The trend was obvious. As Mobutu's mastery of the state became increasingly secure, his legal minions reinterpreted the concept of judicial independence to mean subservience to the MPR. One newspaper described the emerging legal order this way: "In effect, the role of the magistrate in our country is well defined by the party. . . . Thus, in his dual capacity as [party] militant and defender of the law, the magistrate acts according to the directives traced by the MPR."[34]

Judicial independence vitally concerned many magistrates and was a frequent source of barroom discussion in the evenings. A thoughtful, and troubled, judge responded to a question about the main problems facing Zaire's judiciary with a short disquisition on the *abacos* (an acronym for *à bas costume*, or down with suits). Introduced as part of the campaign for Zairian authenticity, the *abacos* is a two-piece masculine garment (trousers and shirt) which replaced the European suit and tie as acceptable formal and business attire.

> There is a certain problem in which justice finds itself checked. It is [judicial] in-dependence. We should have free hands. We are, however, a justice engaged in the Revolution. This liberty is limited by the imposition of the party. It is the same all over where we find national parties. All that we do . . . it cannot be done out-side the ideology of the party. Take wearing an *abacos*, for example. The Code does not yet repress someone who does not wear an *abacos*. If the Code has not yet foreseen that, then it is not an infraction. But considering the political situation, we must busy ourselves with the *abacos*. If a Zairian wears a tie and a European suit, I will prosecute him because I agree with the President-Founder. If everyone began to disobey the President-Founder, where would we be? I render justice, but I render it in conformity with the party.[35]

Despite the party militancy his response seemingly displayed, at other times this magistrate was conspicuously unenthusiastic about the regime's "revolution-ary imperatives." At one juncture he confided that "Mobutu worship" had gone much too far, and, if present trends continued, people would soon be on their knees before the president. In addition, he resented having to go to the airport and participate in *animation* whenever a political dignitary came to Lisala because he believed it beneath his dignity as a magistrate.[36] In short, like many of his colleagues, this judge was often ambivalent about the relationship of the magistra-ture to the more overtly political activities and ideologies of the Zairian state.

A problem closely related to judicial independence concerns the treatment of high-ranking political officials, or their relatives, involved in litigation. One magistrate correctly indicated that such difficulties and inevitably politically sen-sitive matters were universal. He and other local judges were particularly attuned to these problems because President Mobutu and other high-ranking officials had relatives throughout Mongala. "His [Mobutu's] relatives are citizens like any other," he said, "but when they themselves have to deal with justice, we must take care of these matters unlike the others. It is the same thing in your country, I believe. If a relative of [the president] were in a tight corner, his business would be taken care of in a different fashion."[37] Although such things occur everywhere, the degree to which political authorities may intervene in legal matters to aid their kin is usually limited. In Zaire, however, there are no such limitations; it is a government of big men, not laws. From time to time important political officials would thus intervene directly in the judicial process with the result that magistrates had to expend much time, effort, and anguish with little to show for it.

One illustrative case involved a general officer of the FAZ, also a member of the MPR's political bureau, who owned a hotel in Bumba, a small town 150 kilometers from Lisala. Since the general's political and military responsibilities did not allow him to devote any time to this enterprise, he hired three managers. At one juncture the general believed the hotel probably should have been bringing in more money, and he suspected his managers of embezzlement. He therefore dispatched his wife's brother to Bumba to check things over and report back his findings. After completing a financial audit in Bumba, the brother-in-law arrived in Lisala to accuse the three hotel managers of embezzlement. Since the matter concerned one of the most important and powerful men in the republic, the *parquet* immediately opened an investigation and summoned the managers to testify. After an initial inquiry, the investigating magistrate thought something might be amiss, but was not sure where the blame lay. He therefore decided to leave the managers at liberty, provided they report to the *parquet* every morning. A further examination of the books showed the brother-in-law, not the managers, was at fault. By the time this was discovered, however, he had already returned to Kinshasa to speak to the general. Criminal proceedings were then begun against the brother-in-law, but the general dispatched a captain to Lisala to inquire why the three managers were still at large. The magistrate replied they had done nothing wrong and the culprit was probably the general's brother-in-law, now the subject of a full-scale criminal investigation. The criminal charges against the general's relative were sent to a higher court because of the large sums involved, but to the best knowledge of the prosecuting magistrate the dossier he had so carefully compiled remained a dead letter. He had to assume, probably correctly, that the general had intervened to quash the affair.[38]

A case with similar overtones placed one of Lisala's magistrates in a political vise. As public prosecutor, he had arrested both the accountant and head of the department of public works of the Zone of Mobayi-Mbongo for having embezzled funds belonging to the state. The documentation against them appeared impressive. The two suspects, however, accused the investigating magistrate of collaborating with the zone commissioner (a member of the judge's ethnic group) in a personal and ethnically motivated vendetta. The accountant was related to the army general in charge of the Ministry of Veterans' Affairs, and he wasted no time in alerting his highly placed kinsman. Specifically, he accused the magistrate and the zone commissioner of trying to settle a personal score. The general believed the accountant's story and quickly mobilized powerful political personalities to support his cousin. These influential figures pressured the attorney general, who dispatched the magistrate's immediate judicial superior from Mbandaka with instructions to suspend the judge who had compiled the dossier. But when the superior magistrate arrived from Mbandaka, he examined the documentation and determined that the accountant's accusations were unfounded. He therefore decided to fly to Kinshasa to see if judicial officials there would drop the suspension order against the investigating judge and reinstate the case against the accountant and the head of the public works department.[39] Unfortunately, I had to leave Lisala before the denouement, but at the time of my departure the investigating magistrate was still under scrutiny even though he had not yet been suspended. Needless to say, these events left the magistrate demoralized and bitter. Honesty and professionalism do not always pay.

One further example should suffice. In 1975 Zairian media widely publicized what became known as the *coup monté et manqué*. The regime alleged certain civilians and high-ranking members of the armed forces had plotted a coup against Mobutu. Spokesmen for the regime also accused the United States of complicity since some of the officers had trained in the U.S., and the local press was quick to discern the fine hand of the Central Intelligence Agency. The affair had wide-ranging repercussions: expulsion of the American ambassador, removal of a substantial number of Zairian general officers, and dismissal of the chief justice of the Zairian Supreme Court.[40] According to the unconfirmed story circulating on the judicial grapevine, Mobutu wished to have the plotters tried before a military tribunal, but Zairian law maintains soldiers and civilians prosecuted for the same offense must appear before civilian magistrates. The chief justice apparently had the temerity to insist on this point, and Mobutu discharged him. Lisala's magistrates believed this probably indicated that the case against the plotters was weak and that Mobutu would be more likely to get a guilty verdict before a military court. Full details of the 1975 coup have yet to emerge, but even if apocryphal, this tale represents significant beliefs about political interference in judicial affairs and stands as a stark commentary on the relative, and probably shrinking, limits of judicial independence.[41]

Interactions between the political sector and the judiciary are complicated further because since February 1972 the spoken words of the Zairian head of state have had the force of law. After each of Mobutu's public speeches, the minister of justice prepares relevant extracts for promulgation as laws of the land.[42] Now a major source of Zairian law, legislation through Mobutu's spur-of-the-moment remarks creates special difficulties for Zairian justice because presidential asides rarely provide concrete guidance for magistrates who have to prosecute or render judgment. Moreover, it is difficult to relate these presidential edicts to the already existing written Code which forms the basis of Zairian justice. For example, should Mobutu announce that a certain piece of apparel must or must not be worn, as in the case of the *abacos* and neckties, what penalties should magistrates impose on lawbreakers? Inevitably, therefore, Zairian justice must grope in the dark.[43]

The thirteen dissident parliamentarians severely criticized Mobutu's penchant for making law in front of the masses and their analysis is worth attention.

Citizen President-Founder,
   It happens that you improvise in public, often brilliantly moreover. But in your capacity as a politician, You are obliged to recognize the psychology of the crowd so that You can raise its enthusiasm. Do You always resist the demagogy which is a strong temptation in these circumstances? You can also make slips of the tongue

and that has already happened. How can it be understood that these remarks can all constitute the arsenal of Party doctrine without any discrimination? Why do you want all that You say to have the force of law?

Furthermore, it is inadmissible that You continue to modify the laws and the Constitution by speech. Terrorized, the subordinate organs [of party and state] no longer have any choice and are forced to attribute to presidential remarks the force of law even if they hurt the general interest. And these remarks are applicable before the modification of the legal texts. And the conscience is cleared by saying that the Revolution moves more quickly than the modification of the texts.

This conception of things invites arbitrariness.[44]

If anything, these passages understate the case.

By way of example, on 30 December 1974 the president and the political bureau decided to "radicalize" the Zairian Revolution. The subsequent communiqué indicated the state would make major changes in Zairian society to eliminate the ten scourges eating away at the fiber of life. The first scourge, cryptically called "liberty or license," demanded renewed adherence to *Mobutisme* and declared all places in Zaire where President Mobutu had lived and worked would henceforth become national pilgrimage points.[45] As the president's birthplace, Lisala qualified.

In concrete terms this meant the territorial commissioners and the chief of Lisala's Cité had to create special shrines in the parts of town where Mobutu had spent his early years. They made plans to spruce up the already existing votive stone in the courtyard of the hospital where he had been born, as well as to construct something similar on the lot where his parents' house had once stood. The former task presented no untoward difficulty, but the latter request created a serious conflict between magistrates and commissioners.

In late June 1975 the chief of the Cité sent a letter to the present occupant of the presidential lot informing him that she was required to fix up the new pilgrimage point. She asked the citizen to appear at her office so she could assign him a new lot. Because six months had elapsed since announcement of the radicalization and there had been little progress, the subregional commissioner pointedly reminded the zone commissioner and chief that work on the presidential lot had to begin without further delay. In addition, anyone dispossessed would receive help constructing new homes through *salongo*, or community labor.[46] The citizen designated for the signal honor of eviction refused to submit passively to the expropriation. He petitioned the *parquet*, and a magistrate threw out the chief's order of eviction. On 11 July the chief complained to the zone commissioner that although her actions were in complete conformity with the law stipulating undeveloped lots could be withdrawn and attributed to others, the *parquet* had summoned her subordinates in charge of executing the eviction. The chief returned the summonses and instructed her subordinates to ignore them. When the prosecutor's office received the returned and unhonored summonses on the following day, things got nasty. The magistrates told the chief she was hardly in a position to appreciate the character of the judicial dossiers opened in this case and, further, that the *parquet* had the authority to judge requests for the annulment of administrative decisions introduced by individual citizens. They also noted that by returning the summonses she was seriously compromising her subordinates since they could be sentenced to thirty days in jail for failure to appear. Moreover, the judges indicated to the chief that the lot's occupant had filed a complaint charging her subordinates with abusive and arbitrary withdrawal of the lot. The citizen had also shown the magistrates documents indicating he had lived there continuously since 1966, had paid tax on this land each year since then, and had developed the lot. Finally, the magistrates returned the summonses to the chief demanding her subordinates appear before the *parquet* in three days.[47]

Two weeks later, on 23 July 1975, the chief received a congratulatory letter from the subregional commissioner. He lauded her for unceasing efforts "to make Lisala a pilgrimage point worthy of the memory of the birth of the Father of the Zairian Revolution," and said she should not be discouraged in her just path because she benefited from the total support of her hierarchical superiors. Her role was to apply the legal dispositions without worrying about displeasing "certain individuals."[48] Two days later, the magistrates replied directly to the subregional commissioner by noting his support of the chief despite, in their view, the questionable legality of her actions.[49]

Tension and ill feeling between magistrates and commissioners mounted during succeeding weeks and spilled over into other matters. A newly arrived judicial inspector was summarily evicted from his temporary lodgings in the party's hotel, and a new magistrate was refused rooms even though many were available. Furthermore, when the minister of justice arrived in mid-August, local political officials denied him access to the guest house. And when the minister requested transportation to investigate a matter several miles outside town, a commissioner informed him it would not be possible; the subregional commissioner's wife needed the van to do her marketing. Similarly, when the attorney general arrived in Lisala, the subregional commissioner declined to greet or entertain him. Finally, during this period of tension, when even routine and normal courtesy was absent, one of the magistrates mentioned that there was an attempt afoot at the subregion to see that he was "broken."[50]

The affair of the presidential lot dragged on for five years, but the chief and commissioners eventually triumphed.[51] In retrospect, the politicians' victory is not surprising. Theirs was by far the greater power, and it appeared, even then, the magistrates were fighting a rear guard action with little hope of eventual success. This incident illustrates clearly some of the difficulties between the *parquet* and the subregion. It also indicates the regime's penchant for oral law can cause problems. In this particular case one issue was which law would prevail: the politically motivated oral law pronounced on 30 December 1974 as part of the radicalization, or the already existing written code which provided some recourse to the evicted citizen? Regardless of the ultimate disposition of this matter, the case also demonstrates that, within certain limits, magistrates can and do use their positions and knowledge of the law to resist politically inspired attempts to exert arbitrary control.

On the basis of the preceding analysis one can say the professional magistrature constitutes, at least in some instances, a significant institutionalized center of resistance to the state's unfettered exercise of political power. The struggle between courts and commissioners in Lisala is perhaps best envisaged as something akin to what Giddens has termed a dialectic of control, a notion already utilized in analyzing the CND.[52] Because the commissioners' dominance over the magistrates remains incomplete there is a basis for conflictual interaction as both groups strive to lessen areas of uncertainty and insecurity in their respective environments. Commissioners are insecure because they know magistrates can annul some of their decisions and because, as long as this is the case, their total supremacy in the local political arena remains in doubt. From the other side, magistrates resist measures which undermine their role as ultimate arbiters of the law. Their quest, at this point, is to retain a degree of relative autonomy and judicial independence from the more explicitly politicized branches of the state.

Conclusion

Why do magistrates form a pocket of resistance internal to the state? Three reasons are worth retaining. First, the professional magistrature, and even lower-level personnel in judicial administration, are reasonably well sheltered from the influence of politicians by virtue of relatively generous salary scales. They are not necessarily wealthy, but their salaries are at least on a par with those of territorial commissioners. At the official exchange rate prevalent during 1974-75 (Z 1.00 = $2.00), the two highest ranking magistrates in Lisala earned, respectively, $520 and $560 per month. The subregional commissioner and his counterpart at the zone received $540 and $360. The highest ranking secretarial position at the *parquet* carried a monthly salary of $230, while the secretary at the zone earned but $84.[53]

Second, magistrates have more career security than subregional and zone commissioners. Politico-administrative officials hold a five-year political mandate which is revocable at any time. They thus know they need to extract as much profit from their positions as they can, for they labor under a swift and frequently used political ax.[54] Magistrates do not work under quite the same political constraints and are thus under less pressure to accumulate resources during their tenure.

When considered in conjunction, the two preceding points explain at least partially why the magistrature appears to be *relatively* less corrupt than other arms of state power. Judges have the financial resources and career security necessary to resist the financial blandishments of those seeking favorable decisions or other sorts of influence. They are also better able to resist the clientelistic and financial co-optation so characteristic of Zairian political life.[55] Nonetheless, neither the judicial system in general nor the magistrature in particular were entirely free of corruption, as Nguza's remarks cited in epigraph indicate. Some financial pressures do exist, as one magistrate noted when asked if his salary was sufficient. "Logically, yes, because I am a young cadre. But if, for example, I want to build [a house], to have a car, to live a life worthy of a . . . [magistrate], it is not enough."[56]

Some magistrates yielded to the many temptations thrown in their path and one could occasionally hear Lisala's people complaining that money and justice were becoming synonymous. One bureaucrat argued, "if you are before the *parquet* and you have some money, it suffices to pay a bit and your business is forgotten."[57] From time to time one would also hear muted complaints from merchants concerning corruption at the *parquet*,[58] and doubtless there was some. Others would object that the law seemed to be enforced only on the poor, or on those unwilling to bribe legal officials, a trend that was probably reinforced in 1979 when Mobutu ordered plaintiffs in civil and collectivity-level cases to deposit a sum roughly equivalent to two months pay at minimum wages before their affairs would be heard.[59] The dissident parliamentarians castigated the system in the following terms: "Zairian justice is a function of the material capacity of the [person before the court]," and judgments are rendered "not on the ultimate conviction formed from the objective elements of a dossier, but uniquely on the basis of the conclusions of the party who offers the most."[60] But however much corruption existed among Lisala's magistrates, it was vastly less significant, and certainly more unusual, than that prevalent in virtually every other branch of the state. In this sense, too, the magistrature constituted a relatively well insulated pocket of resistance to the *mal zairois* and dialectic of oppression endemic to state and society.[61]

The third, and final, reason why magistrates form a pocket of resistance internal to the state is their educational training and indoctrination in classical European legal ideology. In the words of one student of Zairian law, "Having received a training in occidental law, jurists continue to rely for the most part on occidental law and juridical technique."[62] What else could adequately explain why Lisala's magistrates would "take on" some of the regime's leading political figures when they had little, if anything, to gain and a great deal to lose?

Of Lisala's seven magistrates, only one was a holdover from the First Republic. A former court clerk under the Belgians, he had no university training. The remaining six judges had all gone to either the university in Kinshasa (or the School of National Administration), or had been educated abroad. During their studies most of these magistrates had imbibed a love of the written law, a respect for its workings, and a more acute sense of what the legal power they possessed should, and should not, do. A young magistrate, for example, claimed he did not like to arrest people because,

> When I was at Gemena, I was building a dossier concerning a rape. Two witnesses were cited. In similar cases they [the witnesses] must be made to appear before you. I called for these two witnesses at several points, but they never came. Then I said they should be arrested and brought to Gemena where I would be able to question them about the affair. They had to come 600 kilometers, including 250 on foot. They were at two extremes. One was a twelve-year old boy, the other was a fifty-

year old *papa*. To make them come that way solely to ask them yes or no. . . .
Since then I do not arrest people easily.[63]

Both this comment and some of the incidents related above would make it tempting to describe the Zairian magistrate as a knight on a white horse intent on dispensing humane and compassionate justice based on a written code of law rather than on political expediency. Tempting, but wrong. Even if Zairian magistrates were entirely independent and completely free to enforce the Code as best they saw fit, their role vis-à-vis the population would still be primarily repressive and oppressive. The magistrature remains a branch of state power responsible for enforcing a certain code of behavior and a specific set of values on society at large. The law is coercive and magistrates are most assuredly not defenders of the downtrodden, however tempestuous their relations may be with other arms of the state.

One judge put it this way when commenting on the more serious problems facing Zairian justice. "There is also a big language problem. For example, the prosecutor's office is dead set against a defendant who understands no French. Those who come under the law and those who speak the law have very different ideas."[64] Magistrates spend most of their time on criminal rather than civil cases and therefore deal almost exclusively with people who know nothing about the laws governing them. One judge related that in his three years at Lisala, a defense attorney had never entered his court, and if one ever did his judicial dignity would probably suffer from a visible attack of nerves.[65] Understood but unstated was the assumption that a knowledgeable defense attorney would probably have ample reason to object to how this judge's court normally handled criminal procedures.

Nor, for that matter, should we make too much of the magistrates' stated, and probably sincere, attachment to the written Code. Most of these laws were elaborated under a colonial system not especially noted for its respect for the rights of ordinary Zairians, and recent attempts to reform the Code show little promise of fundamental reorientation. Wyatt MacGaffey furnishes a devastating portrait of how the regime manipulates the law and indicates authorities are now considering a new Code but that "under cover of references to cultural *authenticité*, [it] picks and chooses customs to endorse, rejects others out of hand, and in effect guts customary society in the interests of the bourgeoisie."[66]

The Zairian magistrature is relatively less corrupt than some other arms of state power, but even an honest judge, over the long term, will probably have trouble resisting the system's pressures to become dishonest. Magistrates, too, have human responsibilities and must provide for spouses, children, and families. But an inhumane and thoroughly perverted state often places them in situations where they must ignore sincerely held beliefs to survive amid the buffeting of scarcity and insecurity. Furthermore, if they join the struggle for space by resisting the regime's more outrageous political imperatives through adherence to the Code, the state will sooner or later squash them. Thus, they are buffeted by serious conflicting pressures. Many of Lisala's magistrates acutely felt this moral and professional dilemma and wrestled with it every day. Condemnation is easy; comprehension of a human tragedy more difficult—a point Nguza understands. "I do not hold a grudge against these young magistrates whose texts were imposed upon them by the office of the 'supreme magistrate.' I only regret that their intelligence has been placed in the service of evil."[67]

Returning to a theme evoked earlier, this chapter demonstrated that as a congeries of organized repositories of administrative, coercive, and ideological power, the state cannot possibly act monolithically, or even speak with a single voice. Interstitial crevices exist between the state's various administrative and coercive organs, and we have examined the gulf between courts and commissioners. Since these organizationally distinct components of power grow and decline at different rates, and possess differing values and visions of the shape of society and polity, the picture to emerge is one of a series of imperfectly meshed gears. Conflict and pockets of resistance internal to the state result. This conflict, furthermore, never appears definitively resolved. Although in Lisala and Mongala politico-administrative officials were firmly in control, we may infer the commissioners probably recognized their mastery required constant reassertion and was never entirely secure. The magistrature has continued to resist the supremacy of the commissioners; that much may be seen from recent press reports and the continual need of various authorities, such as Kengo, to reiterate familiar themes: "The independence of the judge . . . must not be considered as a license."[68] In a similar vein, during a trip to Kivu in 1982, the vice-prime minister and minister of political affairs declared that "the Zairian magistrature must be filled out with unconditional *Mobutistes* entirely engaged in the work of national recovery."[69] Magistrates occupy a paradoxical position: both resisting the arbitrary exercise of power by territorial commissioners yet still enforcing an alien and repressive body of law on the citizenry. On the one hand, they are guerrilla partisans sniping at the state from within; on the other, their adherence to the legal code helps maintain and perpetuate the state's dominance over civil society. Their ambiguous position within the state, as well as their ambivalent attitudes toward it, are sources of insecurity both for themselves and for the state they serve.

7

The Insecure State, II

Resistance Without—Religious Groups

It is a comfort to us that our government associates itself with us to bend its knees with us before God. Man is big only when on his knees. It is God who distributes authority. Mr. President, the Church recognizes your authority, for authority comes from God. We will loyally apply the laws that you establish. You can count on us in your work of restoring the peace toward which all so ardently aspire.

—Monsignor Malula, 1965[1]

For decades they have spoken of these riches which do not cease to remain "potential." When [shall we have] a bit of happiness? Payment [is] unceasingly put off. While waiting there is shameless exploitation, organized pillage to the profit of foreigners and their relays, while the majority of the people squat in misery in situations which are sometimes artificially provoked.

—Monsignor Kaseba, June 1981[2]

Wanting to set themselves up as censors of the State and to constitute a sort of counter-power, these churchmen [*religieux*] believe that now they teach us everything. Virtue is theirs; vice, ours.

The blessed and good national conscience is always theirs; the damned are the rest of us.

Disguised popular meetings have replaced the Sunday sermon in certain churches. There our militants are intoxicated to shake their political conviction and the confidence they have in their chief, as well as in the ideals of the party. . . .

From now on I think that in Zaire, churches, temples, mosques can be used only for

> prayer and not for some bad ones who want to
> play at being politicians. . . .
>   Also, in the name of order and national
> unity which I must safeguard in this country, I
> want to say out loud that from this day, I shall
> no longer allow this genre of overt provoca-
> tion. He who has ears, let him hear [*Com-*
> *prenne bien qui pourra*].
>
> —Mobutu Sese Seko, September 1981[3]

Although the state's internal fragmentation virtually presupposes resistance from within as its fortunes ascend and decline, not all causes of the state's insecurity are found in the interstices between organized repositories of administrative, coercive, and ideological power. There are also, at various times and in differing contexts, significant pockets of resistance external to the state which are also part of the dialectical struggle for space. Such resistance does not necessarily exist outside the state's territorial boundaries, although it may, but is usually found in the fabric of civil society. At one extreme, resistance may take the form of armed rebellion; at another, withdrawal or exit. These are neither the only, nor perhaps most likely, possibilities. Groups in society find other ways of adjusting to the state's attempts to impose behavioral rules and normative visions.

This chapter explores three patterns of reaction and accommodation to the *Mobutiste* state. In general, the state has tried to reduce its own insecurity by exerting control over religious groups it fears may ultimately constitute independent sources of power and foci of competing loyalty. The Catholic church, the Kimbanguist church, and the Kitawala group have each reacted differently. As we shall see and as the citations in epigraph attest, the Catholic church first cooperated with, but then resisted the state; the Kimbanguists have collaborated willingly and have even imitated the state; while the Kitawalists have withdrawn and resist even minimal contact. It is crucial to examine, at least briefly, the state's relations with these religious groups to help us delineate more sharply the ambiguous boundary between state and civil society.

The Catholic Church

The Catholic church is by far the most important religious organization in Zaire. Over 50 percent of the population is at least nominally Catholic, and its network of schools educates over 60 percent of the nation's primary school students and more than 40 percent of its secondary students. In addition to the evident ideological power such dominance bestows, the church owns and controls a vast infrastructure of hospitals, clinics, and social programs. It has raw economic power as well. In 1974, for example, the Diocese of Lisala reported total expenditures of roughly $175,000 against an intake of $208,000. Diocesan economic enterprises included farms, ranches, stores, artisans' shops, and schools.[4] In an economically underdeveloped area, these figures inevitably make the church a force of the first magnitude. Moreover, as the state's own economic and social infrastructure has declined, the church's has risen in relative importance. The Catholic church is today Zaire's only truly national institution apart from the state, and it is the only other locus of significant economic, social, and political influence. To understand why, a brief look backward is necessary.

The Catholic church's towering educational dominance stems from the colonial era when the state virtually ceded the colony's educational infrastructure to various missionary orders. In this regard the Belgians went a good deal further than either the French or British. In Zaire, as in Rwanda and Burundi, although there was, and remains, a small Protestant presence, the Catholic church's educational network all but became the state's official educational system.[5] Nonetheless, the relationship between church and state on educational matters was never completely harmonious, for the missionaries were primarily interested in evangelization. The state, on the other hand, wished to train subalterns both for its own administration and for private corporations, to see the "natives" gained a proper appreciation of all the metropole was doing for them, and to ensure Zairians developed proper respect for the authority of the state and the entire colonial establishment. Such different, although largely complementary, goals inevitably meant conflict. The church, for example, did not allow the state to control its utilization of public education subsidies and always resisted the state's attempts to inspect its educational network. As a result, the church created its own corps of educational inspectors, administrators, and principals.[6]

These occasional differences, however, are minimal in comparison to the numerous issues on which church and state worked in concert. The Catholic church was certainly the state's premier ideological apparatus, and helped insure the long-term efficacy of the entire colonial system.[7] Furthermore, Zairians surely perceived the unity of purpose church and state shared. Joseph, later Cardinal, Malula realized this association would cause the church grave problems after independence.

> At the beginning of the evangelization, Church and State walked together. From their collaboration came this abundant harvest. . . . There also resulted from it a disastrous confusion between the two powers. For our people, the Church was the State, and the State was the Church. They considered religion as a matter for the Whites. . . . The two powers are indistinctly accused of colonialism, of wanting to perpetuate their paternalism to maintain Blacks under their dependence. It is time to break these ties.[8]

After 1960, the state tried gradually to reassert its control over education. A new convention between the state and various religious bodies created a coordinated educational network. There were two branches: one secular, the other religious; the latter branch was further divided into Catholic, Protestant, and Kimbanguist sections. The state insisted on paying directly all teachers and personnel in both branches, required national examinations for all students, and saw to it that even schools within the religious sections were open to students regardless of faith.[9] Despite these efforts, the Catholic church remained dominant in education and retained its ideological hold on the popular and political consciousness. A linguistic analysis of the speeches and statements of First Republic politicians demonstrates convincingly the thorough interpenetration of political and religious language. Political discourse between 1960 and 1965 featured a plethora of religious imagery, symbols, and motifs,[10] a trend doubtlessly aided by the education of many first-generation Zairian politicians in Catholic schools and seminaries. Under colonialism, the church was virtually the only avenue of upward mobility for Zairian youth.

Although a fervent supporter of Zairian independence, Malula, by 1960 a bishop, condemned Patrice Lumumba's nationalist government, for in it he perceived both the threat of tyranny and the menace of international communism. Like most Zairians, however, Malula welcomed the Second Republic and, as the first citation in epigraph indicates, promised Mobutu the church's full support. During the new regime's first five years, relations between church and state were generally good. Tensions existed, but both sides usually cooperated. In June 1970, for example, although Cardinal Malula angered the president when his homily, delivered in front of Mobutu and the Belgian monarch, severely took the regime to task for some of its policies, the church nevertheless supported Mobutu's presidential candidacy later that year, largely because he had restored peace and tranquility.

In 1971 some of the regime's specific measures to implement an overarching policy of increased centralization ruptured this entente. The state nationalized and unified the three universities, including Lovanium University in Kinshasa, a Catholic institution. Even more serious was the state's attempt to implant sections of the JMPR in Catholic seminaries. The church objected strongly, yet eventually compromised on a measure banning JMPR sections from major seminaries, but allowing them in minor ones. In 1972 the situation deteriorated further. As part of the campaign for authenticity, all Zairians had to drop their Christian baptismal names in favor of authentic Zairian ones. Cardinal Malula protested this decision and instructed his bishops to ignore it. In retaliation, the regime seized the cardinal's residence in Kinshasa and converted it into JMPR headquarters, stripped him of his national honors, and forced him into exile in the Vatican. The church relented on the name issue, but tensions mounted as the state banned Catholic publications and youth groups.

During 1973 and early 1974 the situation eased as Malula returned from exile and the state gave him another splendid mansion. But by late 1974 and 1975 the conflict between church and state had reemerged more seriously than before. The state decided Christmas would no longer be a Zairian holiday and schools could no longer teach courses in religion. Religious instruction gave way to courses in *Mobutisme*; crucifixes and pictures of the pope in schools, hospitals, and other public buildings relinquished pride of place to portraits of Mobutu. This particular requirement caused much anguish in Mongala where the JMPR removed crucifixes with great gusto. In addition, toward the end of 1974, Political Commissioner Engulu likened the president to a new Messiah, a comparison not calculated to please the clergy. At the end of that year the state decided to complete its control over the educational networks and absorbed them entirely as part of the radicalization.[11]

Throughout this period of strained relations people on both sides of the divide still maintained working, if not cordial, relations. Despite the JMPR's excesses of zeal, relations between church and state in Lisala remained reasonably smooth. Although certain clerics and commissioners bore each other ill will, cooperation still existed at the summit of the local hierarchies. Newly arriving territorial commissioners regularly paid courtesy calls on the bishop, and the latter never had difficulty obtaining an appointment with local political authorities. When the president visited Lisala in 1975, members of the subregional committee of the MPR officially welcomed and greeted him, as is customary. Once in private with the members of the committee, Mobutu wanted to know why the bishop was not part of the state-party's official retinue. He was reportedly angry because of this slight to the churchman and insisted his representatives extend themselves to get along with the bishop.[12]

By 1975 Zaire's economy had fallen on hard times: previously instituted policies such as Zairianization and radicalization went bankrupt; external debt rose dramatically and creditors appeared on the doorstep; copper prices collapsed, as did the standard of living of most Zairians. As the economic situation worsened, more and more officials began extracting resources from the citizenry. Things had become so bad that some clergy started condemning the excesses of the regime. The archbishop of Kananga published a letter to his parishioners that was highly critical of contemporary trends. "At the present hour," he wrote, "we are witnessing an internal colonialism: a class of rich people is in the process of developing whose wealth rests on the misery of millions of citizens; for there exists a large group of those who find themselves rejected on the margins of society and who do not have what they need to live."[13] Similarly, in 1976 the archbishop of Lubumbashi published a scathing pastoral letter denouncing the regime's injustice and corruption, and the following year another letter from all Zairian bishops reiterated the same points.[14]

Despite his rage at these moral, social, and, ultimately, political criticisms, unfavorable economic trends and the aftereffects of his military adventures in Angola and Shaba I forced Mobutu to moderate his stance toward the church. By 1976 it was apparent the state had neither the managerial talent nor the wherewithal to manage the nation's schools, and Mobutu quietly asked the church to step back into the breach. Without fanfare he denationalized the university, and returned the schools to the born again religious educational networks. The church exacted its price. Perhaps fearing the state would, when once again strong, reassert control over education, it demanded approval of a new educational convention. Signed in February 1977, this agreement ceded responsibility for the organization of the schools to the Catholic, Protestant, and Kimbanguist churches and gave them more managerial control than they had possessed before the radicalization. In addition, courses on religion reappeared in the curriculum.[15]

The state's position had clearly weakened, and this was reflected not only in the new educational arrangements, but in other compromises as well. In May 1978 the dean of the MPR's political bureau met with an envoy of the Vatican, and the Zairian press reported the religious emissary had characterized relations between state and church as excellent, especially in light of the recent decision to begin religious broadcasts on national radio.[16] The honeymoon did not last. In July 1978, scarcely a month after the regime had been brought to its knees during Shaba II, the bishops again took to the offensive and stridently denounced the ills besetting Zairian society. But this time, in addition to cataloguing the usual abuses (corruption, violence, injustice, lack of food and pharmaceuticals), they criticized Mobutu's cherished principle of "unity of command" and questioned the efficacy of the state itself.[17] Their document enraged Mobutu, but he was occupied with the aftermath of Shaba II and did not react to the declaration.

In September 1978 the president declared three days of national mourning after the death of Pope John Paul I, an act demonstrating he was still interested in reconciliation, whatever the bishops might write. The following year John Paul II granted Mobutu a papal audience and blessed the president's work of national reconstruction. This was especially important, for, under increasing pressure from his creditors, Mobutu probably realized his "Mobutu Plan" for the reconstruction of Zaire would never be successful without mobilizing the church's economic and social infrastructure. The pope visited Zaire in 1980 and on the eve of his arrival the president married Mama Bobi Ladawa in a Catholic ceremony. Only the Pope's refusal to officiate at the nuptials clouded a successful visit.[18]

This renewed entente ruptured in June 1981 when the bishops published another episcopal letter. This letter, like that of 1978, severely criticized the regime's corruption, brutality, mismanagement, and lack of respect for human dignity. In response, the president sternly warned the Catholic hierarchy not to meddle in politics. (Portions of both the episcopal letter and the president's speech appear in epigraph.) Mobutu retaliated by ordering the JMPR stationed in all places of worship to make sure clergy confined themselves to religious and, presumably, apolitical topics.

In the months following Mobutu's speech several incidents stretched the limits of coincidence. In late November six men tried to assault the bishop of Kindu at Kinshasa; in early December Monsignor Kaseba was beaten with bottles and machetes at the home of friends; finally, on Christmas night Cardinal Malula's residence was attacked and his night watchman killed. The cardinal was elsewhere at the moment, but some hours later soldiers appeared at a diocesan store and demanded to know his whereabouts. They had not found him at home. The inference that political authorities were behind these attacks is hard to resist. The state was clearly no longer in the business of making concessions to the church, and the tension has endured. Shortly before the 1984 presidential elections, Cardinal Malula urged Zairians to consult their consciences before voting, an act the government deemed religious zealotry.[19]

Despite tension and hostility, relations between *Mobutiste* state and Catholic church remain ambiguous. In the first place, although the preceding narrative reads as though the church were monolithic and possessed of a single voice, this was done only to facilitate presentation of the main themes of church-state interaction. There are clear and serious differences of opinion both within the upper reaches of the Catholic hierarchy, as well as between the bishops and many parish priests. By way of example, the 1978 episcopal letter was, on one level, a clear challenge to the Mobutu regime. That letter, however, was the result of an animated and fractious ten-day episcopal conference. The initial draft of the bishops' statement contained a far more radical critique of the Zairian state than the final document; did not distinguish between moral and structural causes of the *mal zairois*; and was much harsher in its condemnation of centralized power and personal rule. In addition, analyses of differences in the two texts indicate at least a significant faction of bishops believed the church's institutional interests were best safeguarded by issuing a moral, rather than structural or class-oriented, critique of the regime. To do otherwise would have made the church liable to renewed attack from the state and would have thus jeopardized its important place in Zairian society.

A probing structural condemnation of the regime, although favored by the lower clergy, which was in most direct contact with the population, could also have ultimately called attention to the ostentatious life-style of certain hierarchs. Even ordinary clergymen live far better than the vast majority of their parishioners and share some of the economic and social privileges of the highest ranking officials of the state.[20] There is another reason why the church may be reluctant to issue a radical structural critique. The church relies on grants from abroad to continue its works in Zaire. As of 1976 not one of Zaire's forty-seven dioceses was financially self-sufficient, and the church thus depended on external subsidies.[21]

In the second place, despite the Catholic hierarchy's periodic criticisms of the state, as an institution the church has remained extremely discrete, for the hierarchy is certainly aware of the risks more overt political activity could bring.[22] In Lisala, for example, even during a period of stress and conflict between church and state, there was concern on both sides that divisions not go too far. Similarly, although Cardinal Malula has periodically criticized the regime, there are nonetheless indications, albeit unconfirmed, that he has instructed his clergy to avoid situations likely to result in public confrontation with the state.[23]

The ambiguous position of the Catholic church is reflected in other ways. On the one hand, individual clergymen who have the best interests of their flock at heart intercede actively on behalf of their congregations when the state's coercive arms threaten unjustified repression. This occurred, as noted in chapter 4, at Maluku when gendarmes began indiscriminate reprisals during a labor dispute. In this instance, the local curé wrote bitter letters of protest to the governor of Kinshasa and other political authorities.[24] Local clergy played a similar role in a women's tax revolt in eastern Zaire, where the curé presented their grievances to the regional governor.[25] On the other hand, the church was more clearly on the side of the state in the wave of strikes affecting schools throughout Zaire in the early 1980s. An unintended effect of the 1977 educational convention had been to place the church between the state and the employees of the school systems which it had again taken over. Since the regime had granted managerial authority to the religious educational networks, it held the church responsible for labor difficulties in Catholic schools. Not wishing to lose its newly won privileges in the educational sector, the Catholic hierarchy intervened in the strike in Kisangani to ensure strikers returned to the classroom—an action assuredly in the interests of the state, not the underpaid teachers.[26]

As the fortunes of the state have worsened, those of the Catholic church have improved. Of the three pillars of colonial society (church, state, company), only the church continues to operate effectively throughout Zaire. In addition to its usual religious role, the church's relative economic strength has risen in importance.[27] In Butembo, eastern Zaire, local businessmen make sure they stay on personally warm terms with the local clergy, regardless of their own faith. To maintain cordial relations is to their advantage because the church can, and does, provide certain facilities, credit, advice, and equipment which are simply unavailable from any other source, including the state. Local entrepreneurs also know the church represents a moral and political influence on consumers and, as businessmen, they have to consider such factors. People in this area also recognize that in the present context the church stands apart as an island of integrity in a sea of corruption and, in consequence, they have far more confidence in it than they do in the state.[28]

Ultimately, however, the conflict between Catholic church and Zairian state is about power. The church is the only institution in Zaire with the strength, will, and independence to question and criticize the regime openly. Furthermore, the church hierarchy is both concerned about conditions of life in Zaire and able to voice its misgivings eloquently. In this regard, and from the state's perspective, it matters not that bishops disagree among themselves, or that conflicts exist within the church, or that many clerics are profoundly ambivalent about assuming a confrontational stance. What does matter is that whatever criticisms and reservations the episcopal conference has expressed are invariably out of line with the regime's ideology, propaganda, and the image it wishes to project at home and abroad. This contributes to the insecurity of the state and cannot be tolerated by it. More fundamentally, the church's independent existence as an important locus of social, educational, economic, and ideological power makes the Zairian state feel insecure. What lies at the heart of the conflict is not so much what the church says or does but, rather, that the church simply exists and has the capacity, within limits, to resist and oppose. Even if this capacity remains unused, it constitutes a significant latent threat to an insecure state.

The Kimbanguist Church

The Kimbanguist church, or the Eglise de Jésus-Christ sur Terre par le Prophète Simon Kimbangu (EJCSK), is an indigenous Zairian religion which emerged from the prophetic actions and charisma of Simon Kimbangu. Kimbangu was born in the Bas-Zairian village of Nkamba, a stronghold of Protestant missionary activity. In 1921 he had a vision and a call to preach the word. Shortly thereafter, while in the throes of a convulsion, he healed a sick child in a neighboring village. News of the cure spread quickly and people flocked to Nkamba. Kimbangu presented himself as a messenger of God, a prophet who preached the word and referred constantly to the scriptures. People in a region suffering from economic depression, and coping with colonialism's societal dislocation and racial discrimination, welcomed a black prophet. Furthermore, populist syncretic movements had long been an integral part of religious life in Central Africa.

The movement quickly became too unwieldy for Kimbangu to manage alone, so he created disciples through a laying on of hands. Although evidence is sparse, some of his disciples conceivably preached an anti-white and anti-colonial message. Colonial authorities, however, were not concerned with religious nuances and perceived the movement as a threat to the region's continued political quiescence. They were further alarmed by the movement's rapid diffusion and the number of converts it attracted. By the end of 1921 colonial administrators had reported converts as far up river as Nouvelle Anvers (now Mankanza) and in the region of Monjamboli (in today's Zone of Bumba). In consequence, the Belgians arrested Kimbangu and imposed the death penalty for hostility against the state. His sentence was remitted to life imprisonment, and he was exiled internally to Lubumbashi where he remained until his death in 1950. Despite, or perhaps because of, the colonial state's hostility, the movement flourished as an illegal, underground religion. The Kimbanguist church was finally legalized on the eve of independence.[29]

There is much disagreement about the exact number of Kimbanguists in Zaire. To outsiders, church leaders claim roughly five million members, but this is surely a deliberate overestimate to inflate the church's prestige. The Kimbanguist church's internal figures indicate no more than 300,000 practicing members. It is nonetheless certain that the influence and importance of this church far outweigh its numbers in relation to both the population as a whole and the two other major recognized religious groups.[30]

In contradistinction to the Catholic church, Kimbanguists have deliberately tried to maintain cordial relations with the Mobutu regime. Because in areas outside Kimbanguism's Bas-Zairian heartland the movement's temporary success was due to the nationalist turmoil of the 1950s, it never succeeded in laying down firm roots in the popular culture. Its presence is thus insecure and its viability remains contingent on collaboration with the state at the national level.[31] More generally, the Kimbanguist church has benefited both from its status as an authentically Zairian religion and from the regime's desire to establish friendly relations with another church to counterbalance its conflict with the Catholics.[32]

Since legalization of the church, leaders of EJCSK have been extremely careful not to offend the powers that be. Wyatt MacGaffey notes this was the case even before Mobutu's accession and characterizes the church's position as political "boot-licking," a harsh but apt term.[33] By and large, the Kimbanguist church has benefited enormously from the Mobutu regime. For example, as part of the state's campaign to dominate society and control the proliferation of schismatic religious sects, in 1971 it passed a law recognizing the three major religions— Catholicism, Protestantism, Kimbanguism—and declared it would no longer tolerate other religious groups. To gain official recognition, sects had to deposit Z 100,000 with the state, a condition few could meet. This ordinance pleased the Kimbanguists because many sects were offshoots of EJCSK and when they were banned, membership in the official Kimbanguist church rose markedly. The campaign for authenticity also worked to the advantage of EJCSK as Mobutu and Diangienda, Simon Kimbangu's son and head of the church, regularly exchanged public praise. To be sure, Kimbanguists lost out when the regime nationalized the religious educational networks in 1974, but that setback was temporary and more than balanced by the other advantages of warm relations with the state. In recent years the Kimbanguist church, although technically apolitical, has fervently supported the *Mobutiste* state and actively uses its religious authority to diffuse the regime's ideological watchwords. The Kimbanguist church has become, for the most part, a *Mobutiste* mouthpiece and one of the state's main ideological supports. In this regard, the roles of the Kimbanguist and Catholic churches have ironically reversed. The Kimbanguists now enjoy the privileged ideological position that the Catholics did throughout the colonial era, while the Catholics have adopted a more confrontational posture—though they remain legal and have not had to go underground.[34]

Good relations between Kimbanguist church and *Mobutiste* state also exist on a more subtle structural plane. There is a striking similarity between the structure of the state and the structure of the Kimbanguist church, and it appears the Kimbanguist hierarchy has specifically adopted certain of the state's administrative practices and organizational modes. This was true even before the advent of the Second Republic and probably stems from the general insecurity the Kimbanguist church still feels as a result of its long period of illegality. During the First Republic, the EJCSK frequently changed its internal administrative structure to match the administrative style of the state then current.[35] This strategy was, to say the least, politically expedient, and perhaps Kimbanguist leaders believed political authorities would find this imitation flattering.

This trend has intensified under Mobutu, and church organization now parallels the administrative division of the state into regions, subregions, zones, and collectivities. As in the political sector, the Kimbanguist leader requires absolute obedience, does not tolerate doctrinal disputes, and insists all communicants be "militant" participants in the life of the church. Members must also carry *cartes de chrétiens*, analogous to the party cards the state requires. In addition, the Kimbanguist church has explicitly copied the state's policy of rotating bureaucrats (church officials) outside their areas of origin to depoliticize ethnicity and centralize power.[36]

Other, more superficial, similarities exist as well. Official visits of Mobutu and Diangienda resemble each other mightily. In one case, both arrived via C-130 aircraft, both brought brass bands, both inspected uniformed guards on arrival. In each instance followers wore shirts and dresses with the leader's picture displayed prominently, and the assembled crowds participated in enthusiastic sessions of *animation*. Moreover, believers refer to both head of state and head of church as the "Guide."[37] In sum, one can speak of a Kimbanguist community that maintains an organization directly parallel to that of the state and preaches doctrines, such as the respect for established authority, that ape those of the state.[38] The Kimbanguists thus appear to have adopted the state as a normative organizational model.

The Kitawalists

The history of Kitawala is intimately linked to the Watch Tower Bible and Tract Society, known colloquially as Jehovah's Witnesses, and many Kitawalist beliefs can be traced ultimately to the influence of the American-based Witnesses. Our knowledge of the history of the Jehovah's Witnesses in Africa is still incomplete, but we do know the movement entered Africa via Capetown about 1906 through the actions of Joseph Booth, a black American missionary, as well as through the black American sailors who made stopovers in South Africa. Given the times, and the black American origin of the movement in Africa, some of Marcus Garvey's influence also trickled through. After Watch Tower's initial penetration of Africa, migrant miners spread the movement throughout Southern Africa. Moving up from the south, Watch Tower entered Shaba around 1923 where it gradually became known as Kitawala, a linguistic deformation of the words Watch Tower.

In Shaba, Watch Tower gradually adapted to prevailing local conditions. Its missionaries preached racial equality, equal pay for equal work, and called for the reversal of the established colonial order to the advantage of the blacks; they announced the imminent arrival of God's Kingdom and the impending struggle for the restitution of Africa to the Africans. When the Kingdom of God was realized, they taught, colonizers would either have to submit to the will of blacks or leave Zaire definitively. But the ideology of these lessons did not contain a specific strategy of revolution, however inflammatory the colonial establishment might have found them.[39]

Watch Tower spread quickly along the Zairian Copperbelt during the 1920s, and by the following decade it had made significant inroads in rural areas, especially as a witchcraft eradication movement. The colonial state, for obvious reasons, did not like the message being preached, and it embarked on a policy of systematic repressive containment through the creation of relegation centers in remote rural areas. Ironically, these centers had exactly the opposite effect: instead of quarantining the movement in a few isolated regions, they aided its propagation. Escapees from these centers often successfully converted the surrounding population to their creed. Even those who remained in confinement had similar successes, for the camps allowed them some liberty of movement since there were far too many detainees to supervise them effectively. The prisoners thus established friendly contact with neighboring villages and their message radiated outward. The colonial government responded with measures that progressively banned the movement, beginning in Shaba in 1937, Haut-Zaire in 1943, Kivu in 1944, Equateur in 1946, Leopoldville in 1948, and culminating in a colony-wide ban in 1949.[40]

Over time, and probably most especially during World War II, Kitawala became more an indigenous African movement and less a branch of the worldwide Watch Tower church. As this process occurred, its message became progressively more radical and correspondingly more distant from that of the parent church. Given Kitawala's decentralized nature and the efforts of Belgian authorities to isolate it, the precise content of Kitawala's ideological message varied from location to location. Nonetheless, there was a common fund of precepts on which most Kitawalists could draw. These included a struggle against sorcery, the purification of society, and the existence of a black God. This last tenet was especially crucial, for it enabled their followers to realize that racial segregation was not God-given, but a device of the colonial state. They denounced all forms of authority as the work of Satan, including taxes, forced labor, and all the other unpleasant aspects of colonial rule. These xenophobic and anti-colonial aspects, its illegality, and clandestine operations were especially important. From this perspective, Jewsiewicki is probably correct to interpret Kitawala and other syncretic religious opposition movements as forms of peasant political consciousness.[41]

During the colonial period Belgians treated Kitawala and the Watch Tower Bible and Tract Society identically. The colonial state saw both as clearly subversive and was not interested in fine distinctions between the two. The order banning Watch Tower in 1949 affected both movements, to the great consternation of the Jehovah's Witnesses. In response, the Witnesses published a tract contesting the indiscriminate merging of Watch Tower and Kitawala, arguing Watch Tower had nothing to do with the antisocial and insubordinate attitude of the Kitawalists, and contending the latter further confused matters by using the name Watch Tower in their propaganda. Watch Tower thus renounced Kitawala and considered it a complete deformation of its teachings. Even in Lisala in 1975, practicing Jehovah's Witnesses bitterly denounced Kitawala and claimed their movement was completely distinct. Nevertheless, although Watch Tower remained a centralized worldwide church, it is fair to view Kitawala as a decentralized and Africanized version of Watch Tower, for it owed its existence to the doctrines of Watch Tower which it adapted to local conditions throughout Zaire. It is, moreover, doubtful Kitawala could have flourished without the doctrinal inspiration and organizational boost initially received from the Witnesses.[42]

Kitawala's illegality and opposition to all forms of alien rule aided its diffusion throughout the colonial period, and in this regard its history resembles Kimbanguism's. It first appeared in Lisala around 1954 and authorities noted it spread "insidiously, and without manifestation of the masses."[43] Undoubtedly, the colonial state was concerned about the growth of Kitawala. In that same year,

M. De Ryck, governor of Equateur, stated, "The situation was calm [but] that does not exclude the proliferation of certain sects, and especially of Kitawala; I have no need to recall to you that this movement, directed against all authority, aims also at weakening our own."[44]

Despite the colonial state's implacable hostility, Kitawala in its various localized guises nevertheless survived Belgian rule. After independence, Kitawalists again reacted primarily to local conditions and stimuli. For example, they participated in some of the rebellions which swept Zaire during the First Republic. In North Shaba they allied with other insurgents to destroy all signs of European influence: churches, schools, hospitals, and public buildings. But their aims were ultimately religious and thus differed profoundly from those of the rest of the rebels with whom they soon came into conflict. In the end, Kitawalist leaders were massacred and their adherents dispersed to avoid both rebels and the Zairian army.[45] Kitawalists have remained hostile to all forms of authority and, in consequence, have run afoul of the centralizing *Mobutiste* state. Mobutu's state, like its colonial predecessor, is intent on exerting and establishing its authority throughout society. Moreover, both the ideological vision and behavioral rules it has tried to impose directly contradict Kitawalist teachings and beliefs. This, we shall see presently, has produced conflict and withdrawal.[46]

For their part, the Jehovah's Witnesses have reacted differently to the imposition of the *Mobutiste* order. Although at times outlawed by the regime, they have nonetheless remained, or tried to remain, within the mainstream of Zairian life. During the mid-1970s they circulated freely in Lisala and sought actively to covert nonbelievers. When queried on this anomalous situation, one territorial official said an "operation" against them had been suspended so the government could count them and thus have a better idea of exactly what it was up against. A man of wide administrative experience, my informant believed Witnesses were numerous in Mongala and the real danger they posed was in their refusal to salute the flag, participate in *salongo*, or pay taxes. He was especially concerned about taxes because he feared the unemployed who were not able to pay would make common cause with the Witnesses and thus cause trouble for the state.[47]

Although at that time there was no coordinated policy to deal with the illegal presence of the Jehovah's Witnesses, local officials thought their presence disturbing and acted against them. The state's representatives generally view citizens who refuse to subscribe to the MPR's current line, even if they are apolitical, with suspicion and hostility. The Jehovah's Witnesses thus caused consternation, for they wish no political affiliation and believe that secular political concerns and symbols detract from their worship. These beliefs obviously run against the idea of an all-inclusive political movement such as the MPR, and Witnesses, contrary to the party line that sees all Zairians as members from birth, reject affiliation with the state. In the words of one administrator:

> In a locality situated 20 kilometers from Lisala, in Ngombe-Doko collectivity, lives a group of Jehovah's Witnesses, composed in large part of youths from 18–23 years

old. The action of these adherents is not aggressive, but rather dangerous because of their uncivic behavior in failing to recognize the legitimately established authority. For them, the slogans of the party . . . just as the honors we render to the national emblems are "insignificant." I arrested three of them and put them in the custody of gendarmes.[48]

They are, in other words, politically passive but militantly apathetic. The Mobutu regime regards them as a threat and territorial officials watch them closely, report on them constantly, and prosecute them whenever possible. Frequently imprisoned without trial, their temples destroyed. Witnesses are harried ceaselessly.[49] To one regional commissioner they were an "obstacle to the common march toward the objectives of the Revolution."[50] In short, the state treats their refusal to participate in party activities as a subversive threat. Their existence and their desire to have nothing to do with this, or any, government contributes to the insecurity of the *Mobutiste* state.

From the mid-1970s the state became increasingly worried about the proliferation of religious groups and attempted repeatedly to control them. In 1979 it amended its 1971 legislation. This new ordinance forbade the existence of any religious group or sect except as a registered nonprofit organization, prevented anyone from either preaching or receiving tithes except in the name of a religious organization registered with the state, and precluded registration for any group whose beliefs did not differ substantially from those of an already registered and thus legally sanctioned religion. As part of its registration campaign, the government published a list of 277 religious groups it had found to be in violation of the law and invited them to deliver the appropriate fees and documentation. Other, probably more realistic, estimates place the number of such sects at around seven hundred.[51] Regardless of the precise number, the state's concern has grown in direct proportion to their proliferation. Mobutu's opening speech to the Third Party Congress in 1982 noted:

> Since these last few years, we have remarked a sort of sudden awakening of religious feelings among many of our compatriots.
> Churches, temples, mosques have grown like mushrooms in no time at all across the entire stretch of the Republic. . . .
> All these sects that we see surging into view these days . . . all that is not serious. We are going to put a bit of order there.[52]

The message came through loud and clear. The congress' closing resolutions called on the president both to inventory all existing religious sects and organizations and to apply rigorously the law governing such matters.[53] Since then, the state's crackdown has continued intermittently. In 1986 Mobutu signed an ordinance dissolving the Jehovah's Witnesses in Zaire. Their activities, he said, "threaten law and order." Similarly, Equateur's governor accused them of "preaching civil disobedience and glorifying the lack of patriotism."[54]

In one sense, the state *should* be concerned with the proliferation of sects because although such schismatic religious movements have long existed and are part of Zairian culture, they nevertheless tend to proliferate in times of societal crisis. In this regard, their appearance constitutes an early warning of political turbulence to come. But the *Mobutiste* state, like its colonial predecessor, has thus far elected to repress rather than to comprehend. It has failed to alleviate the deteriorating social conditions which contribute to the emergence of these movements.

Throughout these difficult years Kitawalists have remained members of decentralized groups who deny all temporal authority. How they have reacted to the state's efforts to bring them into the main currents of national life has depended on their specific situations, geographic location, and the context of local relations with the state's representatives. Thus far their reactions have varied from violent confrontation to peaceful withdrawal. An example of the first option occurred in Shaba in 1979. Reacting to the appearance of FAZ contingents, local Kitawalists, and others, destroyed the state's administrative offices and killed two soldiers. The result was a vicious repression.[55] In Equateur, however, Kitawalists have followed another path. Still denying the validity and legitimacy of the state's authority, they have refused to vote, declined to pay taxes, and failed to present themselves for the national census.[56] They have withdrawn from Zairian politics and society both literally and figuratively.

In 1970, as part of an effort to complete a national census, authorities estimated there were 15,000 Kitawalists in Equateur. Only an estimate was possible because they had withdrawn deep into equatorial rain forest and lived completely isolated from the state and their fellow citizens. The report of the census committee noted such communities existed in the Zones of Befale, Djolu, and Bokungu in Tshuapa Subregion. It also mentioned attempts to reach these settlements proved futile, for the well-protected inhabitants admitted only relatives or others they knew and rejected out of hand the approach of all employees of the state.[57] But in 1973 an enterprising zone commissioner penetrated a Kitawalist community in Bongandanga in Mongala Subregion. His account is instructive.

> [Kitawalists] claim to be 100% servants of God and mortal enemies of money (or riches in general). Since they are busy seeking God, they do not have time to lose for money. Consequently, they will not have the possibility of discharging their CPM and tax obligations. And since the state is deaf in that ear: collision.
>
> Result, the weakest retreats. That is why the Kitawalists are today buried in the inextricable forest of Ilewa at the common limit of the Zones of Bongandanga, Befale, and Djolu. Toward the end of 1973, 5 December exactly, I adventured to go see them in their refuge. After a day's painful march in a perpetually somber forest, we emerged in a clearing which was, at the same time, an immense banana plantation extended over 800 meters in length and 300 meters in width. These banana trees are planted both to hide the anarchists' huts as well as to feed them.
>
> After having pushed us back from their camp, having overwhelmed us with an interrogation which lasted forty-five long minutes, the Kitawalists finished by permitting us access to their village. We were all lodged in a single hut with a formal prohibition from circulating in the camp.
>
> Despite the continuous surveillance exercised on us, we still knew how to deceive

the vigilance of our jailers. By profiting from the liberty accorded Citizen X, the principal *animateur* of our *groupe choc*, to go to see his father who is also an adherent of this religion and who lives in the camp, we had all of the huts in the camp counted. There were 165 in all. The approximate number of the population [is] estimated to be 800 souls. Everyone seemed to be in excellent health.

Very active in agriculture and hunting, the refugees had given their village a very flourishing appearance.

The next morning a discussion was held dealing with the advisability of our interlocutors' stay in the woods. To the question of knowing why they did not want to come out of the forest to establish themselves in a village with their fellow citizens, the Kitawalists answered us, "It is to avoid the persecution of the state which claims taxes." "And if you were exempted?" "It is then that we would want to come out."

We spent a day and two nights in this camp of unhappiness, during which time we were riddled with insect bites of all kinds.

I think that if an official promise came to be given to these recalcitrants, especially to their pastors and evangelists, to exempt them from the CPM, they could be made to come out of the forest.[58]

Direct testimony concerning life in Kitawalist communities is rare for the reasons given in this report. Others who had some contact with them said their camps contain people of many different ethnic groups (Mongo, Kongo, Luba), but their language of communication is Lingala. They have their own schools and dispensaries and are led by their religious leaders, but none of my sources could shed any light on their patterns of political authority or governance. One man who claimed to have visited a Kitawala encampment several times said they do use money—old, pre-Mobutu Congolese francs. They are absolutely unwilling to accept any Zairian currency, with the notable exception of the twenty makuta note bearing a portrait of Patrice Lumumba. (One account of the Kitawalist community in Kisangani also notes their affinity for Lumumba's portrait.) But this version contradicts the report cited above, and I do not know which is correct. All informants agreed on one point, however. Kitawalists firmly reject contact with any manifestation of the state's authority and are willing to fight for their autonomy.[59]

The Kitawalists' relations with the state differ significantly from both the Catholic and Kimbanguist patterns and thus merit commentary. Most obviously, they have withdrawn physically from any contact with the state. As the report above indicates, their refusal to accept any temporal authority placed them on a collision course with the state. Either before or after this collision (and I am not sure which) they withdrew and chose to exit.[60] The commissioner is also correct in his assessment that the weaker party withdrew. The Kitawalists could not directly challenge the state's coercive power and perhaps realized the folly of even trying.

Kitawalists are not unique in opting to exit. Exit has been a commonly pursued strategy throughout Central Africa where people often took flight to avoid colonial demands for manpower, taxes, and labor. The desire of people in French Equatorial Africa to avoid the harsher aspects of alien rule would lead them to pack their belongings and reside in remote areas of the forest or savanna.[61] Similarly, where West Africans lived close to an international boundary, they often crossed the frontier to avoid the onerous burdens of their own colony.[62] Zaire is no different in this regard and there is a long-standing and widespread practice of simply leaving at the first sign of difficulty with the state. Along the Zaire River the Bapoto would load their possessions into canoes and disappear to the large islands in the river when the state promised trouble.[63] In other regions, people would also flee at the approach of a medical team or a census.[64]

The resort to flight at the first sign of meddlesome external authority carried over into the First Republic and was exacerbated by the political turmoil. Ironically, this phenomenon cuts two ways. On the one hand, many people in Kwilu would simply leave their villages at the approach of a truck for this was the only way they could deal with the tyranny of petty functionaries, not to mention the army and gendarmes.[65] On the other hand, however, virtually all the bureaucrats in Lisala recounted macabre tales of their own flight to the forest when they were trying to escape the rebels during the rebellions. This phenomenon has continued in recent years. Mongala's archives are rich in reports from collectivity chiefs complaining they cannot control the movement of their populations who take refuge either on islands in the rivers or in the equatorial forest whenever tax collectors approach.[66] In Kivu, by the end of the 1970s, people were fleeing to the forest both to avoid the demands of the state and to insure their own physical survival. No longer able to obtain even the most ordinary goods in town or village, people began to reside in the forest, where they relied on their fields for survival. In general, accessible roads to any village or town center did not link these settlements.[67] Vansina puts it this way: "In some rural areas, villagers flee the exactions of the military by moving to the inaccessible bush, while others flee to the cities, which are less directly ransomed by the military. Others flee the city where they are starving to try and join their village of origin." It is difficult to quibble with his judgment that these migrations to avoid the long arm of the state and—I would add—the catastrophic consequences of the state's economic policies are clear signs of a growing disaffection and worsening class situation.[68]

Hyden has argued that Tanzanian peasants are powerful because other social classes have not captured them, and, further, their ownership of the means of production, land and labor, enables them to control their means of subsistence and thus exit when it is to their advantage. Furthermore, because of these factors, peasants are only marginally incorporated into the world capitalist economy.[69] Hyden errs, however, in assuming control over subsistence and the ability to exit necessarily indicate power. As the commissioner's report suggests, Kitawalists withdrew because they were powerless in the face of a proximate state. Peasants are not powerful, but the state is weak. Zairian peasants often exit when the state's demands become too great. But when peasants flee to the forest to avoid arbitrary arrest, the descent of a company of soldiers on their village, a new scheme to regroup their villages, or, as in the case of the Kitawalists, to create their own way of life and practice their religion freely, it stretches the point to argue they are powerful merely because in their new location they will be able to hunt and engage in subsistence agriculture.[70]   In these cases the state's weakness and its resulting inability to control its population is a far more compelling explanation than any supposed power of the peasants.

Despite his position in the *Mobutiste* state, the zone commissioner was struck by the "flourishing aspect" of the Kitawalist camp. People were healthy, agricultural produce bountiful. Few, if any, villages in Mongala can make the same boast. Most villages around Lisala would probably appear shabby and unhealthy in comparison. From the perspective of peasants faced with the state's ever-increasing demands on their time and resources, one is thus forced to wonder if exit might not be a workable solution to a harsh problem.

Conclusion

This chapter has examined both the state's attempts to extend its control over religious groups and organizations in civil society and how these groups have coped with the state's pretensions. Three distinct patterns have emerged from this interplay between state and society. First, the Catholic church, historically part of the fabled colonial trinity of church, state, and corporation, has travelled a curious road in its relations with the state. The colonial state ceded educational dominance to missionary groups which were responsible for educating the population and seeing it absorbed the approved religious and moral values. This often consisted of stressing a respect for established authority and hierarchy, whether in state or society. The Catholic church was the main guardian and propagator of the state's ideology. To be sure, there were differences between church and state, but these were insignificant when compared to the overwhelming unity of purpose and agreement these two institutions usually displayed.

Today the Catholic church constitutes the single most powerful and well-organized group in society, and virtually the only one at present able to oppose the state. From the colonial period of ideological cooperation and co-optation, the Catholic church moved into a time of sustained resistance to the *Mobutiste* state. Yet its opposition remains both ambiguous and ambivalent. The Catholic hierarchy doubtlessly realizes its stance toward the regime must be tempered both because some clergy are much less confrontational than others and because many clerics realize their interests may be indissolubly linked to those of the state. Furthermore, we should not overestimate the power of the church; in any serious showdown with the state it will emerge second best. Here, too, there is a dialectic of control at play: the state is anxious to extend its power, but not always able to do so. The state is caught on the horns of a dilemma. It desires to control the church and benefit from its considerable material resources and the social infrastructure it now needs desperately, while, at the same time, it would like to silence its most severe critics. Moreover, the state, rather paradoxically, wishes to gain the moral and intellectual approbation which only the Catholic church in Zaire can bestow.

Second, the Kimbanguist church's reaction to the state's quest for control has been entirely different and, in some regards, a reversal of the Catholic pattern. Long suppressed and outlawed by the colonial state, the Kimbanguist church has no desire to return to confrontation; its emergence into the sun of legality has occurred far too recently. Instead, it has capitalized on its position as an authentic Zairian church and has cooperated actively with the *Mobutiste* state. Moreover, it has consciously imitated certain aspects of the state's organization and policy and put them to its own uses. The structural similarities between this church and the state are striking, and one can only wonder whether, at some future date, this will facilitate a state-controlled interpenetration between the two. For the moment, however, those who rule the state may look on the Kimbanguist church as a religiously tinged, and therefore slightly distorted, mirror image. The reflection, especially when compared to the Catholic church, can only be pleasing.

Third, the Kitawalist reaction is the most radically fundamental. If the Catholic church constitutes an organization in ambivalent opposition to the state and the Kimbanguists have created an organization parallel to the state, then the Kitawalists may have come up with a series of autonomous microtheocracies or counterstates. Kitawalists, like Kimbanguists, suffered as a clandestine and suppressed group during the colonial era. Independence, however, had no effect on their rejection of political power and temporal authority. That the *Mobutiste* state desires authenticity makes it no less temporal and no less political to Kitawalist eyes. So they remain in opposition, but the only way they have been able to continue their resistance is by exiting. In withdrawing to the forest and maintaining their autonomy from the state they have, at least for the moment, been able to preserve both their beliefs and, on the basis of the fragmentary evidence available, a greater level of well-being than found in most Zairian villages. To a beleaguered peasantry the Kitawalist model might represent a minimally viable alternative to the demands of an increasingly rapacious and repressive state. But let us not be too naive. The alternative *is minimal*, and may not be viable much longer. If and when the state develops the power to bring these people back from the forest, it will not hesitate.

Finally, there is no question the Zairian state would like to control and dominate each of these religious groups, but, as our examination of Catholics and Kitawalists has shown, it has been unable to do so. Neither the institutional power of the Catholic church nor the autonomous and independent existence of the Kitawalist communities has been brought to heel. Both have resisted the state; both are caught in the dialectical struggle for autonomous space; and both, therefore, are a source of concern and a constant reminder of the state's impotence. This inability to dominate civil society and its sources of potential organizational foci and alternative ideological initiatives is a striking indication of the Zairian state's weakness and insecurity.

8

The Dialectics of Oppression

> The State does not exist or no longer exists in
> Zaire. It is no more than only a skeleton that
> entertains the illusion.
>
> —Buana Kabue[1]

> Zaire, under your direction, adopted, last Sep-
> tember, a plan . . . implying not only a rein-
> forcement of the liberalization of its economic
> structures, but also courageous austerity
> measures. . . . Recently the International
> Monetary Fund evaluated very positively the
> first results of the new policy that you have in-
> augurated and each day confirms that, thanks
> to your determination and the new impulses
> emanating from your executive council
> [government], Zaire has rediscovered the as-
> cendant phase in its economic life, thus permit-
> ting the development of Zaire's important
> resources in the interests of the country and
> its populations.
>
> —Belgian Prime Minister Martens
> to President Mobutu Sese Seko[2]

Although both the above opinions display radically divergent orientations toward
Zaire and Mobutu, they share the same confusion about the Zairian state. It is
often customary, and certainly facile, to say the truth probably lies somewhere
between these extreme viewpoints. Customary, but wrong, for both commentaries
touch distinct aspects of the same truth. How can we interpret these seemingly
opposing views of the same state? Several major theoretical themes derived from
the analyses presented in previous chapters help generate the response. Insecurity,
scarcity, and the dialectics of oppression; the dialectical struggle for political, social, and economic space; and the coercion of ordinary Zairians caught both at
the confluence of these two dialectics and in the vise of the state's implements of
rule thus merit renewed attention. In addition, I shall present conclusions concerning the general process of state formation, ask why the *Mobutiste* state has

endured for more than twenty years, and discuss the nature of the state in Zaire. Finally, I shall argue for the importance of including a local-level and micropolitical perspective in analyses of the state and reflect on this book's broader theoretical implications.

Insecurity, Scarcity, and the Dialectics of Oppression

Insecurity and scarcity are the twin motors powering a dialectic of oppression. Zaire's political history has changed quickly, and its rulers have realized that the power and positions of today may be gone tomorrow. In Mobutu's system of rule the powerful use political or administrative office to create economic wealth. This usually means officials exploit their power to extract what they can from those in contextually inferior positions in the social hierarchy and, in so doing, create new sources of scarcity. Zairian citizens, already subjected to the harsh conditions of life prevalent in most African countries, are thus caught in the grip of ever increasing insecurity, never knowing when their rulers will appropriate what few resources they have accumulated.

This pervasive insecurity is not limited to the citizenry; the state itself is also insecure. This is certainly not a new observation. Fanon recognized years ago that the bourgeoisie "does not yet possess this good conscience and this tranquillity that only economic power and a grasp of the state system would be able to confer. It does not create a State that reassures the citizen, but one which troubles him."[3] Insecurity is thus writ both large and small; writ large it concerns the state and its rulers, writ small it is about ordinary folk. How is this insecurity manifested?

The CND's repressive and information-gathering tasks contribute to the fear and insecurity faced by Zairians every day. Psychologically and politically insecure rulers have unleashed the political police to assuage their own insecurity, increasingly relying on the CND as the leadership's political legitimacy has eroded. The FAZ, GDN, and JMPR also contribute to the fear and insecurity which villagers and town folk feel, for people know these arms of the state are more likely to steal property than protect it. Similarly, the presence of these forces in the countryside is, at best, a mixed blessing to the regime's politico-administrative officials. Territorial commissioners are insecure because Mobutu can withdraw their appointments at any time. The forces of order contribute to the commissioners' insecurity because the latter cannot control the troops and are always uncertain if the soldiers will be present, or sober, if needed. Magistrates are insecure because they are worried about the place political authorities will ultimately assign them in the self-proclaimed revolutionary order. At the moment, they are fighting a rearguard action to preserve what little judicial independence they retain. They are, moreover, ambivalent about their role both in the *Mobutiste* state and in enforcing alien and repressive laws on people who do not understand them. The unwillingness of magistrates to comply with commissioners on certain issues creates insecurity both for themselves and the state they serve. Their reluctance to embrace some of the regime's more outrageous "revolutionary imperatives" results in the creation of pockets of resistance internal to the state. This, however, offers scant consolation to insecure citizens who must confront a hostile judicial apparatus; one they perceive realistically as part of a repressive state.

Pockets of resistance in the realm of civil society also increase politically defined insecurities. Kitawalists and Jehovah's Witnesses have emphatically rejected the state, and in recent years the Catholic church has moved from ideological support to a more confrontational stance. This, too, increases the state's insecurity, as does its inability to control either population movements (tax flight and withdrawal to the forest) or the citizenry's penchant for retaining firearms (gun control). The absence of control coupled with the state's inability to execute many of its policies contributes dramatically to its rising insecurity. There is much validity in Callaghy's description of the *Mobutiste* state as a "lame Leviathan," but the disability is not only physical, it is also psychological.[4] Furthermore, as the insecurity of the state and its rulers rises, it increasingly recruits the forces of order and state security from either the president's ethnic group or his region. Almost inevitably, citizens from other areas and backgrounds feel excluded from the levers of state power and become apprehensive.[5]

Emphasis on the dialectics of oppression calls attention to the interplay between the insecurity of various organizational arms of the state, on the one hand, and the citizenry's pervasive, and rising, sense of personal insecurity, on the other. There would appear to be two possible political solutions to the question of rising insecurity. First, the state can try to reduce its own insecurity by relying on its coercive arms to repress and intimidate the population. This has been the policy of the *Mobutiste* state. Or one could seek to decrease levels of personal insecurity among the population by creating conditions which would permit greater control of repressive state institutions. For example, the state could make sure the troops are paid and it could prosecute CND agents for violating human rights. Such measures would thereby allow people to enjoy some autonomous political space at the state's expense. Some states, usually democratic ones, protect and nurture this space; the Zairian state smothers it. The result is a struggle for space as the population seeks room to breathe.

The Struggle for Space

Perhaps most frequently seen as a dialectical interplay between social forces favoring centralization and those promoting decentralization, the struggle for space is a long-term historical process that antedates independence. Different types of political configurations dotted the precolonial landscape. Centralized empires and kingdoms such as Luba, Lunda, Kongo, and Kuba existed side by side with an extensive smattering of extremely decentralized and autonomous micropolities such as Ngombe, Upoto, and others. Empires rose and fell as they incorporated these smaller societies and then released them as their powers and vitality waned. Tensions between these modal forms of political organization, centralized administration and small-scale autonomy, were thus present well before the colonial era.[6]

When the Belgians arrived they forcibly placed these hundreds of diverse polities under a centralized state. To be sure, the colonial state evolved considerably, but Belgians aspired to a system of total control. While this goal may have been unattainable, they nevertheless came closer to it than either the French or British. Throughout this period the reality of the repressive, centralized state was reflected in the name Zairians gave to it, *Bula Matari*. Once the nickname of Henry Morton Stanley, *Bula Matari* literally meant "breaker of rocks." Nonetheless, the struggle for space continued under colonial rule, albeit in different forms. Exit remained an option for some; others found solace in religious sects such as Kimbanguism or Kitawala; many refused to comply with the state's regulations and were imprisoned for their troubles.

When the Belgians departed in 1960 they left Zairians with a system much more decentralized than the colonial state had been. The new constitution featured significant degrees of provincial autonomy, and leaders with ethnic bases of political support soon decentralized the state even further. By 1963 First Republic politicians had taken decentralization to an extreme by subdividing most preindependence provinces into ethnically based *provincettes*. After Mobutu seized power in 1965, he progressively eliminated the *provincettes*, removed provincial autonomy, instituted a single state-party, and rebuilt the sinews of the former colonial state. This was most certainly extreme centralization, or recentralization. But this book has shown that significant pockets of decentralization still remain. Even the state's crucial and apparently centralized coercive arms often operate without significant supervision from the center. Sergeants and corporals who command detachments in the countryside are operationally autonomous. Paradoxically, therefore, an effective decentralization, particularly on daily routine, exists under the umbrella of ostensible centralization. From the vantage point of the villagers, this usually means soldiers are free to rampage as the spirit moves them. Similarly, since territorial commissioners, in theory the president's direct representatives in their administrative circumscriptions, can control neither military nor magistrates effectively, many measures the central government promulgates remain dead letters.

Callaghy interprets this dialectic in two ways: first, as a struggle for control pitting the centralizing state against forces and groups in the fabric of civil society; second, as a struggle the centralizing state wages to control its own staff.[7] Much evidence presented here supports these foci, and resistance to the state's control both internal (magistrature and military) and external (Catholic church and Kitawalists) are recurring motifs. No doubt such resistance, whether from within or without, heightens the insecurity of the state and its rulers. From the perspective of the citizenry, however, it is also possible to view this dialectical process as a struggle to retain autonomous political, social, and economic space. We have seen how the state tries to occupy all available space in the hinterland. It suppresses, or at least tries to control, any organizational initiatives which might call forth competing foci of loyalty. Second parties are banned, labor unions co-opted, cultural and religious organizations suppressed or watched closely. People, of course, resist these attempts to the extent possible and struggle against the state.

The proliferation of nonrecognized religious sects; exit to the forest and islands; illegal retention of firearms; occasional wildcat strikes and labor disputes; malicious gossip and cynicism; and the informal economy are all attempts by the powerless to retain some autonomous space and thus cope with, and resist, the state.[8]

This dialectical struggle for space is a long-term, open-ended process of ascent and decline with no preordained conclusion. Furthermore, in many ways it is an integral part of the process of state formation and, in that context, Tilly observes although state formation is an immense and powerful social process, "it is not immanent in particular governments, is not unidirectional, and is not, in any simple sense of the words, a displacement of the 'traditional' by the 'modern.'"[9] I shall address this process presently.

Implements of Rule

People often perceive their state through its methods of rule, and in Zaire attention to the local-level perspective leads naturally to a focus on the state's implements of coercive rule. Much of the state's business up-country is coercion.[10] Coercion exists, and is created, at the confluence of the two dialectics. The dialectic of oppression contributes to coercion in the countryside because the CND, FAZ, GDN, and JMPR foster and maintain a pervasive climate of fear. Members of the state's coercive arms in immediate contact with ordinary citizens use their powers to extract resources from those in contextually inferior positions in the class hierarchy. While their superiors engage in extractive activities to accumulate capital, the rank and file extort to survive. Since superior officers often divert funds destined to pay their salaries, soldiers and gendarmes live off the land—and the backs of the population. Corruption at the top of the polity travels down the line and creates scarcity for those at the bottom. The resulting tensions translate into coercion and extraction. The forces of order and state security employ their firearms, as well as their powers of arrest and detention, to sow fear and terror. Furthermore, even without reference to the state's coercive arms, policies such as the frequent rotation of bureaucrats and the all too common meteoric ascents in, and falls from, Mobutu's favor condition the powerful in various domains to profit from their positions while possible. The weight of the entire system of *Mobutiste* rule thus comes crashing down on the citizenry. To them, the state snarls far more often than it smiles.

The dialectical struggle for space contributes to the prevalence of coercion in two ways. First, because segments of the state ascend and decline at different speeds, organizationally independent power holders can maintain substantial degrees of autonomy vis-à-vis the wishes of those dominating the central state. In other words, even if the state desired to curb the more pernicious activities of its coercive arms (at present a dubious proposition in Zaire), there is every reason to believe it could not. Although some magistrates and commissioners genuinely wish to serve the population and would sincerely like to control the local activities of the state's coercive arms, they remain impotent. This creates even more insecurity for an already insecure state and contributes to a further exacerbation of the dialectic of oppression.

Second, the citizenry's desire for autonomous political space is unquenchable. Zairians, like other peoples, seek the freedom to breathe. As a result, when they confront an oppressive state which permits political participation only on its own terms, they subtly redefine the "political" realm. Attending mass can become a political act, for example. Or they may refuse to participate in *salongo, animation*, or marches of support. The insecure state then reacts with even harsher doses of coercive force. The intersection of the two dialectics, as well as some historical processes involved in the struggle for space, forces consideration of the general process of state formation.

State Formation

In this context Callaghy's superb comparative study of Mobutu's Zaire and absolutist France commands attention. In general, the comparison is subtly done, and, to his credit, Callaghy does not contort his data to conform to his theory. Not only is he well aware of the similarities in these two seemingly disparate social formations, he also displays a keen sense of the important differences. Equally to his credit, he is cognizant of the dangers of teleological assumptions, of assuming that Zaire will somehow travel toward the same outcome of state formation that France did, and he warns his readers of the trap. Despite the similarities, various factors could well alter the present direction of change.[11] In sum, the chance that Zaire will some day resemble today's France, or that it is traveling, or even could travel, in the same direction is probably remote. The emergence of the contemporary form of the French state was not preordained; France as a territorial entity might have disappeared from the face of Europe as did other early attempts at state building. During the period of European absolutism the international system did not insure the continued existence of each and every member—states had to adapt or die. Thus, something resembling a process of "natural selection" occurred.

Precolonial Africa was similar; states arose, flourished, and disappeared subsequently. Since the imposition of the grid-like structure of the contemporary international system of states, Zaire and other states in Africa are no longer faced with a choice between adaptation and extinction. They will continue to exist as territorial units whether or not they change with the times. Consider this counterfactual proposition. Had the Zairian state existed prior to colonial rule, it probably would not have lasted as long as it has because precolonial states did not have the international system to provide ready made legitimacy in the form of international recognition of preset territorial boundaries. Precolonial states were fluid both internally and externally; at present only the internal fluidity remains. Large-scale, continental processes of state formation in Africa have thus been transferred to the much smaller internal arena since the state understood as territorial shell is, for the most part and with but rare exception, no longer open to question. The present international system thus guaranteed the continuity of Zaire as a territorial entity throughout the dissolution of the sinews of the state during the First Republic and the severe challenges posed to the Second. Today only the internal shape of the state as a constellation of administrative, coercive, and ideological power remains in doubt. If we now know why Zaire has endured as a territorial entity, we also need to ask why the *Mobutiste* state has survived as an internal configuration of power. The support and nurture of the international system is certainly an important reason, but only part of a complex equation.

Why Has the *Mobutiste* State Endured?

To answer this question we need to return to some of the ideas and themes first evoked in the general analysis of the triple helix of state, class, and ethnicity, as well as to its more specific treatment of strategies of access and dominance. Although social classes exist in Zaire there are no serious internal class competitors for control of the state.[12] The politico-commercial bourgeoisie governs without serious internal opposition, although they can, and do, squabble among themselves for the fruits of political rule. Giddens argues that exploitation is best conceived as a consequence of domination or power,[13] and the politico-commercial bourgeoisie has made ample use of its power both to harvest the state's economic produce, and to render marginal and impotent any possible opponents. To do this the politico-commercial bourgeoisie uses the sinews of state power to close off possible channels of opposition and employs their ideological armory to provide false hope for citizens that they, or their children, will one day be able to rise in the social hierarchy if only they have faith in their "father." Those who, in other situations, might have formed core oppositional elements find themselves either in sterile exile, seeking solace in the bosom of the Catholic church, or fleeing to the forests. The *Mobutiste* state has made effective opposition impossible at worst, or foolhardy at best.

Young and Turner's excellent analysis of the Mobutu regime pinpoints several explanatory factors. Many people, for example, still think upward mobility is possible through the schools. Although this is actually no longer the case for most, the myth of mobility through education endures. The belief that one's children will be able to rise in the social hierarchy if educated creates and sustains a powerful psychological incentive for going along with the system—no matter how oppressive it has become. In addition, the pervasive ethnically based kinship and clientage system also sustains hope of social mobility for those at the lower end of the social hierarchy.[14] But, as Lemarchand notes, Zairian patronage networks are neither deep nor wide, "and the preservation of class privilege is the principal motive behind the wheeling and dealing going on at the center."[15] Yet belief in social mobility dies hard.

Two other factors help maintain the *Mobutiste* state. The informal economy provides both survival mechanisms for the masses and a safety valve for the state. People must earn a living to survive, and in Zaire today this requires enormous amounts of energy and effort. The "duress of the quotidian," to use Scott's phrase, also inhibits revolt.[16] Finally, the political, economic, and military support the regime enjoys from its allies in the West plays a significant role. At the least, Zaire's continuing support from the IMF, World Bank, and other creditors indicates to its population that the regime has friends abroad. At the most, events such as Shaba I and II demonstrate to Zaire's dispossessed that the state's leadership, if challenged again, could call successfully on powerful outside support.[17]

To these reasons explaining the longevity of the *Mobutiste* state I would add three others emerging from the analyses presented in this book. First, the state tries to occupy all available political space within the system. Mobutu has steadfastly refused to sanction the existence of a second political party, or even an opposition current within the MPR. Furthermore, the state deals with any attempt at organization at lower levels of society by either co-optation into the state-party (youth, labor unions) or suppression. Similarly, the state is likely to deem subversive and threatening any organizational initiatives it cannot control because they might subsequently become foci of potential opposition. This is one reason the Catholic church causes Mobutu such anguish.

Second, Mobutu and his collaborators insure their continued access and dominance by using the state's coercive arms to terrorize and intimidate the population, thus diffusing a pervasive climate of fear. The power of the state is relative. When viewed from abroad it appears the FAZ is teetering on the brink of dissolution whenever it confronts armed opposition; when seen from the perspective of ordinary Zairians, its power is awesome and terrifying. Zairians know, moreover, that the state will use this power to crush opposition ruthlessly whenever and wherever it might appear. It matters little if such opposition is ethnically based or class based, the state will demolish it.

Lastly, the state's clever use of symbols, images, and metaphors aids it in maintaining political quiescence. In this regard, Zaire's rulers skillfully manipulate ethnicity so most Zairians focus on residents of Equateur as the regime's main beneficiaries, thus blaming them for causing society's ills. At the same time, Mobutu and those around him shrewdly convince Equateurians, and others, that present troubles and difficulties are due either to rebels and other bad elements from Kasai and Shaba or to international economic conditions, thus precluding transethnic and social class alliances. But more is involved. Bienen argues perceptively that formal ideologies such as African Socialism, Marxism-Leninism, and—I would add—Authenticity and *Mobutisme* provide weak ideological cement for states in Africa.[18] In this vein, Hyden's observation that many African states seem suspended in midair without firm roots in society is also relevant.[19] Zaire's leaders have sought, perhaps intuitively and unconsciously, to remedy these difficulties with their extensive, albeit occasionally perverse, use of the metaphors of father and family that build on the complex, culturally based moral matrix of legitimate governance. Mobutu and his collaborators know their people and culture extremely well and manipulate this imagery to produce a legitimacy and staying power not wholly dependent on coercion. To be sure, such ideological cement, Zaire's smiling face, can serve larger coercive and extractive ends. The imagery enables Mobutu to present political repression and suppression of legitimate dissent as paternal discipline reluctantly doled out to wayward children in need of correction; it equally permits him to assume the mantle of a generous father and provider to whom his children owe a never-ending debt. The beliefs of the weak are another brick in the fortress of the strong. Mobutu and his cohorts thus make ample use of at least three strategies of access and dominance: coercion, co-optation and the occupation of all available political space, and ideological obfuscation.

The Zairian State

This study's view of the state as a congeries of organized repositories of administrative, coercive, and ideological power subject to, and engaged in, an ongoing process of power accumulation characterized by uneven ascension and uneven decline, coupled with its local-level and micropolitical perspective, have made us aware that the arms of state power are not always under the control of the central state, however high the degree of formal centralization. The state, as Poulantzas reminds us, is not a monolithic entity. Nor does it speak with a single voice. Individual organizational arms of the state may each go its own way, and interstitial crevices exist between them. These organs ascend and decline at varying speeds and have different visions of society and polity. The result resembles a series of imperfectly meshed gears as pockets of resistance internal to the state develop. These notions also lead us back to the relativity of the state's power—perhaps weak to international donors intent on implementing reforms, but massive and overwhelming to the citizenry.

The state is also a fluid and contextual entity whose shape and internal configurations of power are constantly changing. Also changing, therefore, is the line dividing state and civil society as the fortunes and boundaries of the state ebb and flow. The evolving patterns of accommodation between the state and certain religious groups demonstrate these shifts, illustrated by the curious journey of the Catholic church. Once the ideological pillar of colonialism and confused in the popular mind with the colonial state, the church has now assumed a position of opposition to the present-day successor of that state. Once on the inside, it is now on the outside. The Kimbanguist church, however, displays the opposite pattern. Formerly in confrontation with the colonial state, this church now mirrors the state's administrative organization and apes its ideological dogma. These dramatic shifts of position indicate a marked change in the ideological dimensions and boundaries of the state. Moreover, as Bayart suggests, perhaps this fluidity in the boundary between state and civil society renders the standard dichotomy too simple to be of much analytical utility. As conceptions of the state change, so too might conceptions of politics and of what constitutes the political realm. Social groups may not recognize the same phenomena as "political" at the same time.[20]

Interactions between state and civil society should be the object of empirical inquiry before they become the subject of deductive theorizing. Outcomes of these interactions are not predetermined and vary significantly as the state ascends and declines. For example, and as a consequence of this investigation, we might hypothesize that as the state declines, insecure rulers may come to place increasing reliance on the political police as an instrument of rule. Or, as the state declines and its internal political legitimacy erodes, leaders will increasingly attempt to replace it with legitimacy generated from the international system. Or, as the state declines and its leaders become progressively more insecure, they will increasingly limit recruitment to the state's key organs of coercive power to ethnic kinsmen. Or, as the state declines and is no longer able to provide the services it once did, the salience of secondary or informal economic structures will increase. Given our present knowledge, however, all such hypotheses must remain speculative.

I agree with Young and Turner who argue the Zairian state "sees first to its own preservation and nurture" and that "units of the state are committed to securing from their subjects a living for the state itself." But they also maintain that corruption is now "the most visible defining property of the Zairian state," and here I disagree.[21] Corruption is an enormous problem, but it has become so largely because of the social, political, and economic consequences of the dialectic of oppression. Would corruption exist without the dialectic of oppression? Assuredly. Would it have attained such prominence, pervasiveness, and intensity? Assuredly not. Corruption is a cancer but does not itself cause the *mal zairois*. The dialectic of oppression lies at the heart of the problem. Cabral said, "The problem of the nature of the state created after independence is perhaps the secret failure of African independence."[22] Secret no more, the state's failure lies both in its inability and, at times, unwillingness to control the dialectic of oppression and in its active exacerbation of the dialectic's most vicious elements.

Nzongola has justly criticized most academicians for their failure to analyze Zaire's crisis from the vantage point of its main victims, the ordinary folk in cities, towns, and villages.[23] This book is a step, albeit partial, in that direction. It has indicated some basic ingredients necessary for constructing a theory of the state which begins from the population's daily interactions with representatives of the state, and is then elaborated upward. At minimum, such a theory should include an appreciation of the quality of the state's interactions with its people. Are these primarily extractive or redistributive? Does the state facilitate the creation and retention of wealth or, as is true in Zaire, merely siphon it off? Does the population recognize the state's coercive measures as legitimate and necessary or, again the case in Zaire, as arbitrary and unjust? Do people flee from the state or welcome it? Do they see a smile or a snarl? Sustained attention to these ordinary interactions has, in the Zairian context, dictated a concern with the mechanics of coercion.

The local-level perspective also demonstrates that both the optimistic and pessimistic views of the Zairian state contained in epigraph are incomplete; each focuses on but one side of the same coin. Buana Kabue's assertion that the Zairian state is dead is a serious exaggeration. There are certain magistrates, commissioners, and bureaucrats who, despite enormous pressures, still perform conscien-

tiously and who do care about the population. Some branches of the state do put-
ter along and provide what services they can as best they can. These observations, however, must be tempered with the knowledge that the glowing opinions
of Prime Minister Martens are equally exaggerated. To believe the Zairian state
is now capable of achieving both substantial reform and amelioration in the standard of living of its citizens is a dream; too much evidence exists indicating Zairian
leaders remain more interested in accumulation than amelioration. We have seen
how this preference descends the state's hierarchy through the mechanisms of the
dialectic of oppression and results in a reign of terror in the countryside. In this
regard, Mobutu's announcement in November 1986 that he was going to create a
ministry of citizen's rights must be seen for what it is—a charade.[24] The state in
Zaire, as elsewhere in Africa, ascends and declines unevenly. As a result, both
optimists and pessimists are likely to be disappointed and their expectations belied,
a point Young recognized implicitly over twenty years ago when he carefully indicated that the terms commonly employed to describe the so-called Congo Crisis
("chaos," "anarchy") were far too simple to cover the complex processes involved.[25]

The local-level perspective also permits us to get away from the abstractions of
both neo-Marxist and functionalist schools by presenting a view of the state as it
appears in the countryside from the vantage point of those who must endure it as
part of their daily routine; a picture not of what the state should do according to
the dictates of an abstract, elegant theoretical edifice, but of what it does do. The
picture of the dialectic of oppression is unpleasant, but one which the illegally
detained schoolteacher from Moba would recognize. This effort should be seen
as only a tentative step toward the construction of a theory of the state from the
bottom up—one which begins with the tragic realities of life in Zaire, and in much
of the rest of Africa. For only in this way will we ever comprehend the dynamics
of social and political phenomena, the fluid interactions of the strands of the triple
helix, the cultural bases of the moral matrix of legitimate governance that may
well determine political legitimacy, and the reasons why such egregious examples
of exploitation, corruption, and oppression as the Zairian *Mobutiste* state endure.

Notes

Preface

1. On Lisala's history, see Michael G. Schatzberg, *Politics and Class in Zaire: Bureaucracy, Business, and Beer in Lisala* (New York: Africana Publishing Company, 1980) 4–10; and idem, "The Chiefs of Upoto: Political Encapsulation and the Transformation of Tradition in Northwestern Zaire," *Cultures et développement* 12 (1980): 235–69. For the regime's views of Lisala, *Salongo* (Kinshasa), 29 September 1980, 1 and 10 October 1980, 2. In descending order from most to least inclusive unit, Zaire's administrative structure is composed as follows: regions (headed by regional commissioners), subregions (subregional commissioners), zones (zone commissioners), collectivities (chiefs), localities (chiefs), and sublocalities or villages (chiefs or elders).

1. Introduction

1. *Salongo*, 23 May 1983, 8.
2. Amnesty International [AI], *Zaire: Reports of Torture and Killings Committed by the Armed Forces in Shaba Region* (London: AI, 1986), 17–18.
3. This period of Zaire's history has been amply studied. See Crawford Young, *Politics in the Congo: Decolonization and Independence* (Princeton: Princeton University Press, 1965); Jules Gérard-Libois and Benoît Verhaegen, eds., *Congo 1960*, 3 vols. (Brussels: CRISP, 1961); and Jean-Claude Willame, *Patrimonialism and Political Change in the Congo* (Stanford: Stanford University Press, 1972). On private armies, see ibid., 57–76.
4. The definitive study of the Second Republic is Crawford Young and Thomas Turner, *The Rise and Decline of the Zairian State* (Madison: University of Wisconsin Press, 1985). Young and Turner date the crisis from 1974, but there are grounds for disagreement. See Michael G. Schatzberg, review of *The Rise and Decline of the Zairian State*, by Crawford Young and Thomas Turner, *American Political Science Review* 80 (1986): 1389–90.
5. On the economic policy measures see Schatzberg, *Politics and Class*, 121–52; idem, "The State and the Economy: The 'Radicalization of the Revolution' in Mobutu's Zaire," *Canadian Journal of African Studies* 14:2 (1980): 239–57; and Young and Turner, *Rise and Decline*, 326–62. On the catastrophic consequences of Mobutu's grandiose vision of economic development, see Jean-Claude Willame, *Zaire, l'épopée d'Inga: Chronique d'une prédation industrielle* (Paris: L'Harmattan, 1986).
6. See Crawford Young, "Zaire: The Unending Crisis," *Foreign Affairs* 57 (1978): 169–85; Ghislain C. Kabwit, "Zaire: The Roots of the Continuing Crisis," *Journal of Modern African Studies* 17 (1979): 381–407; World Bank, *Zaire: Current Economic Situation and Constraints* (Washington, D.C.: East Africa Regional Office, The World Bank, May 1980); Michael G. Schatzberg, "Zaire," in *The Political Economy of African Foreign Policy: Comparative Analysis*, ed. Timothy M. Shaw and Olajide Aluko (Farnsborough: Gower, 1984), 283–318; and, most recently, Nzongola-Ntalaja, ed., *The Crisis in Zaire: Myths and Realities* (Trenton, N.J.: Africa World Press, 1986).
7. For the complete argument, see Schatzberg, *Politics and Class*, esp., 183–85.
8. Sakombi Inongo, *Lettre ouverte à Nguza Karl-i-Bond* (France: n.p., 1982), 43–44. This little book is a response to Nguza Karl-i-Bond, *Mobutu: Ou l'incarnation du mal zairois* (London: Rex Collings, 1982).

9. Crawford Young, *Ideology and Development in Africa* (New Haven: Yale University Press, 1982), 316.

10. Thomas M. Callaghy, *The State-Society Struggle: Zaire in Comparative Perspective* (New York: Columbia University Press, 1984), 143–44.

11. Field Log, 12 October 1974, 3; Joan Vincent, *African Elite: The Big Men of a Small Town* (New York: Columbia University Press, 1971), 82–83; and Callaghy, *State-Society Struggle*, 449–50.

12. Crawford Young, "Patterns of Social Conflict: State, Class, and Ethnicity," *Daedalus* 111 (1982): 71–98; for historical depth, John Lonsdale, "States and Social Processes in Africa: A Historiographical Survey," *African Studies Review* 24 (1981): 87–138; and also Donald Rothchild and Victor A. Olorunsola, eds., *State versus Ethnic Claims: African Policy Dilemmas* (Boulder, Colo.: Westview, 1983). General, non-Africanist historical overviews may be found in Gianfranco Poggi, *The Development of the Modern State: An Historical Introduction* (Stanford: Stanford University Press, 1978) and, from an anthropological perspective, Ronald Cohen and Elman R. Service, eds., *Origins of the State: The Anthropology of Political Evolution* (Philadelphia: Institute for the Study of Human Issues, 1978). Finally, the recent emergence of a serious body of neo-Marxist literature on the state is treated well in Bob Jessop, *The Capitalist State: Marxist Theory and Methods* (New York: New York University Press, 1982).

13. In some contexts Gramsci means the state to have the restricted meaning of a "politico-juridical organisation in the narrow sense," while in others he perceives it as "the entire complex of practical and theoretical activities with which the ruling class not only justifies and maintains its dominance, but manages to win the active consent of those over whom it rules." Antonio Gramsci, *Selections from the Prison Notebooks of Antonio Gramsci*, ed. and trans. Quintin Hoare and Geoffrey Newell Smith (New York: International Publishers, 1971), 261, 244. Poulantzas observes the state is not an intrinsic entity, but "*a relationship of forces, or more precisely the material condensation of such a relationship among classes and class fractions, such as this is expressed within the State in a necessarily specific form.*" Yet, at later points, he speaks of the state as "an institution destined to reproduce class divisions," as a "mechanism," and as a "*strategic field and process* of intersecting power networks." Nicos Poulantzas, *State, Power, Socialism*, trans. Patrick Camiller (London: Verso, 1980), 128–29, 132, 133, 136. Emphasis in original.

14. On the question of civil society, Gramsci fixed "two major superstructural 'levels': the one that can be called 'civil society', that is the ensemble of organisms commonly called 'private', and that of 'political society' or 'the state'. These two levels correspond on the one hand to the function of 'hegemony' which the dominant group exercises throughout society and on the other hand to that of 'direct domination' or command exercised through the State and 'juridical' government." Yet Gramsci later argued "the general notion of State includes elements which need to be referred back to the notion of civil society (in the manner that one might say that State = political society + civil society, in other words hegemony protected by the armour of coercion)." Gramsci, *Selections from the Prison Notebooks*, 12, 263. Suffice it to say if the state encompasses civil society, then its analytical utility is vastly reduced. Nevertheless, Stanley B. Greenberg, *Race and State in Capitalist Development: Comparative Perspectives* (New Haven: Yale University Press, 1980) and Jean-François Bayart, *L'état au Cameroun* (Paris: Presses de la Fondation Nationale des Sciences Politiques, 1979) have made good use of Gramsci's insights. Also see Jean-François Bayart, "Régime du parti unique et système d'inégalité et de domination au Cameroun: Esquisse," *Cahiers d'études africaines* 18 (1978): 5–35, and the critiques by Leca, Rey, and Bayart's rejoinder in ibid., 37–47, 115–22.

15. Theda Skocpol, *States and Social Revolutions: A Comparative Analysis of France, Russia, and China* (Cambridge: Cambridge University Press, 1979), 14.

16. Anthony Giddens, *A Contemporary Critique of Historical Materialism*, vol. 1,

Power, Property and the State (Berkeley and Los Angeles: University of California Press, 1981), 1:220.

17. For example, Clifford Geertz, *Negara: The Theatre State in Nineteenth Century Bali* (Princeton: Princeton University Press, 1980).

18. Poulantzas, *State, Power, Socialism*, 133, 132.

19. Young and Turner, *Rise and Decline*.

20. Callaghy makes the point cogently in *State-Society Struggle*.

21. Jessop, *The Capitalist State*, 222.

22. Robert H. Jackson and Carl G. Rosberg, "Why Africa's Weak States Persist: The Empirical and the Juridical in Statehood," *World Politics* 35 (1982): 1-24. On specific cases, see Naomi Chazan, *An Anatomy of Ghanaian Politics: Managing Political Recession, 1969-1982* (Boulder, Colo.: Westview, 1983); Mahmood Mamdani, *Imperialism and Fascism in Uganda* (London: Heinemann, 1983); and Samuel Decalo, "Regionalism, Political Decay, and Civil Strife in Chad," *Journal of Modern African Studies* 18 (1980): 23-56.

2. Triple Helix: State, Class, and Ethnicity in Africa

This chapter is a revised version of "The Emerging Trialectic: State, Class, and Ethnicity in Africa" (Paper presented at the Institute of International Studies, University of California, Berkeley, 25 May 1982). I thank Professor Carl G. Rosberg and his colleagues for pushing me to think more systematically about these questions.

1. Interview, Lisala, no. 1, 14 November 1974, 6.

2. "Lettre ouverte au Citoyen Président-Fondateur du Mouvement Populaire de la Révolution, Président de la République par un groupe de parlementaires," in Jean-François Bayart, "La fronde parlementaire au Zaire," *Politique africaine* 3 (1981): 122. The actual figure should read 0.000002 percent.

3. *Salongo*, 14-15 March 1981, 2.

4. Paul Mercier, "Remarques sur la signification du 'tribalisme' en Afrique noire," *Cahiers internationaux de sociologie* 31 (1961): 64-67; Jan Vansina, *Kingdoms of the Savanna* (Madison: University of Wisconsin Press, 1965); Aidan W. Southall, "The Illusion of Tribe," *Journal of Asian and African Studies* 5 (1970): 28-50; Crawford Young, *The Politics of Cultural Pluralism* (Madison: University of Wisconsin Press, 1976); and Enid Schildkrout, *People of the Zongo: The Transformation of Ethnic Identities in Ghana* (Cambridge: Cambridge University Press, 1978). Useful non-Africanist works on ethnicity include John A. Armstrong, *Nations before Nationalism* (Chapel Hill: University of North Carolina Press, 1982); Joseph Rothschild, *Ethnopolitics: A Conceptual Framework* (New York: Columbia University Press, 1981); Charles F. Keyes, ed., *Ethnic Change* (Seattle: University of Washington Press, 1981); Ernest Gellner, *Nations and Nationalism* (Ithaca: Cornell University Press, 1983); and Crawford Young, "The Temple of Ethnicity," *World Politics* 35 (1983): 652-62.

5. Schildkrout, *People of the Zongo*, 16. But Donald L. Horowitz, *Ethnic Groups in Conflict* (Berkeley and Los Angeles: University of California Press, 1985), 51-53; and A.L. Epstein, *Ethos and Identity: Three Studies in Ethnicity* (London: Tavistock, 1978) lean toward the "primordialist" position.

6. Jan Vansina, "Lignage, idéologie et histoire en Afrique équatoriale," *Enquêtes et documents d'histoire africaine* 4 (1980): 143; and idem, "The Peoples of the Forest," in *History of Central Africa*, 2 vols., ed. David Birmingham and Phyllis M. Martin (London: Longman, 1983), 1:75-117.

7. Young, *Politics of Cultural Pluralism*, 12-13.

8. Robin Cohen, "Class in Africa: Analytical Problems and Perspectives," in *The Socialist Register 1972*, ed. Ralph Miliband and John Savile (London: Merlin, 1972), 243.

9. Joel Samoff, "The Bureaucracy and the Bourgeoisie: Decentralization and Class Structure in Tanzania," *Comparative Studies in Society and History* 21 (1979): 50; and idem, "Class, Class Conflict, and the State in Africa," *Political Science Quarterly* 97 (1982): 112–13.

10. Y.-A. Fauré and J.-F. Médard, "Classe dominante ou classe dirigeante?" in *Etat et bourgeoisie en Côte-d'Ivoire*, ed. Y.-A. Fauré and J.-F. Médard (Paris: Karthala, 1982), 146.

11. Adrian J. Peace, *Choice, Class and Conflict: A Study of Southern Nigerian Factory Workers* (Atlantic Highlands, N.J.: Humanities, 1979), 62.

12. Henry Bienen, "The State and Ethnicity: Integrative Formulas in Africa," in *State versus Ethnic Claims: African Policy Dilemmas*, eds. Donald Rothchild and Victor A. Olorunsola (Boulder, Colo.: Westview, 1983), 119.

13. Christopher Leo, *Land and Class in Kenya* (Toronto: University of Toronto Press, 1984), 148.

14. Schatzberg, *Politics and Class*, 31. In the same work I defined social class as the "manifestations of a process by which allied actors obtain or lose, open up or close off, become increasingly or decreasingly conscious of access to life and mobility chances." Ibid., 27–28.

15. J. Clyde Mitchell, *The Kalela Dance: Aspects of Social Relations among Urban Africans in Northern Rhodesia*, Rhodes-Livingston Institute Paper, no. 27 (Manchester: Manchester University Press, 1956), 43.

16. Nelson Kasfir, *The Shrinking Political Arena: Participation and Ethnicity in African Politics, with a Case Study of Uganda* (Berkeley and Los Angeles: University of California Press, 1976), 76; idem, "Explaining Ethnic Participation," *World Politics* 31 (1979): 372–74; and Michael G. Schatzberg, "Ethnicity and Class at the Local Level: Bars and Bureaucrats in Lisala, Zaire," *Comparative Politics* 13 (1981): 461–78.

17. Edmond J. Keller, "Ethiopia: Revolution, Class, and the National Question," *African Affairs* 80 (1981): 548–49.

18. James C. Scott, *Weapons of the Weak: Everyday Forms of Peasant Resistance* (New Haven: Yale University Press, 1985), 43.

19. John Lonsdale, "States and Social Processes," 150–51. Also, Frank Parkin, *Marxism and Class Theory: A Bourgeois Critique* (New York: Columbia University Press, 1979), 42.

20. John S. Saul, *The State and Revolution in Eastern Africa* (New York: Monthly Review Press, 1979), 391–423.

21. Colin Leys, *Underdevelopment in Kenya: The Political Economy of Neo-colonialism 1964–1971* (Berkeley and Los Angeles: University of California Press, 1974), 25.

22. A critical overview of the debate is contained in Bjorn Beckman, "Imperialism and Capitalist Transformation: Critique of a Kenyan Debate," *Review of African Political Economy* 19 (1980): 48–62.

23. Karl Marx, *The Eighteenth Brumaire of Louis Bonaparte*, in *Surveys from Exile*, trans. Ben Fowkes, ed. David Fernbach (New York: Vintage Books, 1976), 239.

24. Claude Rivière, "Dynamique de la stratification sociale en Guinée," (Thèse, Université de Paris V, 1975), 66.

25. Michael A. Cohen, *Urban Policy and Political Conflict in Africa: A Study of the Ivory Coast* (Chicago: University of Chicago Press, 1974), 6, 62.

26. Bonnie Campbell, "The Ivory Coast," in *West African States: Failure and Promise; A Study in Comparative Politics*, ed. John Dunn (Cambridge: Cambridge University Press, 1978), 73, 83.

27. Tessilimi Bakary, "Elite Transformation and Political Succession," in *The Political Economy of Ivory Coast*, ed. I. William Zartman and Christopher Delgado (New York:

Praeger, 1984), 29. Other studies questioning the dominance of indigenous planters are Robert M. Hecht, "The Ivory Coast Economic 'Miracle': What Benefits for Peasant Farmers?" *Journal of Modern African Studies* 21 (1983): 25–53; and the collective effort of Fauré and Médard, *Etat et bourgeoisie*, esp. the essays by Fauré and Médard, and Gastellu and Affou Yapi. The entire debate is reviewed in Jean-François Bayart, "Etat et société civile en Afrique de l'ouest," *Revue française de science politique* 33 (1983): 747–53.

28. Sara Berry, *Fathers Work for Their Sons: Accumulation, Mobility, and Class Formation in an Extended Yoruba Community* (Berkeley and Los Angeles: University of California Press, 1985), 84.

29. Lonsdale, "States and Social Processes," 162.

30. John Markakis, *Ethiopia: Anatomy of a Traditional Polity* (Oxford: Clarendon, 1974), 388.

31. Mwabila Malela, *Travail et travailleurs au Zaïre: Essai sur la conscience ouvrière du prolétariat urbain de Lubumbashi* (Kinshasa: Presses Universitaires du Zaïre, Rectorat, Kinshasa, UNAZA, 1979), 14.

32. Schatzberg, *Politics and Class*.

33. Georges Balandier, *Sens et puissance: Les dynamiques sociales* (Paris: Presses Universitaires de France, 1971), 270–71.

34. I thus prefer to qualify Thomas's statement that "the state is in fact always preeminently a class institution." See Clive Y. Thomas, *The Rise of the Authoritarian State in Peripheral Societies* (New York: Monthly Review Press, 1984), 79.

35. I first used the term "politico-commercial bourgeoisie" in Schatzberg, *Politics and Class*, 176, 209, n. 3. It refers to the dominant Zairian social class which has used political access to build economic wealth. The juxtaposition of elements within the term suggests the historical order of this class' access: initially to the state, then to the economy.

36. Markakis, *Ethiopia*, 389.

37. Mwabila Malela, "Pour une relecture de la sociologie à la lumière de la théorie de dépendance," in *La dépendance de l'Afrique et les moyens d'y remédier: Actes de la 4è session du congrès international des études africaines, Kinshasa, 12–16 décembre 1978*, ed. V. Y. Mudimbe (Paris: Agence de Coopération Culturelle et Technique and Berger-Levrault, 1980), 266–68.

38. Hugues Bertrand, *Le Congo: Formation sociale et môde de développement économique* (Paris: Maspero, 1975), 105–6.

39. Kathleen A. Staudt, "Sex, Ethnic, and Class Consciousness in Western Kenya," *Comparative Politics* 14 (1982): 162–63.

40. Saul, *State and Revolution*, 396.

41. Joel D. Barkan and John J. Okumu, eds., *Politics and Public Policy in Kenya and Tanzania* (New York: Praeger, 1979). On how such networks operate, see Joseph Karimi and Philip Ochieng, *The Kenyatta Succession* (Nairobi: Transafrica, 1980).

42. Donal Cruise O'Brien, *The Mourides of Senegal: The Political and Economic Organization of an Islamic Brotherhood* (Oxford: Clarendon, 1971).

43. Administrative correspondence, 13 April 1972, 25 April 1972, and 26 April 1972.

44. For a good starting point on patron-client relations and political clientelage, see S. N. Eisenstadt and René Lemarchand, eds., *Political Clientelage, Patronage and Development* (Beverly Hills, Calif.: Sage, 1981).

45. Mwabila, *Travail et travailleurs*, 165.

46. Goran Hyden, *No Shortcuts to Progress: African Development Management in Perspective* (Berkeley and Los Angeles: University of California Press, 1983), 114–15.

47. Michaela von Freyhold, *Ujamaa Villages in Tanzania: Analysis of a Social Experiment* (New York: Monthly Review Press, 1979), 32–59.

48. P. M. van Hekken and H. U. E. Thoden van Velzen, *Land Scarcity and Rural Inequality in Tanzania* (The Hague: Mouton, 1972).

49. See Andrew Coulson, *Tanzania: A Political Economy* (Oxford: Clarendon, 1982), 263–71, 319.

50. Bayart, *L'état au Cameroun*, 205.

51. Crawford Young, *Ideology and Development*, 19, 181.

52. Robert H. Bates, *Markets and States in Tropical Africa: The Political Basis of Agricultural Choice* (Berkeley and Los Angeles: University of California Press, 1981), 121.

53. Stanley B. Greenberg, *Race and State in Capitalist Development*, 389–90; and Robert Springborg, *Family, Power, and Politics in Egypt: Sayed Bey Marei—His Clan, Clients, and Cohorts* (Philadelphia: University of Pennsylvania Press, 1982), xxvii.

54. Robert H. Bates, *Essays on the Political Economy of Rural Africa* (Cambridge: Cambridge University Press, 1983), 146–47

55. Poggi, *Development of the Modern State*, 94–95.

56. Samora Machel, "The People's Republic of Mozambique: The Struggle Continues," *Review of African Political Economy* 4 (1975): 19–20 cited in Saul, *State and Revolution*, 11.

57. Bianga bin Waruzi, "Peasant, State and Rural Development in Postindependent Zaire: A Case Study of 'Reforme Rurale' 1970–1980 and its Implications," (Ph.D. diss., University of Wisconsin-Madison, 1982), 80.

58. Discussions with Yahya Sadowski helped me grasp some of these points.

59. Richard A. Joseph, "Democratization under Military Tutelage: Crisis and Consensus in the Nigerian 1979 Elections," *Comparative Politics* 14 (1981): 80.

60. Larry Diamond, "Nigeria in Search of Democracy," *Foreign Affairs* 62 (1984): 905–27.

61. Joseph, "Democratization under Military Tutelage," 91–93, notes most parties were marked with an ethnic imprint, and those with the worst results had the *least* degree of overt ethnic identification.

62. Kanynda Lusanga, "La décentralisation territoriale à l'épreuve de la théorie et des faits," *Cahiers du CEDAF*, no. 2 (1984). It remains to be seen how serious these efforts will be.

63. See Schatzberg, *Politics and Class*, 28–29, for a fuller description.

64. Richard L. Sklar, "The Nature of Class Domination in Africa," *Journal of Modern African Studies* 17 (1979): 537–38.

65. Chazan, *Anatomy of Ghanaian Politics*, 33.

66. Young, *Ideology and Development*, 187; and Goran Hyden, Robert Jackson, and John Okumu, eds., *Development Administration: The Kenyan Experience* (Nairobi: Oxford University Press, 1970).

67. E. A. Brett, *Colonialism and Underdevelopment in East Africa: The Politics of Economic Change 1919–1939* (New York: NOK, 1973), 285.

68. Bayart, *L'état au Cameroun*, 229; and Schatzberg, "Zaire," 283–318.

69. Gavin Kitching, *Class and Economic Change in Kenya: The Making of an African Petite Bourgeoisie 1905–1970* (New Haven: Yale University Press, 1980), 188–99.

70. Morris Szeftel, "Political Graft and the Spoils System in Zambia—The State as a Resource in Itself," *Review of African Political Economy* 24 (1982): 7–8, 20–21.

71. See, too, Schatzberg, *Politics and Class*, 59–98.

72. Steven Langdon, "The Multinational Corporation in the Kenya Political Economy," in *Readings on the Multinational Corporation in Kenya*, ed. Raphael Kaplinsky (Nairobi: Oxford University Press, 1978), 135. Also, Steven W. Langdon, *Multinational Corporations in the Political Economy of Kenya* (New York: St. Martin's, 1981).

73. Langdon, "The Multinational Corporation," 197–98.

74. See Schatzberg, "Zaire," for the complete argument.

75. In 1978 Leys changed his position on the nature of the Kenyan bourgeoisie and essentially adopted Swainson's line of reasoning. Colin Leys, "Capital Accumulation, Class

Formation, and Dependency—The Significance of the Kenyan Case," in *The Socialist Register 1978*, ed. Ralph Miliband and John Savile (London: Merlin, 1978), 248–65; and Nicola Swainson, *The Development of Corporate Capitalism in Kenya 1918–1977* (Berkeley and Los Angeles: University of California Press, 1980). For the other side, see Langdon, "The Multinational Corporation," and Raphael Kaplinsky, "Technical Change and the Multinational Corporation: Some British Multinationals in Kenya," in *Readings on the Multinational Corporation in Kenya*, ed. Raphael Kaplinsky (Nairobi: Oxford University Press, 1978), 134–260.

76. Janet MacGaffey, *Entrepreneurs and Parasites: The Struggle for Indigenous Capitalism in Zaire* (Cambridge: Cambridge University Press, 1988). Also, idem, "Class Relations in a Dependent Economy: Businessmen and Businesswomen in Kisangani, Zaire," (Ph.D. diss., Bryn Mawr College, 1981).

77. Vwakyanakazi Mukohya, "African Traders in Butembo, Eastern Zaire (1960–1980): A Case Study of Informal Entrepreneurship in a Cultural Context of Central Africa," (Ph.D. diss., University of Wisconsin-Madison, 1982) convincingly supports MacGaffey's thesis. Also, Janet MacGaffey, "How to Survive and Become Rich amidst Devastation: The Second Economy in Zaire," *African Affairs* 82 (1983): 351–66.

78. Jean-François Bayart, "Les sociétés africaines face à l'état," *Pouvoirs* 25 (1983): 32–33.

79. Field Log, 8 July 1975, 94.

80. Southall, "Illusion of Tribe," 34, 34–35.

81. Brett, *Colonialism and Underdevelopment*, 66–68.

82. Keller, "Ethiopia: Revolution, Class, and the National Question," 534, 542.

83. J. MacGaffey, *Entrepreneurs and Parasites*, chap. 6.

84. Bertrand, *Le Congo*, 136.

85. Bayart, *L'état au Cameroun*, 61–62, 181; and Ndiva Kofele-Kale, "Ethnicity Regionalism and Political Power: A Post-mortem of Ahidjo's Cameroon," in *The Political Economy of Cameroon*, ed. Michael G. Schatzberg and I. William Zartman (New York: Praeger, 1986), 53–82.

86. After a period of exile and opposition, in 1986 Nguza rallied to the regime and is now Zaire's ambassador to the U.S. Cléophas Kamitatu-Massamba, *La grande mystification du Congo-Kinshasa: Les crimes de Mobutu* (Paris: Maspero, 1971); and idem, *Zaire: Le pouvoir à la portée du peuple* (Paris: L'Harmattan, 1979). On the distribution of plums to First Republic politicians see Schatzberg, *Politics and Class*, 99–152.

87. Richard L. Sklar, "Political Science and National Integration—A Radical Approach," *Journal of Modern African Studies* 5 (1967): 1–11.

88. Markakis, *Ethiopia*, 8.

89. Elikia M'Bokolo, "La triple stratification zairoise," *Monde diplomatique* (November 1981): 21.

90. Cikuru Ng'ashala Batumike, "Une descente aux enfers ou la montagne du désespoir: Témoignage," *Info Zaire*, no. 39 (1983): 23.

91. Leys, *Underdevelopment in Kenya*, 199.

92. Bayart, *L'état au Cameroun*, 269.

93. Naomi Chazan, "Political Culture and Socialization to Politics: A Ghanaian Case," *Review of Politics* 40 (1978): 14; and Ndiva Kofele-Kale, "The Impact of Environment on National Political Culture in Cameroon," in *Values, Identities, and National Integration: Empirical Research in Africa*, ed. John N. Paden (Evanston, Ill.: Northwestern University Press, 1980), 170–71.

94. Pierre Kalck, *Central African Republic: A Failure in Decolonization*, trans. Barbara Thomson (New York: Praeger, 1971), 11; Abner Cohen, *The Politics of Elite Culture: Explorations in the Dramaturgy of Power in a Modern African Society* (Berkeley and Los Angeles: University of California Press, 1981), 18; and Chazan, *Anatomy of Ghanaian Politics*, 235.

95. I. M. Lewis, "The Politics of the 1969 Somalia Coup," *Journal of Modern African Studies* 10 (1972): 383–408; and idem, *A Modern History of Somalia: Nation and State in the Horn of Africa* (London: Longman, 1980), 168, 220.

96. Young, "Patterns of Social Conflict," 71–98; and Schatzberg, "Ethnicity and Class," 465–66.

97. Mwabila, *Travail et travailleurs*, 106.

98. Joel Samoff, "Education in Tanzania: Class Formation and Reproduction," *Journal of Modern African Studies* 17 (1979): 61.

99. Abner Cohen, *The Politics of Elite Culture*, xiii, 128–29, 136–37. Citation, 128–29.

100. Gilbert Comte, "Treize années d'histoire," *Revue française d'études politiques africaines* 8 (1973): 46.

101. André Badibanga, "Je suis le 'Père de la Nation,'" *Revue française d'études politiques africaines* 16 (1980–81): 103–16.

102. Bayart, *L'état au Cameroun*, 253–56. Citation, 255. For more detail on these paternal and familial metaphors in Cameroon and elsewhere in Central Africa, see Michael G. Schatzberg, "The Metaphors of Father and Family," in *The Political Economy of Cameroon*, ed. Michael G. Schatzberg and I. William Zartman (New York: Praeger, 1986), 1–19.

103. Leys, *Underdevelopment in Kenya*, 248.

104. Bayart, *L'état au Cameroun*, 141–82, esp. 173–74. For an elaboration, see Robert H. Jackson and Carl G. Rosberg, *Personal Rule in Black Africa: Prince, Autocrat, Prophet, Tyrant* (Berkeley and Los Angeles: University of California Press, 1982).

105. Elikia, "La triple stratification zairoise," 21.

106. Vansina, "Lignage, idéologie et histoire," 149.

107. Ibid., 148.

108. Mwabila, *Travail et travailleurs*, 123.

109. Schatzberg, *Politics and Class*, 33–58.

110. On the notions of closure and class action see ibid., 28–32.

111. Leys, *Underdevelopment in Kenya*, 199.

112. Mwabila, *Travail et travailleurs*, 171.

113. Christine Obbo, *African Women: Their Struggle for Economic Independence* (London: Zed, 1980), 108–10.

114. Schatzberg, "Ethnicity and Class," 466–67.

115. J. MacGaffey, "Class Relations in a Dependent Economy," 271.

116. Mwabila, *Travail et travailleurs*, 121.

117. Bates, *Markets and States*, 30–44.

3. The State as Ear: Information, Coercion, and the Political Police

This chapter is a much-revised version of "The Long Arm of the Law: Insecurity, Instability, and the Political Police in Zaire" (Paper delivered at the annual meeting of the International Studies Association, Cincinnati, Ohio, 24–27 March 1982).

1. A. Kaseba, *"Notre foi en l'homme image de Dieu": Déclaration du Comité Permanent des Evêques du Zaire* (Kinshasa: Editions du Secrétariat Général de l'Episcopat, 1981), 22–23.

2. Nguza Karl-i-Bond, "Testimony," in U.S. Congress, House, Committee on Foreign Affairs, Subcommittee on Africa, *Political and Economic Situation in Zaire—Fall 1981*, 97th Cong., 1st session, 15 September 1981, 23.

3. In April 1980 the CND was renamed the Centre National de Recherches et d'Investigations (CNRI), and in 1983 it became the Agence National de Documentation. The new names were purely cosmetic, and neither the organization nor its tasks changed.

Moreover, the new names have yet to anchor themselves in the popular consciousness, and many Zairians still refer to the political police as the CND. On this point see Vwakyanakazi Mukohya, "African Traders in Butembo," 67, n. 30. For consistency and convenience, I shall use the old name (CND) throughout.

4. On the extraordinary decline in economic conditions see World Bank, *Zaire: Current Economic Situation*; and Fernand Bezy, Jean-Philippe Peemans, and Jean-Marie Wautelet, *Accumulation et sous-développement au Zaire 1960–1980* (Louvain-la-Neuve: Presses Universitaires de Louvain, 1981).

5. Giddens, *A Contemporary Critique*, 1:5, 1:169.

6. Mobutu Sese Seko, *Petit livre vert: Paroles du Président* (Kinshasa: Edition du Léopard, n.d.), 26 cited in Yabili Yalala Asani, "Droit, révolution et vigilance révolutionnaire," *Jiwe* 3 (1974): 83.

7. Ibid., 84.

8. *Salongo*, 28 October 1978, 3.

9. Administrative correspondence, 11 July 1975.

10. Administrative correspondence, 27 March 1969.

11. Administrative correspondence, 30 October 1971, 6 January 1973.

12. Once interior, and then political affairs, the relevant ministry is now territorial administration.

13. Administrative correspondence, 20 October 1972.

14. Bogumil Jewsiewicki, "L'état et l'accumulation primitive coloniale: La formation du môde de production colonial au Zaire," *Revue française d'histoire d'outre-mer* 68 (1981): 79.

15. Administrative correspondence, 2 February 1968. See, too, administrative correspondence, 12 April 1968, 23 August 1968.

16. Administrative correspondence, 29 December 1970.

17. Administrative correspondence, 12 January 1971.

18. Administrative correspondence, 2 January 1973, 1 March 1973, 14 June 1973.

19. Administrative correspondence, 14 August 1974.

20. Administrative correspondence, 18 June 1975.

21. Administrative correspondence, 6 June 1974.

22. Administrative correspondence, 23 July 1975.

23. Interviews, Lisala, no. 45, 12 August 1975, 3; no. 43, 18 July 1975, 4; and Field Log, 8 July 1974, 94.

24. Interview, Lisala, no. 10, 18 February 1975, 3. Also, interviews, Lisala, no. 2, 19 November 1974, 3; no. 8, 21 February 1975, 6.

25. Administrative correspondence, 2 March 1972.

26. Administrative correspondence, 5 July 1975.

27. Interview, Lisala, no. 33, 13 April 1975, 4; and administrative correspondence, 28 March 1975. MacGaffey uncovered a similar phenomenon in Kisangani. The annual political affairs report for Haut Zaire baldly asserts the "'statistics on manual labor are fantasies and do not reflect reality.'" See J. MacGaffey, "Class Relations in a Dependent Economy," 118.

28. Jan Vansina, personal communication, 24 December 1984.

29. Administrative correspondence, 29 June 1968.

30. Administrative correspondence, 30 April 1968.

31. Administrative correspondence, 11 June 1968.

32. Administrative correspondence, 17 September 1968.

33. Administrative correspondence, 4 February 1969, 18 March 1969.

34. Administrative correspondence, 14 May 1969, ? June 1969, 8 August 1969.

35. Administrative correspondence, 16 April 1970.

36. Administrative correspondence, 16 July 1973.

37. Administrative correspondence, 3 July 1973.

38. Field Log, 20 February 1975, 43.

39. Administrative correspondence, 28 February 1975.

40. Administrative correspondence, 18 April 1975.

41. *Salongo*, 20 June 1982, 2 and 27 September 1982, 3. The official rate of exchange for the unit of currency, the Zaire, was Z 1 = U.S. $2.00 from 1971–75. In 1981 Z 1 = U.S. $0.18. As of 1 April 1987, Z 1 was worth only slightly more than one cent, or Z 94.184 to the dollar. Willame, *Zaire, l'épopée d'Inga*, 7; and *West Africa*, 6 April 1987, 678.

42. Administrative correspondence, 7 May 1975. On these administrative reforms see Michael G. Schatzberg, *"Le mal zairois*: Why Policy Fails in Zaire," *African Affairs* 81 (1982): 337–48.

43. The medical effects refer to malnutrition due to loss of protein and should be obvious. For possible political consequences, see James C. Scott, *The Moral Economy of the Peasant: Rebellion and Subsistence in Southeast Asia* (New Haven: Yale University Press, 1976). In simplified form, Scott argues rural rebellion is likely to occur when landlords or the state violate the peasants' moral right to subsistence.

44. Malulu Mitwensil and Kambidi Nsia-Kinguem, "Le public et l'administration en République du Zaire," *Zaire-Afrique*, no. 143 (March 1980): 167.

45. March and Simon define uncertainty absorption as a process occurring when "inferences are drawn from a body of evidence and the inferences, instead of the evidence itself, are then communicated. . . . Through [this process] . . . the recipient of a communication is severely limited in his ability to judge its correctness." James G. March and Herbert A. Simon, *Organizations* (New York: John Wiley, 1958), 165–66.

46. Administrative correspondence, 25 April 1972.

47. Bogumil Jewsiewicki, "L'expérience d'un Etat-Providence en Afrique noire," *Historical Reflections* 3 (1976): 90.

48. Ali Kalonga, *Le mal zairois* (Brussels: Fati, 1978), 29; and Field Log, 13 September 1975, 117.

49. Emile Janssens, *Au fil d'une vie* (Brussels: Pierre de Mayère, 1973), 59, 61.

50. Ibid., 64. See, too, Emile Janssens, *Histoire de la Force Publique* (Brussels: Ghesquière & Partners, 1979), 193, n. 1.

51. Young, *Politics in the Congo*, 465–70; administrative correspondence, 9 February 1971; Frédéric Vandewalle and Jacques Brassine, *Les rapports secrets de la sûreté congolaise, 1959–1960—Tome premier: Février-octobre 1959* (N.p.: Lucien de Meyer, 1973); and idem, *Les rapports secrets de la sûreté congolaise, 1959–1960—Tome second: Novembre 1959-juin 1960* (N.p.: Lucien de Meyer, 1973).

52. Young, *Politics in the Congo*, 465–70.

53. This allegation has surfaced in several places. Kamitatu-Massamba, *La grande mystification du Congo-Kinshasa*, 45; Kanyonga Mobateli, *Dix ans de régime Mobutu ou les années les plus sombre du Congo/Zaire* (Monthey, Switzerland: Ivy, 1976), 35; and Jules Chomé, *L'ascension de Mobutu: Du sergent Désiré au Général Sese Seko* (Paris: Maspero, 1979), 67.

54. "Ordonnance-loi No. 69–159 du 9 août 1969 fixant les attributions et l'organisation du Centre National de Documentation."

55. "Déclaration de Nguza Karl-i-Bond à Erwin Blumenthal," in *Mobutu Sese Seko, Le Procès: Deuxième Tribunal Russel (Tribunal Permanent des Peuples)*, ed. C. K. Lumuna Sando and Buana Kabue (Brussels: A.F.R.I.C.A. [Association pour la Formation, la Recherche et l'Information sur le Centre de l'Afrique] pour l'Institut de l'Afrique Centrale, 1982), 97.

56. "Aide-mémoire remis par la délégation de l'U.D.P.S. à la délégation du Congrès Américain," August 1983, 8.

57. Until 1982 the subregional committee of the MPR included the subregional commissioner and his assistants, the zone commissioners, the secretary of the JMPR, the chief

magistrate of the tribunal, the head prosecutor, the secretary of the national trade union, and the army commandant. See Schatzberg, *Politics and Class*, 101. The CND has been represented since the 1982 reforms. See Kanynda Lusanga, "La décentralisation territoriale," 57.

58. Administrative correspondence, 9 June 1970.

59. In 1979 Mobutu created a National Security Council under his direct authority and gave it the task of centralizing all security information destined for the president's eyes. Its members were the prime minister; president of the judicial council; the state commissioners (ministers) for foreign affairs, territorial administration, post and telegraph; the chiefs of staff of the army and national gendarmerie; the general administrator of the CND; and the president's special counselor for security affairs. *Salongo*, 7 March 1979, 2 and 30 April 1979, 2.

60. One change did occur in 1980 when the CND became the CNRI. The task of external security became the province of a separate organization called the Service National d'Intelligence. See Comité Zaire, "Les droits de l'homme et les libertés," in *Mobutu Sese Seko, Le Procès: Deuxième Tribunal Russel (Tribunal Permanent des Peuples)*, ed. C. K. Lumuna Sando and Buana Kabue (Brussels: A.F.R.I.C.A. pour l'Institut de l'Afrique Centrale, 1982), 104–5.

61. Young, *Politics in the Congo*, 470.

62. "Aide-mémoire remis par la délégation de l'U.D.P.S.," 2; Buana Kabue, *Citoyen Président: Lettre ouverte au Président Mobutu Sese Seko . . . et aux autres* (Paris: L'Harmattan, 1978), 112; and "Report on the Situation of the Zaire Armed Forces Submitted by Former Prime Minister Nguza," in *Political and Economic Situation in Zaire—Fall 1981*, 46.

63. J. Rothschild, *Ethnopolitics*, 215.

64. Ibid., 217–18.

65. Nguza, "Testimony," 23.

66. See Nguza, *Mobutu*; idem, "Tout un peuple est pris en ôtage," in *Mobutu Sese Seko, Le Procès: Deuxième Tribunal Russel (Tribunal Permanent des Peuples)*, ed. C. K. Lumuna Sando and Buana Kabue (Brussels: A.F.R.I.C.A. pour l'Institut de l'Afrique Centrale, 1982), 71–74; and Buana Kabue, *Citoyen Président*, 34. For a novelist's view of the climate of terror, fear, and insecurity see C. K. Lumuna Sando, *Lovanium: Le Kasala du 4 juin* (Brussels: A.F.R.I.C.A., 1982), esp., 95.

67. Mobutu Sese Seko, speech of 30 June 1977, cited in *Salongo*, 1 July 1977, 3.

68. Mobutu Sese Seko, speech of 4 February 1980, cited in *Salongo*, 5 February 1980, 6–7.

69. On this general point, but in relation to specific measures of economic policy, see Schatzberg, *Politics and Class*, 121–52; and idem, "The State and the Economy," 239–57.

70. Field Log, 22 December 1974, 19–20; 2 January 1975, 21; 17 January 1975, 27.

71. Vwakyanakazi Mukohya, "African Traders in Butembo," 56.

72. J. MacGaffey, "Class Relations in a Dependent Economy," 100–101.

73. Field Log, 7 March 1975, 53–54.

74. Cikuru, "Une descente aux enfers," 17.

75. Poulantzas, *State, Power, Socialism*, 83.

76. Administrative correspondence, 13 September 1971; and République du Zaire, Assemblée Nationale, *Annales Parlementaires*, session ordinaire d'avril 1972, séance du 6 avril 1972, 10.

77. Administrative correspondence, 8 August 1969; and Callaghy, *State-Society Struggle*, 175–76.

78. Coordination Régionale des Ecoles Conventionnées Catholiques, "Réflections," 12 January 1984, *Info Zaire*, nos. 41–42 (1984): 16–17.

79. Cikuru, "Une descente aux enfers," 23.

80. AI, *Political Imprisonment in Zaire: An Amnesty International Special Briefing* (New York: AI, 1983), 4–5 and passim.

81. Telegraphic message, CND Mobayi-Mbongo to Regional Administrator, CND Mbandaka, n.d., but filed under 1975.

82. Administrative correspondence, CND Bumba to Zone Commissioner, Bumba 3 March 1975. Note the correct term is Ngbandi.

83. AI, *Human Rights Violations in Zaire* (London: AI, 1980), 8, and on arbitrary arrest in general, 9–11.

84. Ibid., 6.

85. "Arrêt de travail dans les écoles de la sous-région urbaine de Kisangani," 8 December 1983, *Info Zaire*, nos. 41–42 (1984): 24.

86. AI, *Human Rights Violations in Zaire*, 15.

87. AI, *Political Imprisonment in Zaire*, 8.

88. "Mon calvaire à la C.N.R.I.," *Info Zaire*, nos. 41–42 (1984): 29–30.

89. In addition to the sources already cited, see AI, "The Ill-Treatment and Torture of Political Prisoners at Detention Centers in Kinshasa," AFR 62/32/80, 24 September 1980; Nguza, "Testimony," 7, 19–20; Nguza, *Mobutu*; and the episcopal letter cited in epigraph.

90. Buana Kabue, *Citoyen Président*, 35; and AI, "Arrests and Political Imprisonment in Zaire, August-December 1983," AFR 62/07/84, 8 February 1984, 2.

91. AI, *Human Rights Violations in Zaire*, 19; and Comité Zaire, "Les droits de l'homme et les libertés," 108.

92. Telegraphic message, CND Mobayi-Mbongo to Regional Administrator, CND Mbandaka and Mongala Subregional Commissioner, Lisala, 26 June 1974. Also, telegraphic message, CND Bumba to Regional Administrator, CND Mbandaka and Mongala Subregional Commissioner, Lisala, 24 December 1973.

93. CND Mobayi-Mbongo, "Rapport périodique du 1er au 15 décembre 1973," 15 December 1973.

94. Administrative correspondence, CND Bumba to Zone Commissioner, Bumba, 6 June 1973; administrative correspondence, CND Bumba to Zone Commissioner, Bumba, 28 April 1973; and text of radio message, CND Bumba to Regional Administrator, CND Mbandaka and Mongala Subregional Commissioner, Lisala, 15 November 1973.

95. Telegraphic message, CND Mobayi-Mbongo to Regional Administrator, CND Mbandaka, 7 February 1975; CND Bumba, "Rapport périodique du 10 au 18 octobre 1968," 18 October 1968; telegraphic message, CND Bumba, "Situation journalière," 16 September 1974; telegraphic message, CND Mobayi-Mbongo to Regional Administrator, CND Mbandaka and Mongala Subregional Commissioner, Lisala, 5 June 1974; and telegraphic message, CND Bumba to Regional Administrator, CND Mbandaka and Mongala Subregional Commissioner, Lisala, 4 February 1974. These reports on the local economy were easily verified at stores, bars, and the market.

96. Administrative correspondence, CND Lisala to Inspector of Economic Affairs, Lisala, 2 November 1973.

97. Administrative correspondence, CND Lisala to Mongala Subregional Commissioner, Lisala, 25 October 1971.

98. Administrative correspondence, CND Bumba to Regional Administrator, CND Mbandaka, 19 August 1971.

99. Administrative correspondence, CND Bumba to Regional Administrator, CND Mbandaka, 19 February 1971.

100. Administrative correspondence, CND Bumba to Collectivity Chief, Bumba, 26 September 1973.

101. CND Bumba, "Rapport périodique arreté au 25 septembre 1969," 25 September 1969.

102. See, too, CND Bumba, "Rapport de sécurité," 12 August 1974; administrative correspondence, CND Bumba to Zone Commissioner, Bumba, 7 December 1972; administra-

tive correspondence, CND Bumba to Zone Commissioner, Bumba, 4 February 1975; and administrative correspondence, CND Bumba to Zone Commissioner, Bumba, 9 May 1973.

103. Administrative correspondence, 9 June 1970.

104. Administrative correspondence, 27 January 1970.

105. Administrative correspondence, 23 February 1968. Callaghy notes the same phenomenon in Kivu but relates that CND officials there were accused of sending inaccurate information to Kinshasa. In Mongala, on the other hand, CND reports were usually reliable. See Callaghy, *State-Society Struggle*, 261, 266, 392–93.

106. Administrative correspondence, CND Lisala to Regional Administrator, CND Mbandaka, 16 December 1970.

107. Telegraphic message, CND Bumba to Regional Administrator, CND Mbandaka and Mongala Subregional Commissioner, Lisala, 21 February 1972.

108. Telegraphic message, CND Bumba to Regional Administrator, CND Mbandaka and Mongala Subregional Commissioner, Lisala, 26 May 1974.

109. Telegraphic message, CND Bumba to Regional Administrator, CND Mbandaka and Mongala Subregional Commissioner, Lisala, 24 June 1974.

110. Telegraphic message, CND Bumba to Regional Administrator, CND Mbandaka and Mongala Subregional Commissioner, Lisala, 19 February 1975.

111. On the efficiency of the CND, in addition to the quotation from Nguza cited in epigraph, see Nguza, "Tout un peuple est pris en ôtage," 72; Kalonga, *Le mal zairois*, 18; and Cikuru, "Une descente aux enfers," 14. On disorganization, mismanagement, and corruption, see David J. Gould, *Bureaucratic Corruption in the Third World: The Case of Zaire* (New York: Pergamon, 1980).

112. Callaghy, *State-Society Struggle*, 266.

113. Kalonga, *Le mal zairois*, 54; and Cikuru, "Une descente aux enfers," 19.

114. Cikuru, "Une descente aux enfers," 25.

115. Wyatt MacGaffey, *Modern Kongo Prophets: Religion in a Plural Society* (Bloomington: Indiana University Press, 1983), 155.

116. Giddens, *A Contemporary Critique*, 1:63, 1:120–21.

117. For forms of passive resistance during the colonial period, see Bogumil Jewsiewicki, "Political Consciousness among African Peasants in the Belgian Congo," *Review of African Political Economy* 19 (1980): 23–32.

118. On Guinea, see Jean-Paul Alata, *Prison d'Afrique* (Paris: Seuil, 1976); on South Africa, Gordon Winter, *Inside Boss: South Africa's Secret Police* (Harmondsworth: Penguin, 1981); on Rhodesia and Zimbabwe, Ronald Weitzer, "Continuities in the Politics of State Security in Zimbabwe," in *The Political Economy of Zimbabwe*, ed. Michael G. Schatzberg (New York: Praeger, 1984), 81–118.

119. Thomas Q. Reefe, "The Societies of the Eastern Savanna," in *History of Central Africa*, 2 vols., ed. David Birmingham and Phyllis M. Martin (London: Longman, 1983), 1:182.

120. Bayart, *L'état au Cameroun*, 220–21; Mbu Etonga, "An Imperial Presidency: A Study of Presidential Power in Cameroon," in *An African Experiment in Nation Building: The Bilingual Cameroon Republic since Reunification*, ed. Ndiva Kofele-Kale (Boulder, Colo.: Westview, 1980), 153–55; Bayart, "One-Party Government and Political Development in Cameroon," in Kofele-Kale, ibid., 175; and Richard A. Joseph, "Ruben Um Nyobe and the 'Kamerun' Rebellion," *African Affairs* 73 (1974): 429.

121. Ryszard Kapsuscinski, *The Emperor: Downfall of an Autocrat*, trans. William R. Brand and Katarzyna Mrockowska-Brand (New York: Vintage Books, 1983), 9–12; and Bertrand, *Le Congo*, 72.

122. Mamdani, *Imperialism and Fascism in Uganda*, 43–44; and Tony Avirgan and Martha Honey, *War in Uganda: The Legacy of Idi Amin* (Westport, Conn.: Lawrence Hill, 1982), 30, 150.

123. Marvin Zonis, "Iran: A Theory of Revolution from Accounts of Revolution," *World Politics* 35 (1983): 601.

4. The State as Bandit: Armed Forces, Coercive Force

1. Police Nationale, "Rapport mensuel du mois de juin 1969," Lisala, 25 June 1969.
2. Administrative correspondence, 28 June 1971.
3. Administrative correspondence, 12 March 1975.
4. The quite coercive collectivity police have been treated elsewhere and will receive only tangential mention here. See Schatzberg, *Politics and Class*, 60–82.
5. In August 1984 the GDN gave way to a new organization, the Garde Civile. It remains to be seen if this is a change in more than name only.
6. John Keegan, *The Face of Battle* (Harmondsworth: Penguin, 1976), 330.
7. Maureen Cain, "'An Ironical Departure': The Dilemma of Contemporary Policing," in *Yearbook of Social Policy in Britain, 1976*, ed. K. Jones (London: Routledge and Kegan Paul, 1977), 164. Cited in Otwin Marenin "Policing African States: Toward a Critique," *Comparative Politics* 14 (1982): 381. Marenin's article is an excellent treatment of a long-neglected subject.
8. Young and Turner, *Rise and Decline*, 259; and Bianga, "Peasant, State and Rural Development," 106–20.
9. Young and Turner, *Rise and Decline*, 248–75.
10. Young, *Politics in the Congo*, 441; Janssens, *Histoire de la Force Publique*, 193; and Bryant P. Shaw, *"Force Publique, Force Unique*: The Military in the Belgian Congo, 1914–1939," (Ph.D. diss., University of Wisconsin-Madison, 1984), 1–3, 52.
11. L. H. Gann and Peter Duignan, *The Rulers of Belgian Africa 1884–1914* (Princeton: Princeton University Press, 1979), 66–82; and Shaw, *"Force Publique, Force Unique*," 33, 37.
12. The preceding paragraphs are drawn from Janssens, *Histoire de la Force Publique*, 193; Irving Kaplan, ed., *Zaire: A Country Study* (Washington, D.C.: American University, Foreign Area Studies, 1979), 269–70; Young, *Politics in the Congo*, 458–65; Thomas Turner, "Problems of the Zairian Military" (Paper prepared for the U.S. Department of State, 25 October 1979), 30; and Shaw, *"Force Publique, Force Unique*," 85–86, 108.
13. "Rapport sur la situation à l'intérieur du Territoire de Lisala, mois de mars 1961," Dossier no. 173, National Archives, Kinshasa. More generally, Jules Gérard-Libois and Jean Van Lierde, eds., *Congo 1964* (Brussels: CRISP, 1965), 94–95.
14. Jules Gérard-Libois, ed., *Congo 1966* (Brussels: CRISP, 1967), 26, 116–18; and Schatzberg, *Politics and Class*, 67–71.
15. Forces Armées Zairoises, *L'ère de l'armée nouvelle* (Kinshasa: Cabinet du Département de la Défense, 1973), 33.
16. "Rapport mensuel de mars 1968 du sous-détachement Police Nationale de la Mongala," 24 April 1968.
17. "Rapports mensuels d'avril 1968-février 1970 du sous-détachement Police Nationale de la Mongala"; and "Rapport annuel 1971 du sous-détachement de la Mongala, Police Nationale du Zaire," 29 February 1972.
18. Administrative correspondence, 9 April 1973.
19. Administrative correspondence, 9 December 1972.
20. Administrative correspondence, 2 January 1973.
21. Administrative correspondence, 9 June 1970.
22. Administrative correspondence, 24 October 1969.
23. Administrative correspondence, 23 March 1971 and 24 October 1968.
24. *Salongo*, 3 March 1977, 2.
25. Ibid., 4 May 1978, 4.

26. Administrative correspondence, 14 June 1972.

27. Cikuru, "Une descente aux enfers," 12; and *Salongo*, 1 June 1983, 2. On the *ratis-sage*, see Thomas M. Callaghy, "State-Subject Communication in Zaire: Domination and the Concept of Domain Consensus," *Journal of Modern African Studies* 18 (1980): 486-89.

28. Administrative correspondence, 7 January 1969.

29. *Le militaire et la révolution (le soldat et le peuple)*, texte de la conférence donnée à l'Ecole du Parti, l'Institut Makanda Kabobi, IIè session ordinaire, par le Citoyen Général Molongya Mayikusa, Directeur Général de la Défense Nationale, le 8 mai 1975 (Kinshasa: République du Zaire, Département de la Défense Nationale, 1975), 13.

30. *Salongo*, 6 April 1976, 4.

31. "Entretiens avec le PRP dans le maquis du Zaire," *Info Zaire*, no. 37 (December 1982-February 1983): 5.

32. *Info Zaire Flash*, no. 38-1 (June 1983): 3.

33. AI, *Zaire: Reports of Torture*.

34. "Letter from Curé Father Jansen to the Governor of Kinshasa," 11 February 1983, in AI, *Zaire: Reports of Torture*, 5-7.

35. Nguza, *Mobutu*, 179 and, more generally, 176-85. For the confession of a former executioner, see Kimbana Lulu Kiladio, "Témoignage d'un ancien membre de la police politique de Mobutu," in *Mobutu Sese Seko, Le Procès: Deuxième Tribunal Russel (Tribunal Permanent des Peuples)*, ed. C. K. Lumuna Sando and Buana Kabue (Brussels: A.F.R.I.C.A. pour l'Institut de l'Afrique Centrale, 1982), 79-80.

36. "Le discours présidentiel," *Salongo*, 5 February 1980, 6.

37. Kabwit, "Zaire: The Roots of the Continuing Crisis," 394.

38. Gould, *Bureaucratic Corruption*; and Guy Gran, ed., *Zaire: The Political Economy of Underdevelopment* (New York: Praeger, 1979).

39. "Le discours présidentiel," *Salongo*, 5 February 1980, 7.

40. Field Log, 20 May 1975, 78; AI, *Zaire: Reports of Torture*, 4.

41. David J. Gould, "Patrons and Clients: The Role of the Military in Zairian Politics," in *The Performance of Soldiers as Governors: African Politics and the African Military*, ed. Isaac James Mowoe (Washington, D.C.: University Press of America, 1980), 500-501; and U.S. Congress, House, Committee on Foreign Affairs, *The Impact of U.S. Foreign Policy on Seven African Countries*, 98th Cong., 2nd Session, 24-27 August 1984, 32.

42. Nguza, *Mobutu*, 177-78.

43. Turner, "Problems of the Zairian Military," 18.

44. Interview, Mbandaka, no. 46, 29 August 1975, 3-4.

45. Administrative correspondence, 13 April 1972, 25 April 1972, 26 April 1972; and Field Log, 15 July 1975, 98.

46. Administrative correspondence, 25 September 1972.

47. W. MacGaffey, *Modern Kongo Prophets*, 152, 155.

48. *Salongo*, 3-4 January 1977, 27; and 6 July 1981, 5.

49. Likulia Bolongo, *Droit pénal militaire zairois*, vol. 1., *L'organisation et la compétence des juridictions des forces armées* (Paris: Librairie Générale de Droit et de Jurisprudence, 1977), 1:77-79. Also, interview, Lisala, no. 15, 10 March 1975, 1.

50. Likulia Bolongo, *Droit pénal militaire zairois*, 1:81.

51. Interview, Lisala, no. 23, 16 June 1975, 5.

52. Schatzberg, *Politics and Class*, 162-63; and administrative correspondence, ? February 1969.

53. Interview, Lisala, no. 35, 22 April 1975, 2.

54. "Ordonnance no. 76-182 du 16 juillet 1976 complétant l'ordonnance no. 75-038 du 19 février 1975 portant statut de la Jeunesse du Mouvement Populaire de la Révolution," *Salongo*, 17 December 1976, 2.

55. Administrative correspondence, 6 April 1971; *Salongo*, 19 January 1976, 6.

56. "Rapport annuel d'activités de la JMPR Mongala, exercice 1974," 5 January 1975.
57. Administrative correspondence, 28 June 1972, 12 July 1972, and 16 February 1973.
58. *Salongo*, 27 July 1982, 1 and 21 September 1982, 1.
59. Recall the CND has been renamed several times without any noticeable amelioration in its relations with the population.
60. Shaw, "*Force Publique, Force Unique*," 199–211.
61. Turner, "Problems of the Zairian Military," 25–26.
62. Buana Kabue, *Citoyen Président*, 71.
63. Nguza, *Mobutu*, 181–82; and Buana Kabue, *Citoyen Président*, 112.
64. "Aide-mémoire remis par la délégation de l'U.D.P.S.," 17–18.
65. J. Rothschild, *Ethnopolitics*, 217–18.
66. "Aide-mémoire remis par la délégation de l'U.D.P.S.," 18.
67. Callaghy, "State-Subject Communication in Zaire," 485.
68. Nguza, *Mobutu*, 184.
69. Bianga, "Peasant, State and Rural Development," 280.
70. Avirgan and Honey, *War in Uganda*, 176.
71. "Lettre ouverte au Citoyen Président-Fondateur," 133.
72. On repression after Shaba II, see Comité Zaire, *Zaire: Une aide qui tue* (Brussels: Comité Zaire, 1981), 21; *Info Zaire* no. 4:1 (1978); and C. K. Lumuna Sando, *Zaire: Quel changement pour quelles structures? Misère de l'opposition et faillite de l'Etat* (Brussels: A.F.R.I.C.A., 1980), 148–49. For the Kasongo affair and repression in Bandundu, see Lumuna Sando, *Zaire: Quel changement*, 91; and Rob Buyseniers, *L'église zairoise au service de quelle nation?* (Brussels: A.F.R.I.C.A., 1980), 27–44. On the massacres in Kasai, "Les massacres de Katekelayi et de Luamuela (Kasai Oriental)," *Politique africaine* 6 (1982): 72–106; and Comité Zaire, *Zaire: Une aide qui tue*, 23–25. On all three episodes, Comité Zaire, "Les droits de l'homme et les libertés," 109–11. On Moba and Kalemie, see AI, *Zaire: Reports of Torture*.
73. Schatzberg, "Zaire," 283–318.
74. Young and Turner, *Rise and Decline*, 9.
75. See Callaghy, *State-Society Struggle* for a superb example of this genre which does not fall into this trap.
76. Marenin, "Policing African States," 391.

5. The State as Family, Mobutu as Father: Political Imagery

This is a much different version of "Father and Family: Political Authority in Contemporary Zaire" (Paper delivered at the annual meeting of the Western Political Science Association, Denver, Colorado, 26–28 March 1981).

1. Engulu Baangampongo, "Vigilance et engagement révolutionnaire," exposé aux cadres de la JMPR en session spéciale de l'Institut Makanda Kabobi, N'Sélé, 1 March 1975, 5.
2. *Elima* (Kinshasa), 24 October 1975, 1.
3. Interview, Lisala, no. 58, 21 July 1975, 4.
4. Harry Eckstein and Ted Robert Gurr, *Patterns of Authority: A Structural Basis for Political Inquiry* (New York: John Wiley and Sons, 1975), 22.
5. Harry Eckstein, *The Natural History of Congruence Theory*, Monograph Series in World Affairs, 18:2 (Denver: University of Colorado, 1980), 1; and idem, "A Theory of Stable Democracy," appendix B of *Division and Cohesion in Democracy: A Study of Norway* (Princeton: Princeton University Press, 1966), 234.
6. Eckstein, *Division and Cohesion in Democracy*; Michel Crozier, *The Bureaucratic Phenomenon* (Chicago: University of Chicago Press, 1964); Viviane Isambert-Jamati,

"L'autorité dans l'éducation française," *Archives européennes de sociologie* 6 (1965): 149–66; William R. Schonfeld, *Obedience and Revolt: The French Behavior toward Authority* (Beverly Hills, Calif.: Sage, 1976); Herman Bakvis, "French Canada and the 'Bureaucratic Phenomenon,'" *Canadian Public Administration* 21 (1978): 103–24; and Michael G. Schatzberg, "Conflict and Culture in African Education: Authority Patterns in a Cameroonian Lycée," *Comparative Education Review* 23 (1979): 52–65.

7. Jean-Louis Flandrin, *Families in Former Times* (Cambridge: Cambridge University Press, 1979), 1, cited in Shula Marks and Richard Rathbone, "The History of the Family in Africa: Introduction," *Journal of African History* 24 (1983): 147.

8. Philippe Ariès, *Centuries of Childhood: A Social History of Family Life*, trans. Robert Baldick (New York: Vintage Books, 1962), 356.

9. Thomas M. Callaghy, "State Formation and Absolutism in Comparative Perspective: Seventeenth Century France and Mobutu Sese Seko's Zaire," (Ph.D. diss., University of California, Berkeley, 1979), 167, 292–93; and his *State-Society-Struggle*, 111–37, 419–20.

10. Karl Marx and Frederick Engels, *The German Ideology*, ed. C. J. Arthur (New York: International, 1970), 64.

11. Anthony Giddens, *A Contemporary Critique*, 1:61. Emphasis in original.

12. *Mobutisme* is the "thought, teachings, and actions of the President-Founder of the Mouvement Populaire de la Révolution." See *Mambenga* (Mbandaka), 5 October 1974, 8. M'buze-Nsomi Lobwanabi, *Aux sources d'une révolution* (Kinshasa: Les Presses Africaines, 1977) provides a general overview of the doctrine of authenticity. On local interpretations, see Michael G. Schatzberg, "Fidélité au Guide: The J.M.P.R. in Zairian Schools," *Journal of Modern African Studies* 16 (1978): 417–31. For a Marxist critique, see Nzongola-Ntalaja, "The Authenticity of Neocolonialism: Ideology and Class Struggle in Zaire," *Berkeley Journal of Sociology* 22 (1977–78): 115–30.

13. Jessop, *The Capitalist State*, 149.

14. For details on the sample and interviewing procedures, see Schatzberg, *Politics and Class*, 35–58.

15. Interviews, Lisala, no. 2, 19 November 1974, 5; no. 8, 21 February 1975, 8. Also interviews, Lisala, no. 6, 20 January 1975, 9; no. 57, 6 July 1975, 4.

16. Interviews, Lisala, no. 2, 19 November 1974, 5; no. 37, 3 May 1975, 9; no. 49, 17 June 1975, 6. Also interviews, Lisala, no. 13, 28 February 1975, 4; no. 45, 12 August 1975, 6.

17. Interviews, Lisala, no. 9, 6 February 1975, 5; no. 10, 18 February 1975, 5; and no. 37, 3 May 1975, 9. Also interviews, Lisala, no. 22, 4 June 1975, 5; no. 32, 7 April 1975, 5; no. 48, 29 April 1975, 6.

18. Interview, Lisala, no. 25, 22 November 1974, 2. Also, interviews, Lisala, no. 20, 18 February 1975, 5; no. 14, 6 March 1975, 6; no. 15, 10 March 1975, 5; no. 31, 4 February 1975, 4; no. 39, 11 June 1975, 5–6; no. 42, 17 July 1975, 4; no. 45, 12 August 1975, 6.

19. Interviews, Lisala, no. 26, 27 November 1974, 2; no. 18, 19 March 1975, 5; no. 54, 27 March 1975, 3.

20. Interview, Lisala, no. 4, 7 January 1975, 2.

21. Interviews, Lisala, no. 28, 4 February 1975, 3; no. 35, 22 April 1975, 5; no. 36, 22 March 1975, 10.

22. Interviews, Lisala, no. 34, 17 April 1975, 5; no. 17, 17 March 1975, 6; no. 24, 21 November 1974, 2; no. 27, 3 February 1975, 3; no. 41, 1 July 1975, 5.

23. Administrative correspondence, "Conférence pour les chefs de division régionales," n.d. [1973?].

24. Administrative correspondence, 24 April 1975.

25. "Discours d'orientation prononcé par le Citoyen Madrandele Tanzi, Directeur Politique du M.P.R. lors de l'installation de la commission chargée de la réforme administra-

tive," in *Les réformes administratives au Zaire (1972-1973)*, ed. Mpinga-Kasenda and D. J. Gould (Kinshasa: Presses Universitaires du Zaire, 1975), 41.

26. Mpinga-Kasenda, *L'administration publique du Zaire: L'impact du milieu socio-politique sur sa structure et fonctionnement* (Paris: Pedone, 1973), 214-16.

27. Administrative correspondence, 12 September 1967.

28. Administrative correspondence, 11 December 1973.

29. Interview, Lisala, no. 35, 22 April 1975, 3.

30. Field Log, 1 February 1975, 36. See, too, interview, Lisala, no. 5, 28 March 1975, 8.

31. Bokonga Ekanga Botombele, *Cultural Policy in the Republic of Zaire* (Paris: UNESCO, 1976), 45.

32. *Salongo*, 29 May 1979, 6.

33. Ibid., 16 January 1976, 5.

34. Ibid., 30 April 1976, 2; and 31 January 1976, 2.

35. Ibid., 23 February 1979, 1.

36. Ibid., 15 February 1977, 2.

37. Ibid., 25 June 1976, 1.

38. Ibid., 22 January 1976, 6.

39. Ibid., 1 April 1976, 2; 12 July 1982, 7; 9 September 1978, 1; 27 December 1976, 2; 4 November 1980, 1.

40. Ibid., 22 January 1976, 2.

41. Ibid., 23 October 1977, 3.

42. Ibid., 18 May 1976, 8.

43. Ibid., 14 October 1980, 5.

44. Ibid., 11-12 April 1981, 2.

45. Ibid., 3 September 1982, 2 and 22 April 1983, 1.

46. Ibid., 20 October 1980, 1-4; 21 October 1980, 1; and 16 October 1980, 2.

47. The Bangala are a prototypical case of artificial ethnicity. See Young, *Politics in the Congo*, 242-46; and idem, *The Politics of Cultural Pluralism*, 163-215. But Bangala ethnicity remains controversial. Mumbanza mwa Bawele argues such a group did exist in his, "Y a-t-il des Bangala? Origine et extension du terme," *Zaire-Afrique*, 78 (1973): 471-83.

48. Callaghy, *State-Society Struggle*, 318-30.

49. *Salongo*, 14 January 1976, 5.

50. Ibid., 25 March 1976, 5.

51. V. S. Naipaul, *A Bend in the River* (New York: Alfred A. Knopf, 1979), 257.

52. Fredrik Barth, *Political Leadership among Swat Pathans* (London: Athlone, 1959), 79-80.

53. Marshall Sahlins, *Stone Age Economics* (New York: Aldine, 1972), 133. Emphasis in original.

54. Ibid., 134.

55. Jan Vansina, "Mwasi's Trials," *Daedalus* 111 (1982): 67.

56. Marshall Sahlins, "Poor Man, Rich Man, Big-Man, Chief: Political Types in Melanesia and Polynesia," *Comparative Studies in Society and History* 5 (1963): 285-303.

57. Robert Price, "Politics and Culture in Contemporary Ghana: The Big-Man Small-Boy Syndrome," *Journal of African Studies* 1 (1974): 175-77.

58. "Le discours du Président-Fondateur du Mouvement Populaire de la Révolution à l'occasion de l'ouverture de l'Institut MAKANDA KABOBI à la Cité du Parti le 15 août 1974," *Etudes zairoises*, no. 2 (1974): 203; and Buana Kabue, *Citoyen Président*, 104.

59. Mobutu's interview with *Jeune Afrique*, cited in *Mobutu Sese Seko, Le Procès: Deuxième Tribunal Russel (Tribunal Permanent des Peuples)*, ed. C. K. Lumuna Sando and Buana Kabue (Brussels: A.F.R.I.C.A. pour l'Institut de l'Afrique Centrale, 1982), 196; Comite Zairé, *Zaire: Le dossier de la recolonisation* (Paris: L'Harmattan, 1978), 91;

and Mobutu Sese Seko, "Address to the Conseil National Extraordinaire, Dakar, 14 February 1971," in *Ideologies of Liberation in Black Africa 1856–1970*, ed. J. Ayo Langley (London: Rex Collings, 1979), 727.

60. Mobutu's interview with *Jeune Afrique* in Lumuna Sando and Buana Kabue, *Mobutu Sese Seko, Le Procès*, 197.

61. Nguza Karl-i-Bond, "Dix ans de pouvoir: Idées-forces du Mobutisme," *Studia Diplomatica* 39 (1976): 20. Emphasis added.

62. *Le militaire et la révolution*, 26; and Jan Vansina, personal communication, 24 December 1984.

63. *Info Zaire*, nos. 41–42 (1984): 33.

64. Interview, Lisala, no. 17, 17 March 1975, 2.

65. Vwakyanakazi Mukohya, "African Traders in Butembo," 266–68.

66. Jan Vansina, *Introduction à l'ethnographie du Congo* (Kinshasa: Editions Universitaires du Congo, 1966), 10.

67. David Warren Sabean, "The History of the Family in Africa and Europe: Some Comparative Perspectives," *Journal of African History* 24 (1983): 164; and Megan Vaughn, "Which Family? Problems in the Reconstruction of the History of the Family as an Economic and Cultural Unit," *Journal of African History* 24 (1983): 275, 281.

68. Wyatt MacGaffey, "Lineage Structure, Marriage and the Family amongst the Central Bantu," *Journal of African History* 24 (1983): 174.

69. Joseph C. Miller, "Lineages, Ideology, and the History of Slavery in Western Central Africa," in *The Ideology of Slavery in Africa*, ed. Paul E. Lovejoy (Beverly Hills, Calif.: Sage, 1981), 41–71; Anne Hilton, "Family and Kinship among the Kongo South of the Zaire River from the Sixteenth to the Nineteenth Centuries," *Journal of African History* 24 (1983): 189–206; and Bogumil Jewsiewicki and Mumbanza mwa Bawele, "The Social Context of Slavery in Equatorial Africa during the 19th and 20th Centuries," in Lovejoy, *The Ideology of Slavery*, 73–98.

70. Jan Vansina, "Lignage, idéologie et histoire," 133–55; idem, "Peoples of the Forest," 1:75–117; and Nkiere Bokuna Mpa-Osu, "La parenté comme système idéologique: Essai d'interprétation de l'ordre lignager chez les Basakata," (Ph.D. diss., Université Catholique de Louvain, Institut des Sciences Politiques et Sociales, 1976–77), 6–11.

71. Vansina, "Peoples of the Forest," 1:91; and on the Lunda, Reefe, "Societies of the Eastern Savanna," 1:189–90.

72. G. Hulstaert, *Les Mongo: Aperçu général* (Tervuren: Musée Royal de l'Afrique Centrale, 1961), 35–36; Lokumba Baruti, "Structure et fonctionnement des institutions politiques traditionnelles chez les Lokele (Haut-Zaire)," *Cahiers du CEDAF*, no. 8 (1972): 36; and Mulyumba wa Mamba Itongwa, "Aperçu sur la structure politique des Balega-Basile," *Cahiers du CEDAF*, no. 1 (1978).

73. Ellen Corin, "Vers une réappropriation de la dimension individuelle en psychologie africaine," *Canadian Journal of African Studies* 14 (1980): 142; and idem, "Le père comme modèle de différentiation dans une société clanique matrilinéaire (Yansi, Congo-Kinshasa)," *Psychopathologie africaine* 7 (1971): 205.

74. Nkiere, "La parenté comme système idéologique," 88.

75. André Lux, "Les travailleurs ruraux du Mayombe, ébauche d'une classe sociale?" *Canadian Journal of African Studies* 7 (1973): 441.

76. Shembo Omekenge Shala, "Image paternelle chez le garçon tetela," (Mémoire de licence, UNAZA-Kisangani, 1972) cited in Pierre Erny, *Sur les sentiers de l'université: Autobiographies d'étudiants zairois* (Paris: La Pensée Universelle, 1977), 94–95, 96.

77. Ibid., 96.

78. Corin, "Le père comme modèle de différentiation," 206.

79. Jan Vansina, *The Children of Woot: A History of the Kuba Peoples* (Madison: University of Wisconsin Press, 1978); on larger state structures more generally, idem, *Kingdoms of the Savanna*; and Schatzberg, "Chiefs of Upoto," 235–69.

80. G. Hulstaert, "La société politique Nkundo," *Etudes zairoises*, no. 2 (1974): 98–101.

81. Curtis A. Keim, personal communication, 12 January 1984.

82. William B. Cohen, "The Colonized as Child: British and French Colonial Rule," *African Historical Studies* 3 (1970): 427.

83. Bezy, Peemans, and Wautelet, *Accumulation et sous-développement*, 34–36.

84. Royaume de Belgique, Ministère des Colonies, 2è Direction Générale, *Recueil à l'usage des fonctionnaires et des agents du service territorial au Congo Belge*, 5th ed. (Brussels: Société Anonyme M. Wissenbruch, 1930), 59, 87, 88, 107. Emphasis in original.

85. Jewsiewicki, "L'état et l'accumulation primitive coloniale," 76. For general accounts of missionary activity, see Marvin D. Markowitz, *Cross and Sword: The Political Role of Christian Missions in the Belgian Congo, 1908–1960* (Stanford: Hoover Institution Press, 1973); and David Lagergren, *Mission and State in the Congo: A Study of the Relations between Protestant Missions and the Congo Independent State Authorities with Special Reference to Equator District, 1885–1903*, trans. Owen N. Lee (Uppsala: Gleerup, 1970).

86. Louis Franck cited in Jeremy Greenland, "Western Education in Burundi 1916–1973: The Consequences of Instrumentalism," *Cahiers du CEDAF*, nos. 2–3 (1980): 37.

87. V. Y. Mudimbe, *L'odeur du père: Essai sur des limites de la science et de la vie en Afrique noire* (Paris: Présence Africaine, 1982), 113–14.

88. Kita Kyankenge Masandi, *Colonisation et enseignement: Cas du Zaire avant 1960* (Bukavu: Editions du CERUKI, 1982), 95–96, 100.

89. Ali A. Mazrui, "The Resurrection of the Warrior Tradition in African Political Culture," *Journal of Modern African Studies* 13 (1975): 80.

90. *Recueil d'instructions aux missionnaires publié par la conférence des supérieurs des missions catholiques du Congo belge*, 6th ed. (Louvain: J. Kuyl-Otto, 1930), 15.

91. Congo belge, Inspection Générale de l'Enseignement, *Instructions pour les inspecteurs provinciaux relatives aux programmes à suivre dans les différentes écoles et à leur interprétation* (n.d. [1929?]), 12–13.

92. Congo belge, Inspection Générale de l'Enseignement, *Instructions relatives aux programmes à suivre et aux méthodes à employer dans les écoles de la colonie* (Leo-Kalina: Imprimerie du Gouverment, 1931), 23.

93. In addition to the materials already cited, see Congo belge, Service de l'Enseignement, *Organisation de l'enseignement libre subsidé pour indigènes avec le concours des sociétés de missions chrétiennes; enseignement général pour garçons; programme d'études* (1948), 5, 78.

94. Vicariat Apostolique de Lisala, "L'éducation civique," *Nous . . . Educateurs*, no. 4 (1958): 18.

95. Erny, *Sur le sentiers de l'université*, 87.

96. Catherine Parham, "Our Work with the Girls," *Congo Mission News*, no. 94 (April 1936): 27 cited in John Glenn Barden, *A Suggested Program of Teacher Training for Mission Schools among the Batetela* (New York: Bureau of Publications, Teachers College, Columbia University, 1941), 42.

97. Congo belge, Inspection Générale de l'Enseignement, *Instructions pour les inspecteurs provinciaux de l'enseignement relatives à l'organisation et au fonctionnement des écoles normales* (Boma: Imprimerie du Congo belge, mai 1929), 15.

98. Frère Bernardin, *L'école congolaise: Eléments d'organisation scolaire*, 2d ed. (Bondo: Frères de Saint-Gabriel, 1958), 4.

99. Ibid., 5, 9.

100. Ibid., 32, 33.

101. Herbert F. Weiss, "Comparisons in the Evolution of Pre-Independence Elites in

French-Speaking West Africa and the Congo," in *French-Speaking Africa: The Search for Identity*, ed. William H. Lewis (New York: Walker, 1965), 134.

102. Bernardin, *L'école congolaise*, 35–37.

103. Vicariat Apostolique de Nouvelle Anvers (Scheut), *Cours complet de pédagogie et de méthodologie pour instituteurs enseignant en Lingala (Programme de trois ans) (des écoles normales au Congo)* (Turnhout, Belgium: Henri Proost, 1931), 91, 92.

104. Additional works on colonial education include Barbara Ann Yates, "The Missions and Educational Development in Belgian Africa 1876–1908," (Ph.D. diss., Columbia University, 1967); idem, "African Reactions to Education: The Congolese Case," *Comparative Education Review* 15 (1971): 158–71; idem, "The Triumph and Failure of Mission Vocational Education in Zaire 1879–1908," *Comparative Education Review* 20 (1976): 193–208; idem, "Shifting Goals of Industrial Education in the Congo, 1878–1908," *African Studies Review* 21 (1978): 33–48; Mumbanza mwa Bawele, "Les établissements d'enseignement public à l'époque de l'E.I.C.: La colonie scolaire de Nouvelle-Anvers (1892–1913)," *Etudes d'histoire africaine* 8 (1976): 87–129; Johannes Fabian, "Missions and the Colonization of African Languages: Developments in the Former Belgian Congo," *Canadian Journal of African Studies* 17 (1983): 165–87; and, for the influence of Belgian paternalism on the universities, Benoît Verhaegen, *L'enseignement universitaire au Zaire: De Lovanium à l'UNAZA 1958–1978* (Paris: L'Harmattan, 1978).

105. Bruce Fetter, "L'Union Minière du Haut-Katanga, 1920–1940: La naissance d'une sous-culture totalitaire," *Cahiers du CEDAF*, no. 6 (1973).

106. L. Mottoulle, *Politique sociale de l'Union Minière du Haut-Katanga pour sa main d'oeuvre indigène et ses résultats au cours de vingt années d'application* (Brussels: Institut Royal Colonial Belge, Section des Sciences Morales et Politiques, 14:3, 1946), 5. For a work which underscores the contradictions of corporate paternalism in a slightly different context, see Charles van Onselin, *Chibaro: African Mine Labour in Southern Rhodesia 1900–1933* (London: Pluto, 1976), 151, 193–94.

107. Willame, *Patrimonialism and Political Change*, 79.

108. Schatzberg, *Politics and Class*, 183–85.

109. W. D'Hondt, M. Magabe, and G. Wehmuller, "La perception du rôle du père par les adolescents de la ville de Bukavu," *Cahiers du CEDAF*, no. 8 (1979): 36.

110. Richard Sennett, *Authority* (New York: Vintage Books, 1980), 82.

111. Claude Meillassoux, *Maidens, Meal and Money: Capitalism and the Domestic Community* (Cambridge: Cambridge University Press, 1981), 47, 86. The citation is from idem, "The Social Organisation of the Peasantry: The Economic Basis of Kinship," *Journal of Peasant Studies* 1 (1973): 88.

112. Sennett, *Authority*, 86.

113. Nzongola-Ntalaja, "The Continuing Struggle for National Liberation in Zaire," *Journal of Modern African Studies* 17 (1979): 609.

114. Vansina, "Lignage, idéologie et histoire," 149.

115. Sennett, *Authority*, 71.

116. Vansina, "Peoples of the Forest," 1:84.

117. Gellner, *Nations and Nationalism*, 11.

118. Abner Cohen, *Two-Dimensional Man: An Essay on the Anthropology of Power and Symbolism in Complex Society* (Berkeley and Los Angeles: University of California Press, 1974), 32.

119. Idem, *The Politics of Elite Culture*, 151. For a linguistic approach, see Lowell Dittmer, "Political Culture and Political Symbolism: Toward a Theoretical Synthesis," *World Politics* 29 (1977): 552–83.

120. Vansina, "Lignage, idéologie et histoire," 149.

121. Fouad Ajami, *The Arab Predicament: Arab Political Thought and Practice since 1967* (Cambridge: Cambridge University Press, 1981), 131.

122. Jomo Kenyatta, *Facing Mount Kenya: The Tribal Life of the Gikuyu* (New York: Vintage Books, n.d.), 182.

123. Vansina, "Lignage, idéologie et histoire."

124. Sennett, *Authority*, 162.

125. J. Gérard-Libois and Jean Van Lierde, eds., *Congo 1965* (Brussels: CRISP, 1966), 412; and J. Gérard-Libois, *Congo 1966*, 103.

126. Young and Turner, *Rise and Decline*, 7; and my review in *American Political Science Review* 80 (1986): 1390.

127. *Le MPR a huit ans* (Kinshasa: Département de l'Orientation Nationale, 1975), 23.

128. Kamitatu-Massamba, *Zaire: Le pouvoir à la portée du peuple*, 146–49.

129. Nguza Karl-i-Bond, *Le Zaire de demain: Réflexion pour la IIIè République du Congo* (Antwerp: Soethoudt, 1983), 72.

130. Interview, Lisala, no. 2, 19 November 1974, 4.

131. Interviews, Lisala, no. 5, 28 March 1975, 6; no. 13, 28 February 1975, 3; no. 20, 15 January 1975, 4; no. 39, 11 June 1975, 5.

132. Mobutu Sese Seko, "Speech before the MPR's Second Ordinary Congress," Kinshasa, November 1977, 14–15.

133. Kapuscinski, *The Emperor*, 33–34.

134. Interview, Lisala, no. 5, 28 March 1975, 7.

135. *Salongo*, 4 March 1981, 2.

136. Ibid., 29 April 1981, 3. For other examples of this discourse and metaphors, see *Salongo*, 25 June 1982, 4; 13 December 1982, 3.

137. Nguza, "Tout un peuple est pris en ôtage," 73.

138. Kanyonga Mobateli, *Dix ans de régime Mobutu*, 33.

139. Sakombi Inongo, *Lettre ouverte à Nguza Karl-i-Bond*, 63.

140. Ibid., 71.

141. National Council of Churches in the USA, Africa Committee, "Zaire Symposium," Washington, D.C., 2 November 1983. I attended this gathering and took notes on the more interesting dialogues.

142. Babudaa Malibato, *Education et instruction civiques: Le citoyen dans la communauté nationale*, 3è secondaire, manuel conforme au programme de la République du Zaire (Kinshasa: BEC, 1974), 16, 72.

143. James C. Scott, *Weapons of the Weak*, 338.

6. The Insecure State, I: Resistance Within—The Magistrature

Chapters 6 and 7 grew from "The Insecure State in Zaire: Resistance Within, Resistance Without" (Paper presented at the annual meeting of the American Political Science Association, Denver, Colorado, 2–5 September 1982).

1. Mobutu Sese Seko, Speech before the Second Ordinary Congress of the MPR, November 1977, 15–16.

2. Nguza, "Tout un peuple est pris en ôtage," 73.

3. When the colonial period ended, Zaire had only 207 judges; by 1974 there were 643 magistrates at subregional, regional, and national tribunals. Congo belge, *Statistiques relatives à l'année 1959; Bulletin annuel des statistiques du Congo belge 1959* (Cambridge: Chadwyck-Healy, 1981), 8; and République du Zaire, Commission Permanente de l'Administration Publique, "Répartition des agents de l'état par grade, par département et région d'affectation," 24 October 1974, computer printout.

4. Young, *Politics in the Congo*, 420–23; Young and Turner, *Rise and Decline*, 14; and Callaghy, *State-Society Struggle*, 361–68.

5. Bob Jessop, "On Recent Marxist Theories of Law, the State, and Juridico-Political Ideology," *International Journal of the Sociology of Law* 8 (1980): 339–68.

6. Wyatt MacGaffey, *Religion and Society in Central Africa: The BaKongo of Lower Zaire* (Chicago: University of Chicago Press, 1986), 17.

7. Ibid., 214.

8. Martin Chanock, *Law, Custom and Social Order: The Colonial Experience in Malawi and Zambia* (Cambridge: Cambridge University Press, 1985).

9. Despite its tendency to accept unquestioningly both the Code and Belgian motives, John H. Crabb, *The Legal System of Congo-Kinshasa* (Charlottesville, Va.: Michie, 1970), provides useful information. For example, 41–45, 89.

10. André Durieux, "Exposé descriptif et synthétique des institutions politiques, administratives et judiciaires du Congo Belge et du Ruanda-Urundi," in *Encyclopédie du Congo Belge*, 3 vols. (Brussels: Editions Bieleveld, n.d. [1950?]), 3:536–40.

11. P. Piron, *L'indépendance de la magistrature et le statut des magistrats* (Brussels: Académie Royale des Sciences Coloniales, Classe des Sciences Morales et Politiques, 5:5, 1956), 11–12.

12. Cited in ibid., 7.

13. Jean-Luc Vellut, "Hégémonies en construction: Articulations entre état et entreprises dans le bloc colonial belge (1908–1960)," *Canadian Journal of African Studies* 16 (1982): 327.

14. Young, *Politics in the Congo*, 420–23.

15. Administrative correspondence, 17 March 1970.

16. Interview, Lisala, no. 23, 16 June 1975, 4.

17. Interview, Lisala, no. 22, 4 June 1975, 4.

18. Field Log, 9 April 1975, 66.

19. Interview, Lisala, no. 23, 16 June 1975, 4–5.

20. Ibid.

21. Administrative correspondence, 2 January 1974.

22. *Salongo*, 14 October 1978, 3.

23. Callaghy, *State-Society Struggle*, 274.

24. Administrative correspondence, 28 February 1972.

25. Interview, Lisala, no. 14, 6 March 1975, 3.

26. Administrative correspondence, 16 June 1975.

27. Interview, Lisala, no. 14, 6 March 1975, 3; and Field Log, 7 March 1975, 52–53.

28. Interview, Lisala, no. 23, 16 June 1975, 4; and also interview, Lisala, no. 22, 4 June 1975, 3.

29. Interview, Lisala, no. 14, 6 March 1975, 4.

30. Antoine Rubbens, *L'indépendance des magistrats dans la République démocratique du Congo (Constitution-Loi-Statut)* (Brussels: Académie Royale des Sciences d'Outre-Mer, Classe des Sciences Morales et Politiques, n.s. 34:4, 1966), 40.

31. Idem, *Le droit judiciaire congolais*, vol. 1, *Le pouvoir, l'organisation et la compétence judiciaires* (Kinshasa and Brussels: Université Lovanium and Ferd. Larcier, 1970), 1:183.

32. Bayona-Ba-Meya Muna Kivimba, "L'indépendance de la magistrature en République du Zaire," *Annales de la faculté de droit* 1 (1972): 36.

33. Kengo wa Dondo, "L'organisation et le fonctionnement de la justice dans la République du Zaire," *Revue juridique du Zaire* 49 (1973): 247.

34. *Salongo*, 18 March 1976, 5.

35. Interview, Lisala, no. 23, 16 June 1975, 3.

36. Field Log, 22 December 1974, 19.

37. Interview, Lisala, no. 23, 16 June 1975, 4.

38. Field Log, 15 July 1975, 98–99.

39. Field Log, 20 May 1975, 76–77.

40. For the diplomatic aspects, see Elise Forbes Pachter, "Our Man in Kinshasa: U.S. Relations with Mobutu, 1970–1983, Patron Client Relations in the International Sphere,"

(Ph.D. diss., School of Advanced International Studies, The Johns Hopkins University, 1987), 199–247.

41. Field Log, 15 July 1975, 98.

42. Johan M. Pauwels, "La réforme du droit civil au Zaire—Comment concilier tradition et développement?" *Journal of African Law* 17 (1973): 222, n. 2; Buana Kabue and C. K. Lumuna Sando, "Introduction à la politique zairoise," in *Mobutu Sese Seko, Le Procès: Deuxième Tribunal Russel (Tribunal Permanent des Peuples)*, ed. C. K. Lumuna Sando and Buana Kabue (Brussels: A.F.R.I.C.A. pour l'Institut de l'Afrique Centrale, 1982), 37; and Johan M. Pauwels and Walter Pintens, *La législation zairoise relative au nom: Droit et authenticité africaine* (Brussels: Académie Royale des Sciences d'Outre-Mer, Classe des Sciences Morales et Politiques, Mémoires, n.s., 47:2, 1983), 10.

43. Interview, Lisala, no. 14, 6 March 1975, 4.

44. Bayart, "La fronde parlementaire au Zaire," 103.

45. For the text see "La deuxième révolution mobutienne," *Zaire* (Kinshasa), 6 January 1975, 20–22. For an overview, see Schatzberg, "The State and the Economy," 239–57.

46. Administrative correspondence, 26 June 1975, 5 July 1975. *Salongo* tends to be rather coercive.

47. Administrative correspondence, 11 July 1975, 12 July 1975. The law in question was the Loi Foncière no. 71/009 of 31 December 1971, the Loi Bakajika. See Margaret A. Turner, "Housing in Zaire: How the System Works and How the People Cope," (Ph.D. diss., University of Wisconsin-Madison, 1985), 195, 225, n. 30.

48. Administrative correspondence, 23 July 1975.

49. Administrative correspondence, 25 July 1975.

50. Field Log, 11 August 1975, 109 and 18 August 1975, 111.

51. *Salongo*, 14 October 1980, 5.

52. Giddens, *A Contemporary Critique*, 1:63.

53. Various interviews, Lisala, 1974–75.

54. For an elaboration of just how much they stand to lose, see Schatzberg, *Politics and Class*, 52–53, esp. table 8.

55. Gould, *Bureaucratic Corruption*.

56. Interview, Lisala, no. 23, 16 June 1975, 2.

57. Interview, Lisala, no. 19, 11 April 1975, 5.

58. Field Log, 20 July 1975, 102; 14 July 1975, 98; and 8 February 1975, 38.

59. Wyatt MacGaffey, "The Policy of National Integration in Zaire," *Journal of Modern African Studies* 20 (1982): 98.

60. "Aide-Mémoire remis par la délégation de l'U.D.P.S.," 15.

61. For a dismal view of Zairian justice, see the novel by Muamba Kanyinda, *La pourriture* (Kinshasa: Editions Edimaf, 1978). For comparative perspectives, see Mamdani, *Imperialism and Fascism in Uganda*, 44; and Coulson, *Tanzania: A Political Economy*, 221.

62. J. M. Pauwels, "Vingt années de législation zairoise 1960–1980," *Penant* 92 (1982): 11.

63. Interview, Lisala, no. 23, 16 June 1975, 6–7.

64. Interview, Lisala, no. 22, 4 June 1975, 3.

65. Field Log, 11 July 1975, 97.

66. W. MacGaffey, "The Policy of National Integration," 93–94.

67. Nguza, *Mobutu*, 74.

68. *Salongo*, 13 March 1978, 13.

69. Ibid., 30–31 January 1982, 10.

7. The Insecure State, II: Resistance Without—Religious Groups

1. Gérard-Libois and Van Lierde, *Congo 1965*, 449.
2. Kaseba, *"Notre foi en l'homme image de Dieu,"* 21.
3. *Salongo*, 15 September 1981, 5.
4. Callaghy, *State-Society Struggle*, 303–4. Figures from the Diocese of Lisala were taken from Association Diocèse de Lisala, "Etat de recettes et de dépenses—Année 1974," 2 February 1975.
5. Pierre Erny, *Ecoles d'église en Afrique noire: Poids du passé et perspectives d'avenir* (Fribourg: Nouvelle Revue de Science Missionnaire, 1982), 50.
6. Kita Kyankenge Masandi, *Colonisation et enseignement*, 27–72, esp., 65–66.
7. Jewsiewicki, "L'état et l'accumulation primitive," 76.
8. J. Malula, "L'âme bantoue face à l'Evangile," *Vivante Afrique* 198 (1958): 12–13, cited in Erny, *Ecoles d'église en Afrique noire*, 77.
9. Erny, *Ecoles d'église en Afrique noire*, 109–10.
10. Nyunda ya Rubango, "Les principales tendances du discours politiques zairois (1960–1965)," *Cahiers du CEDAF*, no. 7 (1980): 37ff.
11. This summary of church-state relations under Mobutu is drawn from: Rob Buyseniers, *L'église zairoise*; Callaghy, *State-Society Struggle*, 303–7; Leo Goovaerts, "L'église et l'état au Zaire à l'épreuve de l'authenticité," *Cultures et développement* 7 (1975): 243–82; Kenneth Lee Adelman, "The Church-State Conflict in Zaire: 1969–1974," *African Studies Review* 18 (1975): 102–16; "Les relations entre l'église et l'état au Zaire," *Etudes africaines du CRISP*, no. 145 (28 December 1972); and administrative correspondence, 21 March 1975.
12. Interview, Mbandaka, no. 72, 29 August 1975, 2–3.
13. Monsignor Bakole wa Ilunga, *Paroles de vie aux chrétiens de l'Archidiocèse de Kananga* (Kananga: Archdiocese of Kananga, 11 February 1975), 20. Also, idem, *Paths of Liberation: A Third World Spirituality*, trans. Matthew J. O'Connell (Maryknoll: Orbis Books, 1984).
14. Monsignor Kabanga, *Je suis un homme: Lettre pastorale de Carême 1976* (Lubumbashi: Archdiocese of Lubumbashi, March 1976); and *"Tous solidaires et responsables": Lettre pastorale des évêques du Zaire* (25 February 1977), in *Documentation et Information*, 28 June 1978, 590–97.
15. *Salongo*, 1 March 1977, 5; Buyseniers, *L'église zairoise*, 6–7; and Erny, *Ecoles d'église en Afrique noire*, 111–12.
16. *Salongo*, 4 May 1978, 2.
17. For the text of the declaration see Buana Kabue, *Citoyen Président*, 220–31.
18. *Salongo*, 30 September 1978, 5 and 1–7 May 1980. Also, Buyseniers, *L'église zairoise*, 7–9; and Jonathan Kwitney, *Endless Enemies: The Making of an Unfriendly World* (New York: Congdon & Weed, 1984), 90.
19. Odungo Nyangayo, "Mobutu Jails Archbishop and Raps the Catholic Church," *New African*, no. 171, December 1981, 31; Jean Savoie, "L'église au Zaire: Dénoncer la corruption, cela comporte des risques," *La revue nouvelle*, nos. 5–6 (1982): 549–50; Sylvain Camara, "Le Zaire et la puissance: deuxième partie," *Revue française d'études politiques africaines* 18 (1983): 48–49; and *Wall Street Journal*, 7 August 1984.
20. See Buyseniers, *L'église zairoise*, 45–63, 74–75; and "L'église et l'état," *Info Zaire*, no. 3 (1979): 6–11.

21. J.A. Cardinal Malula, *L'église de Dieu qui est à Kinshasa vous parle* (Kinshasa: Editions St. Paul d'Afrique, 1976), 29.

22. B. Jewsiewicki, "Introduction," *Canadian Journal of African Studies* 18 (1984): 10–11.

23. Letter from Malula to a parish priest in Kinshasa, typescript, 17 August 1983 in which Malula instructs subordinates not to hold thanksgiving masses for the thirteen dissident parliamentarians, and to make sure people do not congregate outside church after mass to discuss politics. I do not know if this letter is genuine.

24. The correspondence is reproduced in *Info Zaire Flash*, no. 38–1 (June 1983).

25. Catharine Newbury, "Ebutumwa Bw'Emiogo: The Tyranny of Cassava, A Women's Tax Revolt in Eastern Zaire," *Canadian Journal of African Studies* 18 (1984): 35–54.

26. *Info Zaire*, no. 41 (1984).

27. Philippe Borel, "Divisions et faiblesses d'une opposition privée de stratégie politique," *Monde diplomatique*, September 1981.

28. Vwakyanakazi Mukohya, "African Traders in Butembo," 245, 308.

29. Efraim Andersson, *Messianic Popular Movements in the Lower Congo* (Uppsala: Almqvist & Wiksells, 1958), 29–67, 223–33; Willy de Craemer, Jan Vansina, and Renée Fox, "Religious Movements in Central Africa: A Theoretical Study," *Comparative Studies in Society and History* 18 (1976): 458–75, esp., 465; Susan Asch, *L'église du prophète Kimbangu: De ses origines à son rôle actuel au Zaire (1921–1981)* (Paris: Karthala, 1983), 15–42; and Royaume de Belgique, Chambre des Représentants, *Rapport sur l'administration du Congo Belge pendant l'année 1921* (Brussels: Chambre des Représentants, 1921), 117.

30. Susan Asch, "Contradictions internes d'une institution religieuse: L'EJCSK au Zaire," *Archives des sciences sociales des religions* 52 (1981): 106. The other officially recognized religious groups are the Catholic church and the Eglise du Christ au Zaire, an umbrella organization of Protestant denominations which I shall not consider here.

31. Wyatt MacGaffey, "The Implantation of Kimbanguism in Kisangani, Zaire," *Journal of African History* 23 (1983): 382.

32. Asch, "Contradictions internes," 102.

33. W. MacGaffey, *Modern Kongo Prophets*, 64.

34. Asch, *L'église du prophète Kimbangu*, 70–77, 132, 134; and W. MacGaffey, *Modern Kongo Prophets*, 64–66.

35. W. MacGaffey, *Modern Kongo Prophets*, 62.

36. Susan Asch, "Etude socio-démographique de l'implantation et la composition actuelles de la congrégation kimbanguist (Zaire)," *Cahiers du CEDAF*, nos. 1–2 (1982): 11–12, 27–34, 38, 42.

37. André Droogers, "Kimbanguism at the Grass Roots: Beliefs in a Local Kimbanguist Church," *Journal of Religion in Africa* 11 (1980): 204–5.

38. W. MacGaffey, *Modern Kongo Prophets*, 189.

39. Mwene-Batende, *Mouvements messianiques et protestation sociale: Le cas du Kitawala chez les Kumu du Zaire* (Kinshasa: Faculté de Théologie Catholique, 1982), 129–93. Also see Karen E. Fields, *Revival and Rebellion in Colonial Central Africa* (Princeton: Princeton University Press, 1985), 91–94.

40. Sholto Cross, "The Watch Tower Movement in South Central Africa, 1908–1945," (D.Phil. thesis, Oxford University, 1973), 409–14; Field Log, 13 September 1975, 117; Mwene-Batende, *Mouvements messianiques et protestation sociale*, 139–41; Roger Anstey, *King Leopold's Legacy: The Congo under Belgian Rule 1908–1960* (London: Oxford University Press, 1966), 134; and confidential letter from Equateur's governor, R. Spitaels, to all District Commissioners and Territorial Administrators, no. 221/62/48, 9 June 1958.

41. B. Jewsiewicki, "Modernisation ou destruction du village africain; L'économie

politique de la 'modernisation agricole' au Congo Belge," *Cahiers du CEDAF*, no. 5 (1983): 63–64, 69–70.

42. See Mwene-Batende, "Le Kitawala dans l'évolution socio-politique récente: Cas du groupe Belukela dans la ville du Kisangani," *Cahiers des religions africaines* 10 (1976): 91–92; Kuama Mobwa, "L'extension du Kitawala à la Province de l'Equateur," *Cahiers de l'I.S.P. Gombe*, série B 1 (1980): 76–77; and J. R. Hooker, "Witnesses and Watchtower in the Rhodesias and Nyasaland," *Journal of African History* 6 (1965): 92.

43. Royaume de Belgique, Chambre des Représentants, *Rapport sur l'administration du Congo Belge pendant l'année 1954* (Brussels: Chambre des Représentants, 1954), 69.

44. Province de l'Equateur, *Conseil de Province 1954*, 1ère partie, "Allocution du Président, le Gouverneur de Province, M. De Ryck," 23 March 1954, 5.

45. Guy Bernard, "La contestation des églises nationales au Congo," *Canadian Journal of African Studies* 5 (1971): 155.

46. Jacques E. Gérard, *Les fondements syncrétiques du Kitawala* (Brussels: CRISP and Le Livre Africain, 1969); Robert Kaufmann, *Millénarisme et acculturation* (Brussels: Editions de l'Institut de Sociologie de l'Université Libre de Bruxelles, 1964), 79–101; Daniel Biebuyck, "La société Kumu face au Kitawala," *Zaire* 11 (1957): 7–40; W. de Mahieu, "Les Komo et le Kitawala," *Cahiers des religions africaines* 10 (1976): 51–66; Njangu Canda-Ciri, "Le Kimbanguisme et le Kitawala: Etude comparative," *Antennes, revue de CERUKI (Centre de Recherches Universitaires du Kivu)* 5 (1977): 25–39; Sholto Cross, "Social History and Millenarial Movements: The Watch Tower in South Central Africa," *Social Compass* 24 (1977): 83–95; idem, "Kitawala, Conspiracies, and the Sûreté: An Historiological Enquiry," *Enquêtes et documents d'histoire africaine* 2 (1977): 67–85; and Maurice Lovens, "La révolte de Masisi-Lubutu (Congo Belge, janvier-mai 1944)," *Cahiers du CEDAF*, nos. 3–4 (1974): 14, 27, 40, 42.

47. Field Log, 6 November 1974, 7–8; and interview, Lisala, no. 37, 3 May 1975, 8.

48. Zone de Lisala, "Rapport mensuel—mois de mars 1975," 7 April 1975.

49. Administrative correspondence, 15 March 1975, 20 March 1975, 8 November 1974.

50. Administrative correspondence, 2 October 1970.

51. Vansina, "Mwasi's Trials," 63; W. MacGaffey, *Modern Kongo Prophets*, 43; *Salongo*, 5 January 1979, 9; and Kazumba K. Tshiteya, "Le discours savant et le développement du sous-développement au Zaire," *Canadian Journal of African Studies* 18 (1984): 59.

52. *Salongo*, 8 December 1982, 6.

53. Ibid., 13 December 1982, 5.

54. *West Africa*, 24 March 1986, 648; and ibid., 14 April 1986, 796.

55. Comité Zaire, "Les droits de l'homme et les libertés," 111.

56. Mwene-Batende, *Mouvements messianiques et protestation sociale*, 268.

57. Administrative correspondence, 7 July 1970.

58. "Rapport semestriel sur la marche de l'administration de la Zone de Bongandanga et les collectivités la composant," 15 December 1974, 19–20. *Animateur* of the *groupe choc* is the leader of a political cheerleading group.

59. Field Log, 8 July 1975, 94–95; interview, Lisala, no. 37, 3 May 1975, 8; and W. MacGaffey, "The Implantation of Kimbanguism," 391.

60. On the notion of exit, see Albert O. Hirschman, "Exit, Voice, and the State," *World Politics* 31 (1978): 90–107.

61. Phyllis M. Martin, "The Violence of Empire," in *History of Central Africa*, 2 vols., ed. David Birmingham and Phyllis M. Martin (London: Longman, 1983), 2:22; and Ralph A. Austin and Rita Headrick, "Equatorial Africa under Colonial Rule," in ibid., 2:37.

62. A. I. Asiwaju, "Migrations as Revolt: The Example of the Ivory Coast and the Upper Volta before 1945," *Journal of African History* 17 (1976): 577–94.

63. Schatzberg, "Chiefs of Upoto," 247.

64. Bogumil Jewsiewicki, "Rural Society and the Belgian Colonial Economy," in *His-*

tory of Central Africa, 2 vols., ed. David Birmingham and Phyllis M. Martin (London: Longman, 1983), 2:121.

65. Benoît Verhaegen, *Rébellions au Congo*, 2 vols. (Brussels: CRISP, 1966), 1:62.
66. Administrative correspondence, 18 January 1971, 26 August 1972.
67. Bezy, Peemans, and Wautelet, *Accumulation et sous-développement*, 155.
68. Vansina, "Mwasi's Trials," 60.
69. Goran Hyden, *Beyond Ujamaa in Tanzania: Underdevelopment and an Uncaptured Peasantry* (Berkeley and Los Angeles: University of California Press, 1980).
70. Interview, Lisala, no. 39, 11 June 1975, 5; and administrative correspondence, 18 January 1971, 14 June 1972.

8. The Dialectics of Oppression

1. Buana Kabue, *Citoyen Président*, 23.
2. *Le Soir* (Brussels), 14–15 July 1984, 3.
3. Frantz Fanon, *Les damnés de la terre* (Paris: Maspero, 1968), 108.
4. Callaghy, *State-Society Struggle*, 231, 409. Also see Bianga, "Peasant, State and Rural Development," 73–74.
5. Cikuru, "Une descente aux enfers," 29.
6. Michael G. Schatzberg, "The Struggle for Space: The Dialectics of Autonomy in Zaire" (Paper presented to the Annual Meeting of the African Studies Association, Madison, Wisconsin, 29 October-2 November 1986).
7. Callaghy, *State-Society Struggle*, 231–32, 233–333.
8. Catharine Newbury, "Survival Strategies in Rural Zaire: Realities of Coping with Crisis," in *The Crisis in Zaire: Myths and Realities*, ed. Nzongola-Ntalaja (Trenton, N.J.: Africa World Press, 1986), 99–112; and Scott, *Weapons of the Weak*, 282.
9. Charles Tilly, "Foreword," to Anton Blok, *The Mafia of a Sicilian Village, 1860–1960: A Study of Violent Peasant Entrepreneurs* (New York: Harper & Row, 1974), xxi.
10. Thomas, *Rise of the Authoritarian State*, 89.
11. Callaghy, *State-Society Struggle*, 229, 416–18.
12. Ibid., 193.
13. Giddens, *A Contemporary Critique*, 1:60.
14. Young and Turner, *Rise and Decline*, 135–37, 160.
15. René Lemarchand, "Bringing Factions Back into the State," in *The Crisis in Zaire: Myths and Realities*, ed. Nzongola-Ntalaja (Trenton, N.J.: Africa World Press, 1986), 63–64.
16. Scott, *Weapons of the Weak*, 247; also see Janet MacGaffey, "Fending-for-Yourself: The Organization of the Second Economy in Zaire," in *The Crisis in Zaire: Myths and Realities*, ed. Nzongola-Ntalaja (Trenton, N.J.: Africa World Press, 1986), 141–56; and her *Entrepreneurs and Parasites*.
17. Thomas M. Callaghy, "The International Community and Zaire's Debt Crisis," in *The Crisis in Zaire: Myths and Realities*, ed. Nzongola-Ntalaja (Trenton, N.J.: Africa World Press, 1986), 221–43; and Winsome J. Leslie, "The World Bank and Zaire," in ibid., 245–63. Also, Young and Turner, *Rise and Decline*, 135–37; and Pachter, "Our Man in Kinshasa."
18. Bienen, "State and Ethnicity," 121–22.
19. Hyden, *No Shortcuts to Progress*, 19, 195.
20. Jean-François Bayart, "L'énonciation du politique," *Revue française de science politique* 35 (1985): 367, 369.
21. Young and Turner, *Rise and Decline*, 244, 183.
22. Amilcar Cabral, *Return to the Source: Selected Speeches* (New York: Monthly Review Press, 1973), 84.

23. Nzongola-Ntalaja, "Crisis and Change in Zaire, 1960–1985," in *The Crisis in Zaire: Myths and Realities*, ed. Nzongola-Ntalaja (Trenton, N.J.: Africa World Press, 1986), 10.

24. *West Africa*, 10 November 1986, 2382.

25. Young, *Politics in the Congo*, 351, 354, 357.

Bibliography

Adelman, Kenneth Lee. "The Church-State Conflict in Zaire: 1969–1974." *African Studies Review* 18 (1975): 102–16.
Administrative correspondence. Archives, Mongala Subregion, Political Affairs Department, Lisala.
"Aide-mémoire remis par la délégation de l'U.D.P.S. à la délégation du Congrès Américain." August 1983. Typescript.
Ajami, Fouad. *The Arab Predicament: Arab Political Thought and Practice since 1967.* Cambridge: Cambridge University Press, 1981.
Alata, Jean-Paul. *Prison d'Afrique.* Paris: Seuil, 1976.
Amnesty International [AI]. *Human Rights Violations in Zaire.* London: AI, 1980.
_____. "The Ill-Treatment and Torture of Political Prisoners at Detention Centers in Kinshasa." AFR 62/32/80, 24 September 1980.
_____. *Political Imprisonment in Zaire: An Amnesty International Special Briefing.* New York: AI, 1983.
_____. "Arrests and Political Imprisonment in Zaire, August-December 1983." AFR 62/07/84, 8 February 1984.
_____. *Zaire: Reports of Torture and Killings Committed by the Armed Forces in Shaba Region.* London: AI, 1986.
Andersson, Efraim. *Messianic Popular Movements in the Lower Congo.* Uppsala: Almqvist & Wiksells, 1958.
Anstey, Roger. *King Leopold's Legacy: The Congo under Belgian Rule 1908–1960.* London: Oxford University Press, 1966.
Ariès, Philippe. *Centuries of Childhood: A Social History of Family Life.* Translated by Robert Baldick. New York: Vintage Books, 1962.
Armstrong, John A. *Nations before Nationalism.* Chapel Hill: University of North Carolina Press, 1982.
"Arrêt de travail dans les écoles de la sous-région urbaine de Kisangani," 8 December 1983. *Info Zaire,* nos. 41–42 (1984): 20–27.
Asch, Susan. "Contradictions internes d'une institution religieuse: L'EJCSK au Zaire." *Archives des sciences sociales des religions* 52 (1981): 99–124.
_____. "Etude socio-démographique de l'implantation et la composition actuelles de la congrégation kimbanguist (Zaire)." *Cahiers du CEDAF,* nos. 1–2 (1982).
_____. *L'église du prophète Kimbangu: De ses origines à son rôle actuel au Zaire (1921–1981).* Paris: Karthala, 1983.
Asiwaju, A. I. "Migrations as Revolt: The Example of the Ivory Coast and the Upper Volta before 1945." *Journal of African History* 17 (1976): 577–94.
Association Diocèse de Lisala. "Etat de recettes et de dépenses—Année 1974," 2 February 1975.
Austin, Ralph A., and Rita Headrick. "Equatorial Africa under Colonial Rule." In *History of Central Africa,* 2 vols., edited by David Birmingham and Phyllis M. Martin, 2:27–94. London: Longman, 1983.
Avirgan, Tony, and Martha Honey. *War in Uganda: The Legacy of Idi Amin.* Westport, Conn.: Lawrence Hill, 1982.
Babudaa Malibato. *Education et instruction civiques: Le citoyen dans la communauté nationale.* 3è secondaire, manuel conforme au programme de la République du Zaire. Kinshasa: BEC, 1974.

Badibanga, André. "Je suis le 'Père de la Nation.'" *Revue française d'études politiques africaines* 16 (1980–81): 103–16.

Bakary, Tessilimi. "Elite Transformation and Political Succession." In *The Political Economy of Ivory Coast*, edited by I. William Zartman and Christopher Delgado, 21–55. New York: Praeger, 1984.

Bakole wa Ilunga. *Paroles de vie aux chrétiens de l'Archidiocèse de Kananga.* Kananga: Archdiocese of Kananga, 11 February 1975.

———. *Paths of Liberation: A Third World Spirituality.* Translated by Matthew J. O'Connell. Maryknoll: Orbis Books, 1984.

Bakvis, Herman. "French Canada and the 'Bureaucratic Phenomenon.'" *Canadian Public Administration* 21 (1978): 103–24.

Balandier, Georges. *Sens et puissance: Les dynamiques sociales.* Paris: Presses Universitaires de France, 1971.

Barden, John Glenn. *A Suggested Program of Teacher Training for Mission Schools among the Batetela.* New York: Bureau of Publications, Teachers College, Columbia University, 1941.

Barkan, Joel D., and John J. Okumu, eds. *Politics and Public Policy in Kenya and Tanzania.* New York: Praeger, 1979.

Barth, Fredrik. *Political Leadership among Swat Pathans.* London: Athlone, 1959.

Bates, Robert H. *Markets and States in Tropical Africa: The Political Basis of Agricultural Choice.* Berkeley and Los Angeles: University of California Press, 1981.

———. *Essays on the Political Economy of Rural Africa.* Cambridge: Cambridge University Press, 1983.

Bayart, Jean-François. "Régime du parti unique et système d'inégalité et de domination au Cameroun: Esquisse." *Cahiers d'études africaines* 18 (1978): 5–35.

———. *L'état au Cameroun.* Paris: Presses de la Fondation Nationale des Sciences Politiques, 1979.

———. "One-Party Government and Political Development in Cameroon." In *An African Experiment in Nation Building: The Bilingual Cameroon Republic since Reunification*, edited by Ndiva Kofele-Kale, 159–87. Boulder, Colo.: Westview, 1980.

———. "La fronde parlementaire au Zaire." *Politique africaine* 3 (1981): 90–139.

———. "Etat et société civile en Afrique de l'ouest." *Revue française de science politique* 33 (1983): 747–53.

———. "Les sociétés africaines face à l'état." *Pouvoirs* 25 (1983): 23–39.

———. "L'énonciation du politique." *Revue française de science politique* 35 (1985): 343–73.

Bayona-Ba-Meya Muna Kivimba. "L'indépendance de la magistrature en République du Zaire." *Annales de la faculté de droit* 1 (1972): 19–36.

Beckman, Bjorn. "Imperialism and Capitalist Transformation: Critique of a Kenyan Debate." *Review of African Political Economy* 19 (1980): 48–62.

Bernard, Guy. "La contestation des églises nationales au Congo." *Canadian Journal of African Studies* 5 (1971): 145–56.

Bernardin, Frère. *L'école congolaise: Eléments d'organisation scolaire.* 2d ed. Bondo: Frères de Saint-Gabriel, 1958.

Berry, Sara. *Fathers Work for Their Sons: Accumulation, Mobility, and Class Formation in an Extended Yoruba Community.* Berkeley and Los Angeles: University of California Press, 1985.

Bertrand, Hugues. *Le Congo: Formation sociale et môde de développement économique.* Paris: Maspero, 1975.

Bezy, Fernand, Jean-Phillippe Peemans, and Jean-Marie Wautelet. *Accumulation et sous-développement au Zaire 1960–1980.* Louvain-la-Neuve: Presses Universitaires de Louvain, 1981.

Bianga bin Waruzi. "Peasant, State and Rural Development in Postindependent Zaire: A

Case Study of 'Reforme Rurale' 1970–1980 and Its Implications." Ph.D. diss., University of Wisconsin-Madison, 1982.

Biebuyck, Daniel. "La société Kumu face au Kitawala." *Zaire* 11 (1957): 7–40.

Bienen, Henry. "The State and Ethnicity: Integrative Formulas in Africa." In *State versus Ethnic Claims: African Policy Dilemmas*, edited by Donald Rothchild and Victor A. Olorunsola, 100–26. Boulder, Colo.: Westview, 1983.

Birmingham, David, and Phyllis M. Martin, eds. *History of Central Africa.* 2 vols. London: Longman, 1983.

Bokonga Ekanga Botombele. *Cultural Policy in the Republic of Zaire.* Paris: UNESCO, 1976.

Borel, Philippe. "Divisions et faiblesses d'une opposition privée de stratégie politique." *Monde diplomatique*, September 1981.

Brett, E. A. *Colonialism and Underdevelopment in East Africa: The Politics of Economic Change 1919–1939.* New York: NOK, 1973.

Buana Kabue. *Citoyen Président: Lettre ouverte au Président Mobutu Sese Seko . . . et aux autres.* Paris: L'Harmattan, 1978.

Buana Kabue and C. K. Lumuna Sando. "Introduction à la politique zairoise." In *Mobutu Sese Seko, Le Procès: Deuxième Tribunal Russel (Tribunal Permanent des Peuples)*, edited by C. K. Lumuna Sando and Buana Kabue, 19–60. Brussels: A.F.R.I.C.A. [Association pour la Formation, la Recherche et l'Information sur le Centre de l'Afrique] pour l'Institut de l'Afrique Centrale, 1982.

Buyseniers, Rob. *L'église zairoise au service de quelle nation?* Brussels: A.F.R.I.C.A., 1980.

Cabral, Amilcar. *Return to the Source: Selected Speeches.* New York: Monthly Review Press, 1973.

Callaghy, Thomas M. "State Formation and Absolutism in Comparative Perspective: Seventeenth Century France and Mobutu Sese Seko's Zaire." Ph.D. diss., University of California, Berkeley, 1979.

⸻. "State-Subject Communication in Zaire: Domination and the Concept of Domain Consensus." *Journal of Modern African Studies* 18 (1980): 469–92.

⸻. *The State-Society Struggle: Zaire in Comparative Perspective.* New York: Columbia University Press, 1984.

⸻. "The International Community and Zaire's Debt Crisis." In *The Crisis in Zaire: Myths and Realities*, edited by Nzongola-Ntalaja, 221–43. Trenton, N.J.: Africa World Press, 1986.

Camara, Sylvain. "Le Zaire et la puissance: Deuxième partie." *Revue française d'études politiques africaines* 18 (1983): 38–61.

Campbell, Bonnie. "The Ivory Coast." In *West African States: Failure and Promise; A Study in Comparative Politics*, edited by John Dunn, 66–116. Cambridge: Cambridge University Press, 1978.

Centre National de Documentation (CND). Bumba, "Rapport périodique du 10 au 18 octobre 1968," 18 October 1968.

⸻. Bumba, "Rapport périodique arreté au 25 septembre 1969," 25 September 1969.

⸻. Mobayi-Mbongo, "Rapport périodique du 1er au 15 décembre 1973," 15 December 1973.

⸻. Bumba, "Rapport de sécurité," 12 August 1974.

⸻. Bumba, "Situation journalière," 16 September 1974.

Chanock, Martin. *Law, Custom and Social Order: The Colonial Experience in Malawi and Zambia* (Cambridge: Cambridge University Press, 1985.

Chazan, Naomi. "Political Culture and Socialization to Politics: A Ghanaian Case." *Review of Politics* 40 (1978): 3–31.

⸻. *An Anatomy of Ghanaian Politics: Managing Political Recession, 1969–1982.* Boulder, Colo: Westview, 1983.

Chomé, Jules. *L'ascension de Mobutu: Du sergent Désiré au Général Sese Seko.* Paris: Maspero, 1979.

Cikuru Ng'ashala Batumike. "Une descente aux enfers ou la montagne du désespoir: Témoignage." *Info Zaire*, no. 39 (1983): 4–32.

Cohen, Abner. *Two-Dimensional Man: An Essay on the Anthropology of Power and Symbolism in Complex Society.* Berkeley and Los Angeles: University of California Press, 1974.

_____. *The Politics of Elite Culture: Explorations in the Dramaturgy of Power in a Modern African Society.* Berkeley and Los Angeles: University of California Press, 1981.

Cohen, Michael A. *Urban Policy and Political Conflict in Africa: A Study of the Ivory Coast.* Chicago: University of Chicago Press, 1974.

Cohen, Robin. "Class in Africa: Analytical Problems and Perspectives." In *The Socialist Register 1972*, edited by Ralph Miliband and John Savile, 231–55. London: Merlin, 1972.

Cohen, Ronald, and Elman R. Service, eds. *Origins of the State: The Anthropology of Political Evolution.* Philadelphia: Institute for the Study of Human Issues, 1978.

Cohen, William B. "The Colonized as Child: British and French Colonial Rule." *African Historical Studies* 3 (1970): 427–31.

Comité Zaire. *Zaire: Le dossier de la recolonisation.* Paris: L'Harmattan, 1978.

_____. *Zaire: Une aide qui tue.* Brussels: Comité Zaire, 1981.

_____. "Les droits de l'homme et les libertés." In *Mobutu Sese Seko, Le Procès: Deuxième Tribunal Russel (Tribunal Permanent des Peuples)*, edited by C. K. Lumuna Sando and Buana Kabue, 102–11. Brussels: A.F.R.I.C.A. pour l'Institut de l'Afrique Centrale, 1982.

Comte, Gilbert. "Treize années d'histoire." *Revue française d'études politiques africaines* 8 (1973): 39–57.

Congo belge. Inspection Générale de l'Enseignement. *Instructions pour les inspecteurs provinciaux de l'enseignement relatives à l'organisation et au fonctionnement des écoles normales.* Boma: Imprimerie du Congo belge, mai 1929.

_____. *Instructions pour les inspecteurs provinciaux relatives aux programmes à suivre dans les différentes écoles et à leur interprétation.* Leo-Kalina: Imprimerie du Gouvernment, n.d. (1929?).

_____. *Instructions relatives aux programmes à suivre et aux méthodes à employer dans les écoles de la colonie.* Leo-Kalina: Imprimerie du Gouvernment, 1931.

_____. Service de l'Enseignement. *Organisation de l'enseignement libre subsidé pour indigènes avec le concours des sociétés de missions chrétiennes; enseignement général pour garçons; programme d'études.* 1948.

_____. *Statistiques relatives à l'année 1959; Bulletin annuel des statistique du Congo belge 1959.* Cambridge: Chadwyck-Healy, 1981.

Coordination Régionale des Ecoles Conventionnées Catholiques. "Réflections," 12 January 1984. *Info Zaire*, nos. 41–42 (1984): 13–19.

Corin, Ellen. "Le père comme modèle de différentiation dans uns société clanique matrilinéaire (Yansi, Congo-Kinshasa)." *Psychopathologie africaine* 7 (1971): 185–224.

_____. "Vers une réappropriation de la dimension individuelle en psychologie africaine." *Canadian Journal of African Studies* 14 (1980): 135–56.

Coulson, Andrew. *Tanzania: A Political Economy.* Oxford: Clarendon, 1982.

Crabb, John H. *The Legal System of Congo-Kinshasa.* Charlottesville, Va.: Michie, 1970.

Cross, Sholto. "The Watch Tower Movement in South Central Africa, 1908–1945." D.Phil. thesis, Oxford University, 1973.

_____. "Social History and Millenarial Movements: The Watch Tower in South Central Africa." *Social Compass* 24 (1977): 83–95.

_____ . "Kitawala, Conspiracies, and the Sûreté: An Historiological Enquiry." *Enquêtes et documents d'histoire africaine* 2 (1977): 67–85.
Crozier, Michel. *The Bureaucratic Phenomenon.* Chicago: University of Chicago Press, 1964.
Cruise O'Brien, Donal. *The Mourides of Senegal: The Political and Economic Organization of an Islamic Brotherhood.* Oxford: Clarendon, 1971.
Decalo, Samuel. "Regionalism, Political Decay, and Civil Strife in Chad." *Journal of Modern African Studies* 18 (1980): 23–56.
De Craemer, Willy, Jan Vansina, and Renée Fox. "Religious Movements in Central Africa: A Theoretical Study." *Comparative Studies in Society and History* 18 (1976): 458–75.
D'Hondt, W., M. Magabe, and G. Wehmuller. "La perception du rôle du père par les adolescents de la ville de Bukavu." *Cahiers du CEDAF*, no. 8 (1979): 18–37.
Diamond, Larry. "Nigeria in Search of Democracy." *Foreign Affairs* 62 (1984): 905–27.
"Discours d'orientation prononcé par le Citoyen Madrandele Tanzi, Directeur Politique du M.P.R. lors de l'installation de la commission chargée de la réforme administrative." In *Les réformes administratives au Zaire (1972–1973)*, edited by Mpinga-Kasenda and D. J. Gould, 35–42. Kinshasa: Presses Universitaires du Zaire, 1975.
Dittmer, Lowell. "Political Culture and Political Symbolism: Toward a Theoretical Synthesis." *World Politics* 29 (1977): 552–83.
Droogers, André. "Kimbanguism at the Grass Roots: Beliefs in a Local Kimbanguist Church." *Journal of Religion in Africa* 11 (1980): 188–211.
Durieux, André. "Exposé descriptif et synthétique des institutions politiques, administratives et judiciaires du Congo Belge et du Ruanda-Urundi." In *Encyclopédie du Congo Belge*, 3 vols., 3:515–54. Brussels: Bieleveld, n.d. (1950?).
Eckstein, Harry. "A Theory of Stable Democracy." Appendix B of *Division and Cohesion in Democracy: A Study of Norway*, 223–88. Princeton: Princeton University Press, 1966.
_____ . *The Natural History of Congruence Theory.* Monograph Series in World Affairs, 18:2. Denver: University of Colorado, 1980.
Eckstein, Harry, and Ted Robert Gurr. *Patterns of Authority: A Structural Basis for Political Inquiry.* New York: John Wiley & Sons, 1975.
Eisenstadt, S. N., and René Lemarchand, eds. *Political Clientelage, Patronage and Development.* Beverly Hills, Calif.: Sage, 1981.
Elikia M'Bokolo. "La triple stratification zairoise." *Monde diplomatique*, November 1981.
Engulu Baangampongo. "Vigilance et engagement révolutionnaire." Exposé aux cadres de la JMPR en session spéciale de l'Institut Makanda Kabobi, N'Sélé, 1 March 1975.
"Entretiens avec le PRP dans le maquis du Zaire." *Info Zaire*, no. 37 (1982–83): 3–25.
Epstein, A. L. *Ethos and Identity: Three Studies in Ethnicity.* London: Tavistock, 1978.
Erny, Pierre. *Sur les sentiers de l'université: Autobiographies d'étudiants zairois.* Paris: La Pensée Universelle, 1977.
_____ . *Ecoles d'église en Afrique noire: Poids du passé et perspectives d'avenir.* Fribourg: Nouvelle Revue de Science Missionnaire, 1982.
Fabian, Johannes. "Missions and the Colonization of African Languages: Developments in the Former Belgian Congo." *Canadian Journal of African Studies* 17 (1983): 165–87.
Fanon, Frantz. *Les damnés de la terre.* Paris: Maspero, 1968.
Fauré, Y.-A. and J.-F. Médard. "Classe dominante ou classe dirigeante?" In *Etat et bourgeoisie en Côte-d'Ivoire*, edited by Y.-A. Fauré and J.-F. Médard, 125–47. Paris: Karthala, 1982.
_____ , eds. *Etat et bourgeoisie en Côte-d'Ivoire.* Paris: Karthala, 1982.
Fetter, Bruce. "L'Union Minière du Haut-Katanga, 1920–1940: La naissance d'une sous-culture totalitaire." *Cahiers du CEDAF*, no. 6 (1973).

Fields, Karen E. *Revival and Rebellion in Colonial Central Africa.* Princeton: Princeton University Press, 1985.

Forces Armées Zairoises. *L'ère de l'armée nouvelle.* Kinshasa: Cabinet du Département de la Défense, 1973.

Freyhold, Michaela von. *Ujamaa Villages in Tanzania: Analysis of a Social Experiment.* New York: Monthly Review Press, 1979.

Gann, L. H. and Peter Duignan. *The Rulers of Belgian Africa 1884–1914.* Princeton: Princeton University Press, 1979.

Geertz, Clifford. *Negara: The Theatre State in Nineteenth Century Bali.* Princeton: Princeton University Press, 1980.

Gellner, Ernest. *Nations and Nationalism.* Ithaca: Cornell University Press, 1983.

Gérard, Jacques E. *Les fondements syncrétiques du Kitawala.* Brussels: CRISP [Centre de Recherche et d'Information Socio-politiques] and Le Livre Africain, 1969.

Gérard-Libois, Jules, ed. *Congo 1966.* Brussels: CRISP, 1967.

Gérard-Libois, Jules, and Jean Van Lierde, eds. *Congo 1964.* Brussels: CRISP, 1965.

———, eds. *Congo 1965.* Brussels: CRISP, 1966.

Gérard-Libois, Jules, and Benoît Verhaegen, eds. *Congo 1960.* 3 vols. Brussels: CRISP, 1961.

Giddens, Anthony. *A Contemporary Critique of Historical Materialism.* Vol. 1, *Power, Property and the State.* Berkeley and Los Angeles: University of California Press, 1981.

Goovaerts, Leo. "L'église et l'état au Zaire à l'épreuve de l'authenticité." *Cultures et développement* 7 (1975): 243–82.

Gould, David J. *Bureaucratic Corruption in the Third World: The Case of Zaire.* New York: Pergamon, 1980.

———. "Patrons and Clients: The Role of the Military in Zairian Politics." In *The Performance of Soldiers as Governors: African Politics and the African Military,* edited by Isaac James Mowoe, 465–511. Washington, D.C.: University Press of America, 1980.

Gramsci, Antonio. *Selections from the Prison Notebooks of Antonio Gramsci.* Edited and translated by Quintin Hoare and Geoffrey Newell Smith. New York: International Publishers, 1971.

Gran, Guy, ed. *Zaire: The Political Economy of Underdevelopment.* New York: Praeger, 1979.

Greenberg, Stanley B. *Race and State in Capitalist Development: Comparative Perspectives.* New Haven: Yale University Press, 1980.

Greenland, Jeremy. "Western Education in Burundi 1916–1973: The Consequences of Instrumentalism." *Cahiers du CEDAF,* nos. 2–3 (1980).

Hecht, Robert M. "The Ivory Coast Economic 'Miracle': What Benefits for Peasant Farmers?" *Journal of Modern African Studies* 21 (1983): 25–53.

Hekken, P. M. van, and H. U. E. Thoden van Velzen. *Land Scarcity and Rural Inequality in Tanzania.* The Hague: Mouton, 1972.

Hilton, Anne. "Family and Kinship among the Kongo South of the Zaire River from the Sixteenth to the Nineteenth Centuries." *Journal of African History* 24 (1983): 189–206.

Hirschman, Albert O. "Exit, Voice, and the State." *World Politics* 31 (1978): 90–107.

Hooker, J. R. "Witnesses and Watchtower in the Rhodesias and Nyasaland." *Journal of African History* 6 (1965): 91–106.

Horowitz, Donald L. *Ethnic Groups in Conflict.* Berkeley and Los Angeles: University of California Press, 1985.

Hulstaert, G. *Les Mongo: Aperçu général.* Tervuren: Musée Royal de l'Afrique Centrale, 1961.

———. "La société politique Nkundo." *Etudes zairoises,* no. 2 (1974): 85–107.

Hyden, Goran. *Beyond Ujamaa in Tanzania: Underdevelopment and an Uncaptured Peasantry.* Berkeley and Los Angeles: University of California Press, 1980.
_____. *No Shortcuts to Progress: African Development Management in Perspective.* Berkeley and Los Angeles: University of California Press, 1983.
Hyden, Goran, Robert Jackson, and John Okumu, eds. *Development Administration: The Kenyan Experience.* Nairobi: Oxford University Press, 1970.
Isambert-Jamati, Viviane. "L'autorité dans l'éducation française." *Archives européennes de sociologie* 6 (1965): 149–66.
Jackson, Robert H., and Carl G. Rosberg. "Why Africa's Weak States Persist: The Empirical and the Juridical in Statehood." *World Politics* 35 (1982): 1–24.
_____. *Personal Rule in Black Africa: Prince, Autocrat, Prophet, Tyrant.* Berkeley and Los Angeles: University of California Press, 1982.
Janssens, Emile. *Au fil d'une vie.* Brussels: Pierre de Mayère, 1973.
_____. *Histoire de la Force Publique.* Brussels: Ghesquière & Partners, 1979.
Jessop, Bob. "On Recent Marxist Theories of Law, the State, and Juridico-Political Ideology." *International Journal of the Sociology of Law* 8 (1980): 339–68.
_____. *The Capitalist State: Marxist Theory and Methods.* New York: New York University Press, 1982.
Jewsiewicki, B[ogumil]. "L'expérience d'un Etat-Providence en Afrique noire." *Historical Reflections* 3 (1976): 79–103.
_____. "Political Consciousness among African Peasants in the Belgian Congo." *Review of African Political Economy* 19 (1980): 23–32.
_____. "L'état et l'accumulation primitive coloniale: La formation du môde de production colonial au Zaire." *Revue française d'histoire d'outre-mer* 68 (1981): 71–91.
_____. "Modernisation ou destruction du village africain: L'économie politique de la 'modernisation agricole' au Congo Belge." *Cahiers du CEDAF*, no. 5 (1983).
_____. "Rural Society and the Belgian Colonial Economy." In *History of Central Africa,* 2 vols., edited by David Birmingham and Phyllis M. Martin, 2:95–125. London: Longman, 1983.
_____. "Introduction." *Canadian Journal of African Studies* 18 (1984): 8–12.
Jewsiewicki, B., and Mumbanza mwa Bawele. "The Social Context of Slavery in Equatorial Africa during the 19th and 20th Centuries." In *The Ideology of Slavery in Africa,* edited by Paul E. Lovejoy, 73–98. Beverly Hills, Calif.: Sage, 1981.
Joseph, Richard A. "Ruben Um Nyobe and the 'Kamerun' Rebellion." *African Affairs* 73 (1974): 428–48.
_____. "Democratization under Military Tutelage: Crisis and Consensus in the Nigerian 1979 Elections." *Comparative Politics* 14 (1981): 75–100.
Kabanga (Monsignor). *Je suis un homme: Lettre pastorale de Carême 1976.* Lubumbashi: Archdiocese of Lubumbashi, March 1976.
Kabwit, Ghislain C. "Zaire: The Roots of the Continuing Crisis." *Journal of Modern African Studies* 17 (1979): 381–407.
Kalck, Pierre. *Central African Republic: A Failure in Decolonization.* Translated by Barbara Thomson. New York: Praeger, 1971.
Kalonga, Ali. *Le mal zairois.* Brussels: Fati, 1978.
Kamitatu-Massamba, Cléophas. *La grande mystification du Congo-Kinshasa: Les crimes de Mobutu.* Paris: Maspero, 1971.
_____. *Zaire: Le pouvoir à la portée du peuple.* Paris: L'Harmattan, 1979.
Kanynda Lusanga. "La décentralisation territoriale zairoise à l'épreuve de la théorie et des faits." *Cahiers du CEDAF*, no. 2 (1984).
Kanyonga Mobateli. *Dix ans de régime Mobutu ou les années les plus sombre du Congo/Zaire.* Monthey, Switzerland: Ivy, 1976.
Kaplan, Irving, ed. *Zaire: A Country Study.* Washington, D.C.: American University, Foreign Area Studies, 1979.

Kaplinsky, Raphael. "Technical Change and the Multinational Corporation: Some British Multinationals in Kenya." In *Readings on the Multinational Corporation in Kenya*, edited by Raphael Kaplinsky, 201-60. Nairobi: Oxford University Press, 1978.

Kapsuscinski, Ryszard. *The Emperor: Downfall of an Autocrat.* Translated by William R. Brand and Katarzyna Mrockowska-Brand. New York: Vintage Books, 1983.

Karimi, Joseph, and Philip Ochieng. *The Kenyatta Succession.* Nairobi: Transafrica, 1980.

Kaseba, A. *"Notre foi en l'homme image de Dieu": Déclaration du Comité Permanent des Evêques du Zaire.* Kinshasa: Editions du Secrétariat Général de l'Episcopat, 1981.

Kasfir, Nelson. *The Shrinking Political Arena: Participation and Ethnicity in African Politics, with a Case Study of Uganda.* Berkeley and Los Angeles: University of California Press, 1976.

_____. "Explaining Ethnic Participation." *World Politics* 31 (1979): 365-88.

Kaufmann, Robert. *Millénarisme et acculturation.* Brussels: Editions de l'Institut de Sociologie de l'Université Libre de Bruxelles, 1964.

Kazumba K. Tshiteya. "Le discours savant et le développement du sous-développement au Zaire." *Canadian Journal of African Studies* 18 (1984): 59-60.

Keegan, John. *The Face of Battle.* Harmondsworth: Penguin, 1976.

Keller, Edmond J. "Ethiopia: Revolution, Class, and the National Question." *African Affairs* 80 (1981): 519-49.

Kengo wa Dondo. "L'organisation et le fonctionnement de la justice dans la République du Zaire." *Revue juridique du Zaire* 49 (1973): 245-60.

Kenyatta, Jomo. *Facing Mount Kenya: The Tribal Life of the Gikuyu.* New York: Vintage Books, n.d.

Keyes, Charles F., ed. *Ethnic Change.* Seattle: University of Washington Press, 1981.

Kimbana Lulu Kiladio. "Témoignage d'un ancien membre de la police politique de Mobutu." In *Mobutu Sese Seko, Le Procès: Deuxième Tribunal Russel (Tribunal Permanent des Peuples)*, edited by C. K. Lumuna Sando and Buana Kabue, 79-80. Brussels: A.F.R.I.C.A. pour l'Institut de l'Afrique Centrale, 1982.

Kita Kyankenge Masandi. *Colonisation et enseignement: Cas du Zaire avant 1960.* Bukavu: Editions du CERUKI, 1982.

Kitching, Gavin. *Class and Economic Change in Kenya: The Making of an African Petite Bourgeoisie 1905-1970.* New Haven: Yale University Press, 1980.

Kofele-Kale, Ndiva. "The Impact of Environment on National Political Culture in Cameroon." In *Values, Identities, and National Integration: Empirical Research in Africa*, edited by John N. Paden, 151-72. Evanston, Ill.: Northwestern University Press, 1980.

_____. "Ethnicity, Regionalism and Political Power: A Post-mortem of Ahidjo's Cameroon." In *The Political Economy of Cameroon*, edited by Michael G. Schatzberg and I. William Zartman, 53-82. New York: Praeger, 1986.

Kuama Mobwa. "L'extension du Kitawala à la Province de l'Equateur." *Cahiers de l'I.S.P. Gombe*, série B 1 (1980): 75-101.

Kwitney, Jonathan. *Endless Enemies: The Making of an Unfriendly World.* New York: Congdon & Weed, 1984.

"La deuxième révolution mobutienne." *Zaire* (Kinshasa), 6 January 1975, 20-22.

Lagergren, David. *Mission and State in the Congo: A Study of the Relations between Protestant Missions and the Congo Independent State Authorities with Special Reference to Equator District, 1885-1903.* Translated by Owen N. Lee. Uppsala: Gleerup, 1970.

Langdon, Steven W. "The Multinational Corporation in the Kenya Political Economy." In *Readings on the Multinational Corporation in Kenya*, edited by Raphael Kaplinsky, 134-200. Nairobi: Oxford University Press, 1978.

_____. *Multinational Corporations in the Political Economy of Kenya.* New York: St. Martin's, 1981.

"Le discours du Président-Fondateur du Mouvement Populaire de la Révolution à l'occasion de l'ouverture de l'Institut MAKANDA KABOBI à la Cité du Parti le 15 août 1974." *Etudes zairoises*, no. 2 (1974): 197–207.

"L'église et l'état." *Info Zaire*, no. 3 (1979): 6–11.

Lemarchand, René. "Bringing Factions Back into the State." In *The Crisis in Zaire: Myths and Realities*, edited by Nzongola-Ntalaja, 51–66. Trenton, N.J.: Africa World Press, 1986.

Le militaire et la révolution (le soldat et le peuple); texte de la conférence donnée à l'Ecole du Parti, l'Institut Makanda Kabobi, IIè session ordinaire, par le Citoyen Général Molongya Mayikusa, Directeur Général de la Défense Nationale, le 8 mai 1975. Kinshasa: République du Zaire, Département de la Défense Nationale, 1975.

Le MPR a huit ans. Kinshasa: Département de l'Orientation Nationale, 1975.

Leo, Christopher. *Land and Class in Kenya*. Toronto: University of Toronto Press, 1984.

Leslie, Winsome J. "The World Bank and Zaire." In *The Crisis in Zaire: Myths and Realities*, edited by Nzongola-Ntalaja, 245–63. Trenton, N.J.: Africa World Press, 1986.

"Les massacres de Katekelayi et de Luamuela (Kasai Oriental)." *Politique africaine* 6 (1982): 72–106.

"Les relations entre l'église et l'état au Zaire." *Etudes africaines du CRISP*, no. 145 (28 December 1972).

"Lettre ouverte au Citoyen Président-Fondateur du Mouvement Populaire de la Révolution, Président de la République par un groupe de parlementaires." In "La fronde parlementaire au Zaire," edited by Jean-François Bayart, 94–139. *Politique africaine* 3 (1981): 90–139.

Lewis, I. M. "The Politics of the 1969 Somalia Coup." *Journal of Modern African Studies* 10 (1972): 383–408.

_____ . *A Modern History of Somalia: Nation and State in the Horn of Africa*. London: Longman, 1980.

Leys, Colin. *Underdevelopment in Kenya: The Political Economy of Neo-colonialism, 1964–1971*. Berkeley and Los Angeles: University of California Press, 1974.

_____ . "Capital Accumulation, Class Formation, and Dependency—The Significance of the Kenyan Case." In *The Socialist Register 1978*, edited by Ralph Miliband and John Savile, 248–65. London: Merlin, 1978.

Likulia Bolongo. *Droit pénal militaire zairois*. Vol. 1, *L'organisation et la compétence des juridictions des forces armées*. Paris: Librairie Générale de Droit et de Jurisprudence, 1977.

Lokumba Baruti. "Structure et fonctionnement des institutions politiques traditionnelles chez les Lokele (Haut-Zaire)." *Cahiers du CEDAF*, no. 8 (1972).

Lonsdale, John. "States and Social Processes in Africa: A Historiographical Survey." *African Studies Review* 24 (1981): 139–225.

Lovens, Maurice. "La révolte de Masisi-Lubutu (Congo Belge, janvier-mai 1944)." *Cahiers du CEDAF*, nos. 3–4 (1974).

Lumuna Sando, C. K. *Zaire: Quel changement pour quelles structures? Misère de l'opposition et faillite de l'Etat*. Brussels: A.F.R.I.C.A., 1980.

_____ . *Lovanium: Le Kasala du 4 juin*. Brussels: A.F.R.I.C.A., 1982.

Lux, André. "Les travailleurs ruraux du Mayombe, ébauche d'une classe sociale?" *Canadian Journal of African Studies* 7 (1973): 433–54.

MacGaffey, Janet. "Class Relations in a Dependent Economy: Businessmen and Businesswomen in Kisangani, Zaire." Ph.D. diss., Bryn Mawr College, 1981.

_____ . "How to Survive and Become Rich amidst Devastation: The Second Economy in Zaire." *African Affairs* 82 (1983): 351–66.

_____ . "Fending-for-Yourself: The Organization of the Second Economy in Zaire." In

The Crisis in Zaire: Myths and Realities, edited by Nzongola-Ntalaja, 141–56. Trenton, N.J.: Africa World Press, 1986.

_____. *Entrepreneurs and Parasites: The Struggle for Indigenous Capitalism in Zaire.* Cambridge: Cambridge University Press, 1988.

MacGaffey, Wyatt. "The Policy of National Integration in Zaire." *Journal of Modern African Studies* 20 (1982): 87–105.

_____. "The Implantation of Kimbanguism in Kisangani, Zaire." *Journal of African History* 23 (1982): 381–94.

_____. *Modern Kongo Prophets: Religion in a Plural Society.* Bloomington: Indiana University Press, 1983.

_____. "Lineage Structure, Marriage and the Family amongst the Central Bantu." *Journal of African History* 24 (1983): 173–87.

_____. *Religion and Society in Central Africa: The BaKongo of Lower Zaire.* Chicago: University of Chicago Press, 1986.

Mahieu, W. de. "Les Komo et le Kitawala." *Cahiers des religions africaines* 10 (1976): 51–66.

Malula, J. A. (Cardinal). *L'église de Dieu qui est à Kinshasa vous parle.* Kinshasa: Editions St. Paul d'Afrique, 1976.

Malulu Mitwensil and Kambidi Nsia-Kinguem. "Le public et l'administration en République du Zaire." *Zaire-Afrique*, no. 143 (1980): 165–80.

Mamdani, Mahmood. *Imperialism and Fascism in Uganda.* London: Heinemann, 1983.

March, James G. and Herbert A. Simon. *Organizations.* New York: John Wiley, 1958.

Marenin, Otwin. "Policing African States: Toward a Critique." *Comparative Politics* 14 (1982): 379–96.

Markakis, John. *Ethiopia: Anatomy of a Traditional Polity.* Oxford: Clarendon Press, 1974.

Markowitz, Marvin D. *Cross and Sword: The Political Role of Christian Missions in the Belgian Congo, 1908–1960.* Stanford: Hoover Institution Press, 1973.

Marks, Shula, and Richard Rathbone. "The History of the Family in Africa: Introduction." *Journal of African History* 24 (1983): 145–61.

Martin, Phyllis M. "The Violence of Empire." In *History of Central Africa*, 2 vols., edited by David Birmingham and Phyllis M. Martin, 2:1–26. London: Longman, 1983.

Marx, Karl. *The Eighteenth Brumaire of Louis Bonaparte.* In *Surveys From Exile*, translated by Ben Fowkes, edited by David Fernbach, 143–249. New York: Vintage Books, 1976.

Marx, Karl and Frederick Engels. *The German Ideology.* Edited by C. J. Arthur. New York: International Publishers, 1970.

Mazrui, Ali A. "The Resurrection of the Warrior Tradition in African Political Culture." *Journal of Modern African Studies* 13 (1975): 67–84.

Mbu Etonga. "An Imperial Presidency: A Study of Presidential Power in Cameroon." In *An African Experiment in Nation Building: The Bilingual Cameroon Republic since Reunification*, edited by Ndiva Kofele-Kale, 133–57. Boulder, Colo.: Westview, 1980.

M'buze-Nsomi Lobwanabi. *Aux sources d'une révolution.* Kinshasa: Les Presses Africaines, 1977.

Meillassoux, Claude. "The Social Organisation of the Peasantry: The Economic Basis of Kinship." *Journal of Peasant Studies* 1 (1973): 81–90.

_____. *Maidens, Meal and Money: Capitalism and the Domestic Community.* Cambridge: Cambridge University Press, 1981.

Mercier, Paul. "Remarques sur la signification du 'tribalisme' en Afrique noire." *Cahiers internationaux de sociologie* 31 (1961): 61–80.

Miller, Joseph C. "Lineages, Ideology, and the History of Slavery in Western Central

Africa." In *The Ideology of Slavery in Africa*, edited by Paul E. Lovejoy, 41–71. Beverly Hills, Calif,: Sage, 1981.

Mitchell, J. Clyde. *The Kalela Dance: Aspects of Social Relations among Urban Africans in Northern Rhodesia.* Rhodes-Livingston Institute Paper, No. 27. Manchester: Manchester University Press, 1956.

Mobutu Sese Seko. "Address to the Conseil National Extraordinaire, Dakar, 14 February 1971." In *Ideologies of Liberation in Black Africa 1856–1970*, edited by J. Ayo Langley, 722–33. London: Rex Collings, 1979.

"Mon calvaire à la C.N.R.I." *Info Zaire*, nos. 41–42 (1984): 29–30.

Mottoulle, L. *Politique sociale de l'Union Minière du Haut-Katanga pour sa main d'oeuvre indigène et ses résultats au cours de vingt années d'application.* Brussels: Institut Royal Colonial Belge, Section des Sciences Morales et Politiques, 14:3, 1946.

Mpinga-Kasenda. *L'administration publique du Zaire: L'impact du milieu socio-politique sur sa structure et fonctionnement.* Paris: Pedone, 1973.

Muamba Kanyinda. *La pourriture.* Kinshasa: Editions Edimaf, 1978.

Mudimbe, V. Y. *L'odeur du père: Essai sur des limites de la science et de la vie en Afrique noire.* Paris: Présence Africaine, 1982.

Mulyumba wa Mamba Itongwa. "Aperçu sur la structure politique des Balega-Basile." *Cahiers du CEDAF*, no. 1 (1978).

Mumbanza mwa Bawele. "Y a-t-il des Bangala? Origine et extension du terme." *Zaire-Afrique*, no. 78 (1973): 471–83.

――――. "Les établissements d'enseignement public à l'époque de l'E.I.C.: La colonie scolaire de Nouvelle-Anvers (1892–1913)." *Etudes d'histoire africaine* 8 (1976): 87–129.

Mwabila Malela. *Travail et travailleurs au Zaire: Essai sur la conscience ouvrière du prolétariat urbain de Lubumbashi.* Kinshasa: Presses Universitaires du Zaire, Rectorat, Kinshasa, UNAZA, 1979.

――――. "Pour une relecture de la sociologie à la lumière de la théorie de dépendance." In *La dépendance de l'Afrique et les moyens d'y remédier: Actes de la 4è session du congrès international des études africaines, Kinshasa, 12–16 décembre 1978*, edited by V. Y. Mudimbe, 263–70. Paris: Agence de Coopération Culturelle et Technique and Berger-Levrault, 1980.

Mwene-Batende. "Le Kitawala dans l'évolution socio-politique récente: Cas du groupe Belukela dans la ville du Kisangani." *Cahiers des religions africaines* 10 (1976): 81–105.

――――. *Mouvements messianiques et protestation sociale: Le cas du Kitawala chez les Kumu du Zaire.* Kinshasa: Faculté de Théologie Catholique, 1982.

Naipaul, V. S. *A Bend in the River.* New York: Alfred A. Knopf, 1979.

Newbury, Catharine. "Ebutumwa Bw'Emiogo: The Tyranny of Cassava, A Women's Tax Revolt in Eastern Zaire." *Canadian Journal of African Studies* 18 (1984): 35–54.

――――. "Survival Strategies in Rural Zaire: Realities of Coping with Crisis." In *The Crisis in Zaire: Myths and Realities*, edited by Nzongola-Ntalaja, 99–112. Trenton, N.J.: Africa World Press, 1986.

Nguza Karl-i-Bond. "Dix ans de pouvoir: Idées-forces du Mobutisme." *Studia Diplomatica* 39 (1976): 3–39.

――――. "Testimony." In *Political and Economic Situation in Zaire—Fall 1981*, 1–30. U.S. Congress, House, Committee on Foreign Affairs, Subcommittee on Africa, 97th Cong., 1st session, 15 September 1981.

――――. "Report on the Situation of the Zaire Armed Forces Submitted by Former Prime Minister Nguza." In *Political and Economic Situation in Zaire—Fall 1981*, 37–51. U.S. Congress, House, Committee on Foreign Affairs, Subcommittee on Africa, 97th Cong., 1st session, 15 September 1981.

――――. *Mobutu: Ou l'incarnation du mal zairois.* London: Rex Collings, 1982.

_____. "Déclaration de Nguza Karl-i-Bond à Erwin Blumenthal." In *Mobutu Sese Seko, Le Procès: Deuxième Tribunal Russel (Tribunal Permanent des Peuples)*, edited by C. K. Lumuna Sando and Buana Kabue, 96–101. Brussels: A.F.R.I.C.A. pour l'Institut de l'Afrique Centrale, 1982.

_____. "Tout un peuple est pris en ôtage." In *Mobutu Sese Seko, Le Procès: Deuxième Tribunal Russel (Tribunal Permanent des Peuples)*, edited by C. K. Lumuna Sando and Buana Kabue, 71–74. Brussels: A.F.R.I.C.A. pour l'Institut de l'Afrique Centrale, 1982.

_____. *Le Zaire de demain: Réflexion pour la IIIè République du Congo*. Antwerp: Soethoudt & Co., 1983.

Njangu Canda-Ciri. "Le Kimbanguisme et le Kitawala: Etude comparative." *Antennes, Revue de CERUKI (Centre de Recherches Universitaires du Kivu)* 5 (1977): 25–39.

Nkiere Bokuna Mpa-Osu. "La parenté comme système idéologique: Essai d'interprétation de l'ordre lignager chez les Basakata." Ph.D. diss., Université Catholique de Louvain, Institut des Sciences Politiques et Sociales, 1976–77.

Nyunda ya Rubango. "Les principales tendances du discours politiques zairois (1960–1965)." *Cahiers du CEDAF*, no. 7 (1980).

Nzongola-Ntalaja. "The Authenticity of Neocolonialism: Ideology and Class Struggle in Zaire." *Berkeley Journal of Sociology* 22 (1977–78): 115–30.

_____. "The Continuing Struggle for National Liberation in Zaire." *Journal of Modern African Studies* 17 (1979): 595–614.

_____. "Crisis and Change in Zaire, 1960–1985." In *The Crisis in Zaire: Myths and Realities*, edited by Nzongola-Ntalaja, 3–25. Trenton, N.J.: Africa World Press, 1986.

_____, ed. *The Crisis in Zaire: Myths and Realities*. Trenton, N.J.: Africa World Press, 1986.

Obbo, Christine. *African Women: Their Struggle for Economic Independence*. London: Zed, 1980.

Odungo Nyangayo. "Mobutu Jails Archbishop and Raps the Catholic Church." *New African*, no. 171 (December 1981): 31.

Onselin, Charles van. *Chibaro: African Mine Labour in Southern Rhodesia 1900–1933*. London: Pluto, 1976.

"Ordonnance no. 76-182 du 16 juillet 1976 complétant l'ordonnance no. 75-038 du 19 février 1975 portant statut de la Jeunesse du Mouvement Populaire de la Révolution."

"Ordonnance no. 69-159 du 9 août 1969 fixant les attributions et l'organisation du Centre National de Documentation."

Pachter, Elise Forbes. "Our Man in Kinshasa: U.S. Relations with Mobutu, 1970–1983, Patron Client Relations in the International Sphere." Ph.D. diss., School of Advanced International Studies, The Johns Hopkins University, 1987.

Parkin, Frank. *Marxism and Class Theory: A Bourgeois Critique*. New York: Columbia University Press, 1979.

Pauwels, J. M. "La réforme du droit civil au Zaire—Comment concilier tradition et développement?" *Journal of African Law* 17 (1973): 216–26.

_____. "Vingt années de législation zairoise 1960-1980." *Penant* 92 (1982): 6–31.

Pauwels, J. M., and Walter Pintens. *La législation zairoise relative au nom: Droit et authenticité africaine*. Brussels: Académie Royale des Sciences d'Outre-Mer, Classe des Sciences Morales et Politiques, Mémoires, n.s., 47:2, 1983.

Peace, Adrian J. *Choice, Class and Conflict: A Study of Southern Nigerian Factory Workers*. Atlantic Highlands, N.J.: Humanities, 1979.

Piron, P. *L'indépendance de la magistrature et le statut des magistrats*. Brussels: Académie Royale des Sciences Coloniales, Classe des Sciences Morales et Politiques, 5:5, 1956.

Poggi, Gianfranco. *The Development of the Modern State: An Historical Introduction.* Stanford: Stanford University Press, 1978.

Police Nationale. "Rapport mensuel de mars 1968 du sous-détachement Police Nationale de la Mongala," 24 April 1968.

––––––. "Rapport mensuel du mois de juin 1969," Lisala, 25 June 1969.

––––––. "Rapports mensuels d'avril 1968-février 1970 du sous-détachement Police Nationale de la Mongala."

––––––. "Rapport annuel 1971 du sous-détachement de la Mongala, Police Nationale du Zaire," 29 February 1972.

Poulantzas, Nicos. *State, Power, Socialism.* Translated by Patrick Camiller. London: Verso, 1980.

Price, Robert. "Politics and Culture in Contemporary Ghana: The Big-Man Small-Boy Syndrome." *Journal of African Studies* 1 (1974): 173–204.

Province de l'Equateur. *Conseil de Province 1954,* 1ère partie. "Allocution du Président, le Gouverneur de Province, M. De Ryck." 23 March 1954.

"Rapport annuel d'activités de la JMPR Mongala, exercice 1974," 5 January 1975.

"Rapport semestriel sur la marche de l'administration de la Zone de Bongandanga et les collectivités la composant," 15 December 1974.

"Rapport sur la situation à l'intérieur du Territoire de Lisala, mois de mars 1961," dossier no. 173, National Archives, Kinshasa.

Recueil d'instructions aux missionnaires publié par la conférence des supérieurs des missions catholiques du Congo belge. 6th ed. Louvain: J. Kuyl-Otto, 1930.

Reefe, Thomas Q. "The Societies of the Eastern Savanna." In *History of Central Africa,* 2 vols., edited by David Birmingham and Phyllis M. Martin, 1:160–204. London: Longman, 1983.

République du Zaire, Assemblée Nationale. *Annales Parlementaires.* Session ordinaire d'avril 1972, séance du 6 avril 1972.

––––––. Commission Permanente de l'Administration Publique. "Répartition des agents de l'état par grade, par département et région d'affectation." Computer printout, 24 October 1974.

Rivière, Claude. "Dynamique de la stratification sociale en Guinée." Thèse, Université de Paris V, 1975.

Rothchild, Donald, and Victor A. Olorunsola, eds. *State versus Ethnic Claims: African Policy Dilemmas.* Boulder, Colo.: Westview, 1983.

Rothschild, Joseph. *Ethnopolitics: A Conceptual Framework.* New York: Columbia University Press, 1981.

Royaume de Belgique, Chambre des Représentants. *Rapport sur l'administration du Congo Belge pendant l'année 1921.* Brussels: Chambre des Représentants, 1921.

––––––. *Rapport sur l'administration du Congo Belge pendant l'année 1954.* Brussels: Chambre des Représentants, 1954.

––––––. Ministère des Colonies, 2è Direction Générale. *Recueil à l'usage des fonctionnaires et des agents du service territorial au Congo Belge.* 5th ed. Brussels: Société Anonyme M. Wissenbruch, 1930.

Rubbens, Antoine. *L'indépendance des magistrats dans la République démocratique du Congo (Constitution-Loi-Statut).* Brussels: Académie Royale des Sciences d'Outre-Mer, Classe des Sciences Morales et Politiques, n.s. 34:4, 1966.

––––––. *Le droit judiciaire congolais.* Vol. 1, *Le pouvoir, l'organisation et la compétence judiciaires.* Kinshasa and Brussels: Université Lovanium and Ferd. Larcier, 1970.

Sabean, David Warren. "The History of the Family in Africa and Europe: Some Comparative Perspectives." *Journal of African History* 24 (1983): 163–71.

Sahlins, Marshall. "Poor Man, Rich Man, Big-Man, Chief: Political Types in Melanesia and Polynesia." *Comparative Studies in Society and History* 5 (1963): 285–303.

––––––. *Stone Age Economics.* New York: Aldine, 1972.

Sakombi Inongo. *Lettre ouverte à Nguza Karl-i-Bond*. France: n.p., 1982.

Salongo (Kinshasa), 1970–1983.

Samoff, Joel. "The Bureaucracy and the Bourgeoisie: Decentralization and Class Structure in Tanzania." *Comparative Studies in Society and History* 21 (1979): 30–62.

_____. "Class, Class Conflict, and the State in Africa." *Political Science Quarterly* 97 (1982): 105–27.

_____. "Education in Tanzania: Class Formation and Reproduction." *Journal of Modern African Studies* 17 (1979): 47–69.

Saul, John S. *The State and Revolution in Eastern Africa*. New York: Monthly Review Press, 1979.

Savoie, Jean. "L'église au Zaire: Dénoncer la corruption, cela comporte des risques." *La revue nouvelle*, nos. 5–6 (1982): 549–50.

Schatzberg, Michael G. Field Log. 5 October 1974 - 27 October 1975.

_____. Interviews. Lisala, Mbandaka, Kinshasa, nos. 1–73, 1974–75. Memorial Library, University of Wisconsin-Madison.

_____. "Fidélité au Guide: The J.M.P.R. in Zairian Schools." *Journal of Modern African Studies* 16 (1978): 417–31.

_____. "Conflict and Culture in African Education: Authority Patterns in a Cameroonian Lycée." *Comparative Education Review* 23 (1979): 52–65.

_____. *Politics and Class in Zaire: Bureaucracy, Business, and Beer in Lisala*. New York: Africana Publishing Company, 1980.

_____. "The Chiefs of Upoto: Political Encapsulation and the Transformation of Tradition in Northwestern Zaire." *Cultures et développement* 12 (1980): 235–69.

_____. "The State and the Economy: The 'Radicalization of the Revolution' in Mobutu's Zaire." *Canadian Journal of African Studies* 14 (1980): 239–57.

_____. "Ethnicity and Class at the Local Level: Bars and Bureaucrats in Lisala, Zaire." *Comparative Politics* 13 (1981): 461–78.

_____. "*Le mal zairois*: Why Policy Fails in Zaire." *African Affairs* 81 (1982): 337–48.

_____. "Zaire." In *The Political Economy of African Foreign Policy: Comparative Analysis*, edited by Timothy M. Shaw and Olajide Aluko, 283–318. Farnsborough: Gower, 1984.

_____. "The Metaphors of Father and Family." In *The Political Economy of Cameroon*, edited by Michael G. Schatzberg and I. William Zartman, 1–19. New York: Praeger, 1986.

_____. Review of *The Rise and Decline of the Zairian State*, by Crawford Young and Thomas Turner. *American Political Science Review* 80 (1986): 1389–90.

_____. "The Struggle for Space: The Dialectics of Autonomy in Zaire." Paper presented at the annual meeting of the African Studies Association, Madison, Wisconsin, 29 October - 2 November 1986.

Schildkrout, Enid. *People of the Zongo: The Transformation of Ethnic Identities in Ghana*. Cambridge: Cambridge University Press, 1978.

Schonfeld, William R. *Obedience and Revolt: The French Behavior toward Authority*. Beverly Hills, Calif.: Sage, 1976.

Scott, James C. *The Moral Economy of the Peasant: Rebellion and Subsistence in Southeast Asia*. New Haven: Yale University Press, 1976.

_____. *Weapons of the Weak: Everyday Forms of Class Resistance*. New Haven: Yale University Press, 1985.

Sennett, Richard. *Authority*. New York: Vintage Books, 1980.

Shaw, Bryant P. "*Force Publique, Force Unique*: The Military in the Belgian Congo, 1914–1939." Ph.D. diss., University of Wisconsin-Madison, 1984.

Sklar, Richard L. "Political Science and National Integration—A Radical Approach." *Journal of Modern African Studies* 5 (1967): 1–11.

_____ . "The Nature of Class Domination in Africa." *Journal of Modern African Studies* 17 (1979): 531–52.

Skocpol, Theda. *States and Social Revolutions: A Comparative Analysis of France, Russia, and China.* Cambridge: Cambridge University Press, 1979.

Southall, Aidan W. "The Illusion of Tribe." *Journal of Asian and African Studies* 5 (1970): 28–50.

Springborg, Robert. *Family, Power, and Politics in Egypt: Sayed Bey Marei—His Clan, Clients, and Cohorts.* Philadelphia: University of Pennsylvania Press, 1982.

Staudt, Kathleen A. "Sex, Ethnic, and Class Consciousness in Western Kenya." *Comparative Politics* 14 (1982): 149–67.

Swainson, Nicola. *The Development of Corporate Capitalism in Kenya 1918–1977.* Berkeley and Los Angeles: University of California Press, 1980.

Szeftel, Morris. "Political Graft and the Spoils System in Zambia—The State as a Resource in Itself." *Review of African Political Economy* 24 (1982): 4–21.

Thomas, Clive Y. *The Rise of The Authoritarian State in Peripheral Societies.* New York: Monthly Review Press, 1984.

Tilly, Charles. "Foreword." In *The Mafia of a Sicilian Village, 1860–1960: A Study of Violent Peasant Entrepreneurs,* by Anton Blok, xiii-xxiv. New York: Harper & Row, 1974.

"Tous solidaires et responsables": Lettre pastorale des évêques du Zaire. In *Documentation et Information* (28 June 1978): 590–97.

Turner, Margaret A. "Housing in Zaire: How the System Works and How the People Cope." Ph.D. diss., University of Wisconsin-Madison, 1985.

Turner, Thomas. "Problems of the Zairian Military." Paper prepared for the U.S. Department of State, 25 October 1979.

U.S. Congress, House, Committee on Foreign Affairs. *The Impact of U.S. Foreign Policy on Seven African Countries.* 98th Cong., 2nd Session, 24–27 August 1984.

Vandewalle, Frédéric, and Jacques Brassine. *Les rapports secrets de la sûreté congolaise, 1959–1960—Tome premier: Février-octobre 1959.* N.p.: Lucien de Meyer, 1973.

_____ . *Les rapports secrets de la sûreté congolaise, 1959–1960—Tome second: Novembre 1959-juin 1960.* N.p.: Lucien de Meyer, 1973.

Vansina, Jan. *Kingdoms of the Savanna.* Madison: University of Wisconsin Press, 1965.

_____ . *Introduction à l'ethnographie du Congo.* Kinshasa: Editions Universitaires du Congo, 1966.

_____ . *The Children of Woot: A History of the Kuba Peoples.* Madison: University of Wisconsin Press, 1978.

_____ . "Lignage, idéologie et histoire en Afrique équatoriale." *Enquêtes et documents d'histoire africaine* 4 (1980): 133–55.

_____ . "Mwasi's Trials." *Daedalus* 111 (1982): 49–70.

_____ . "The Peoples of the Forest." In *History of Central Africa,* 2 vols., edited by David Birmingham and Phyllis M. Martin, 1:75–117. London: Longman, 1983.

Vaughn, Megan. "Which Family? Problems in the Reconstruction of the History of the Family as an Economic and Cultural Unit." *Journal of African History* 24 (1983): 275–83.

Vellut, Jean-Luc. "Hégémonies en construction: Articulations entre état et entreprises dans le bloc colonial belge (1908–1960)." *Canadian Journal of African Studies* 16 (1982): 313–30.

Verhaegen, Benoît. *Rébellions au Congo.* 2 vols. Brussels: CRISP, 1966, 1969.

_____ . *L'enseignement universitaire au Zaire: De Lovanium à l'UNAZA 1958–1978.* Paris: L'Harmattan, 1978.

Vicariat Apostolique de Lisala. "L'éducation civique." *Nous . . . Educateurs,* no. 4 (1958): 17–20.

Vicariat Apostolique de Nouvelle Anvers (Scheut). *Cours complet de pédagogie et de méthodologie pour instituteurs enseignant en Lingala (Programme de trois ans) (des écoles normales au Congo)*. Turnhout, Belgium: Henri Proost & Cie, 1931.

Vincent, Joan. *African Elite: The Big Men of a Small Town*. New York: Columbia University Press, 1971.

Vwakyanakazi Mukohya. "African Traders in Butembo, Eastern Zaire (1960–1980): A Case Study of Informal Entrepreneurship in a Cultural Context of Central Africa." Ph.D. diss., University of Wisconsin-Madison, 1982.

Weiss, Herbert F. "Comparisons in the Evolution of Pre-Independence Elites in French-Speaking West Africa and the Congo." In *French-Speaking Africa: The Search for Identity*, edited by William H. Lewis, 130–42. New York: Walker & Company, 1965.

Weitzer, Ronald. "Continuities in the Politics of State Security in Zimbabwe." In *The Political Economy of Zimbabwe*, edited by Michael G. Schatzberg, 81–118. New York: Praeger, 1984.

Willame, Jean-Claude. *Patrimonialism and Political Change in the Congo*. Stanford: Stanford University Press, 1972.

_____. *Zaire, l'épopée d'Inga: Chronique d'une prédation industrielle*. Paris: L'Harmattan, 1986.

Winter, Gordon. *Inside Boss: South Africa's Secret Police*. Harmondsworth: Penguin, 1981.

World Bank. *Zaire: Current Economic Situation and Constraints*. Washington, D.C.: East Africa Regional Office, The World Bank, May 1980.

Yabili Yalala Asani. "Droit, révolution et vigilance révolutionnaire." *Jiwe* 3 (1974): 77–105.

Yates, Barbara Ann. "The Missions and Educational Development in Belgian Africa 1876–1908." Ph.D. diss., Columbia University, 1967.

_____. "African Reactions to Education: The Congolese Case." *Comparative Education Review* 15 (1971): 158–71.

_____. "The Triumph and Failure of Mission Vocational Education in Zaire 1879–1908." *Comparative Education Review* 20 (1976): 193–208.

_____. "Shifting Goals of Industrial Education in the Congo, 1878–1908." *African Studies Review* 21 (1978): 33–48.

Young, Crawford. *Politics in the Congo: Decolonization and Independence*. Princeton: Princeton University Press, 1965.

_____. *The Politics of Cultural Pluralism*. Madison: University of Wisconsin Press, 1976.

_____. "Zaire: The Unending Crisis." *Foreign Affairs* 57 (1978): 169–85.

_____. *Ideology and Development in Africa*. New Haven: Yale University Press, 1982.

_____. "Patterns of Social Conflict: State, Class, and Ethnicity." *Daedalus* 111 (1982): 71–98.

_____. "The Temple of Ethnicity." *World Politics* 35 (1983): 652–62.

Young, Crawford, and Thomas Turner. *The Rise and Decline of the Zairian State*. Madison: University of Wisconsin Press, 1985.

Zone de Lisala. "Rapport mensuel—mois de mars 1975," 7 April 1975.

Zonis, Marvin. "Iran: A Theory of Revolution from Accounts of Revolution." *World Politics* 35 (1983): 586–606.

Index

Abacos, 106
Ahidjo, Ahmadou, 22, 92
Ajami, Fouad, 91–92
Amin, Idi, 51, 67
Amnesty International, 44
Angola, 3, 55
Animation, 78–79, 106, 124
Ariès, Philippe, 72
Armed forces: corruption in, 56–57, 59–60, 62–63, 138; fear of, 67–68, 135, 138, 141; interference with civilian administration by, 60–62; lack of civilian control of, 69–70; and legal system, 63–64; recruitment in, 65–67; relative strength of, 67–69. *See also* Collectivity police; Forces Armées Zairoises; Gendarmerie Nationale; Jeunesse du Mouvement Populaire de la Révolution
Authenticity, 5, 113, 118, 141. *See also* Ideology
Awolowo, Chief, 18

Balandier, Georges, 13
Bandundu massacre, 68
Barre, Siad, 25
Barth, Fredrik, 79
Bates, Robert H., 16, 17
Bayart, Jean-François, 16, 26, 142
Bayona-Ba-Meya, 105
Berlin Conference, 7
Berry, Sara, 12–13
Bertrand, Hugues, 14
Bienen, Henry, 9, 141
Biya, Paul, 92
Bobozo, General, 14, 60–61
Bokanga, Ekanga Botombele, 76
Bokassa, 26
Bolikango, Jean, 32
Booth, Joseph, 125
Brett, E. A., 21
Buana Kabue, 134, 143
Bula Matari, 137
Burundi, 13, 117

Cabral, Amilcar, 143
Callaghy, Thomas M., 4, 66–67, 73, 100, 104, 136, 137, 139
Cameroon, 22–23, 24–25, 26, 51, 92
Campbell, Bonnie, 12
Cartes de chrétiens, 124
Catholic church, 85–88, 116–22; educational system of, 85–88, 117–18, 119; relationship with government, 118–22, 132, 136, 142
Central African Republic, 16, 25, 26
Centre National de Documentation (CND), 30–31, 38–40, 49–50; arrest and imprisonment by, 43–44; intimidation by, 41–43, 135, 138; surveillance and information gathering by, 42–43, 45–47; symbolic reassurance function of, 47–48; torture by, 44–45. *See also* Information-gathering
Chanock, Martin, 100
Chazan, Naomi, 19, 25
Class: and independent bourgeoisie, 20–21; vs. ethnicity, 9–10, 13–14; fluidity of, 9–11; and labor unions, 14–15; and political clientelage, 14; and social mobility, 140; and state, 12–13, 16–17, 28
CND. *See* Centre National de Documentation
Cohen, Abner, 26, 90
Cohen, Michael, 12
Cohen, Robin, 9
Collectivity police, 52, 55. *See also* Armed forces
Colonial Charter, 101
Colonialism, 19; centralization under, 137; courts under, 100–101; and ethnicity, 21–22; gun control under, 35; ideology of, 84–88; lack of indigenous bourgeoisie under, 12; religious groups under, 85–88, 118, 125–27
Colonies Agricoles pour Rélegués Dangereux, 38
Communications. *See* Centre National de Documentation; Information-gathering
Congo Crisis, 2, 144
Contribution personnelle minimum (CPM), 61, 129, 130
Copper, 2–3, 4
Corps des Activistes pour la Défense de la Révolution, 65. *See also* Jeunesse du Mouvement Populaire de la Révolution
Corruption, 19–20, 111–12, 143; in armed forces, 56–57, 59–60, 62–63, 138
Coup monté et manqué, 108
Courts. *See* Magistrature

De Ryck, M., 126–27
Dikonda, Professor, 44

Eckstein, Harry, 72
Eglise de Jésus-Christ sur Terre par le Prophète Simon Kimbangu (EJCSK), 116, 122–25, 132–33, 142
Egypt, 17, 91–92
Ekafera, 38
Elima, 71
Engels, Frederick, 73
Engulu Baangampongo, 71, 76, 94, 118
Equateur, 23–24, 66
Ethiopia, 10, 13–14, 22, 95
Ethnicity, 8–11, 141; and the armed forces, 66; vs. class, 9–10, 13–14; under colonialism, 21–

22; and insecurity and scarcity, 28; and political clientelage, 14; and social mobility, 140; and state, 10–11, 21–25, 28
Eyadema, 26

Fanon, Frantz, 135
FAZ. *See* Forces Armées Zairoises
First Republic, 2, 3, 22, 35; armed forces under, 54–55; decentralization under, 137; Kitawalists during, 127; legal system during, 105
Force Publique, 35, 53–54, 55, 65
Forces Armées Zairoises (FAZ), 52–53; corruption in, 59–60, fear of, 67–68, 135, 138, 141; government lack of control of, 69–70; presidential gifts to officers of, 60, 79–80; recruitment in, 66; reorganization of, 55; violence against population by, 1–2, 55, 57–59, 67–68. *See also* Armed forces
France, 73, 139
Franck, Louis, 86

Gabon, 26
Garvey, Marcus, 125
GDN. *See* Gendarmerie Nationale
Gellner, Ernest, 90
Gendarmerie Nationale (GDN), 53; corruption in, 56–57, 59–60; fear of, 67–68, 135, 138; government lack of control of, 69–70; as judicial police officers, 63; organization of, 55; quality of personnel of, 55–56; recruitment in, 66; violence against population by, 57–59, 67–68. *See also* Armed forces
Ghana, 16, 19, 25, 80
Giddens, Anthony, 4–5, 31, 50, 73, 111, 140
Gramsci, Antonio, 4
Greenberg, Stanley B., 17
"Guide," the, 124–25. *See also* Mobutu Sese Seko
Guinea, 12, 16
Gun control, 35–38, 136. *See also* Centre Nationale de Documentation; Information-gathering
Gurr, Ted Robert, 72

Hekken, P. M. van, 15
Houphouët-Boigny, Félix, 26
Hyden, Goran, 131, 141

Idiofa massacre, 68
Ideology, 5, 25–27, 141–42. *See also* Authenticity; *Mobutisme*; Paternalism
Independent State, 53, 100
Information-gathering: and communications within government, 33–35, 37–38; and government surveillance, 31–35, 42–43, 45–47; re gun control, 35–38. *See also* Centre Nationale de Documentation
International Monetary Fund (IMF), 20, 134, 141
Ivory Coast, 9, 12, 26

Jackson, Robert H., 7
Janssens, Emile, 38
Jehovah's Witnesses, 125, 126, 127–28, 136
Jessop, Bob, 6
Jeunesse du Mouvement Populaire de la

Révolution (JMPR), 32, 52, 58; abuses by, 64–65; corruption in, 59–60; fear of, 135, 138; government lack of control of, 69; presence in church institutions, 118, 120; purposes of, 68. *See also* Armed forces
Jewsiewicki, B., 126
John Paul I, Pope, 120
John Paul II, Pope, 120

The Kalela Dance, 9–10
Kalemie, FAZ in, 68
Kamitatu-Massamba, Cleophas, 23, 94
Kanyonga Mobateli, 96
Kaplinsky, Raphael, 20
Kasai Oriental massacre, 68
Kaseba, A., 30, 115, 120
Kasongo affair, 68
Katekelayi massacre, 68
Keegan, John, 53
Keita, Modibo, 16
Keller, Edmond J., 10
Kengo wa Dondo, 105, 114
Kenya, 9, 11, 14, 19, 20, 21
Kenyatta, Jomo, 15, 26–27, 92
Kimbangu, Diangienda, 124
Kimbangu, Simon, 122–23, 124
Kimbanguist church, 116, 122–25, 132–33, 142
Kisangani teachers' strike, 43, 44–45, 68
Kitawalists, 125–32; history of, 125–27; relationship with Mobutu's government, 116, 127, 129–32, 133, 136
Kitching, Gavin, 19
Kofele-Kale, Ndiva, 25

Labor unions, 14–15
Ladawa, Mama Bobi, 78, 120
Langdon, Steven W., 20
Lemarchand, René, 140
Leo, Christopher, 9
Leopold II, King, 53, 100
Leys, Colin, 11, 20, 24, 26–27, 28
Lisala, ix, 24
Lonsdale, John, 10, 13
Lovanium University, 118
Luamuela massacre, 68
Lumumba, Patrice, 118

MacGaffey, Janet, 20–21, 28
MacGaffey, Wyatt, 100, 113, 123
Machel, Samora, 17
Magistrature, 99–114; administrative independence of, 102; ambiguous position of, 113–14, 135–36; and arrest and detention, 103; as center of resistance, 110–13; corruption in, 111–12; history of, 100–102; judicial review of lower court decisions by, 104–105; and the MPR, 105–106; and presidential edicts, 108–10; training of, 112–13; treatment of political officials by, 104, 106–108
Mali, 16
Maluku steel mill, 58–59, 68
Malula, Joseph, 115, 117, 118, 120, 121
Marenin, Otwin, 69
Markakis, John, 13–14, 23
Martens, 134, 144

Marx, Karl, 12, 73
Matip, Mayi, 22, 23
Mazrui, Ali A., 86
Mba, Leon, 26
Meillassoux, Claude, 89, 92
Mercier, Paul, 9
Mitchell, J. Clyde, 9–10
Moba, FAZ violence in, 1–2, 68
Mobutisme, 5, 109, 141. *See also* Ideology
Mobutu, Mama, 77–78
Mobutu Plan, 120
Mobutu Sese Seko, 1, 8, 138; and armed forces, 55, 58, 59, 65–66, 68; attitude toward church, 115–16, 119, 120, 128; attitude toward second political party, 141; and Bobozo, 61; centralization policies of, 2–3, 18, 69, 137; and CND, 39, 40, 41; creation of ministry of citizens' rights, 144; criticism of bureaucrats by, 94–95; and Diangienda, 124; edicts of, 108–109; ethnic alliances of, 23, 65–66; as father-chief, 78, 94; as father and gift-giver, 71, 79–81; as father and head of family, 72, 76–78, 90–91; and the judiciary, 99, 105–106; and Nguza, 81; popularity of, 2–3; promise of M. to relinquish power, 92–93; response to dissent, 26, 95–96; vigilance of, 32, 49. *See also* Paternalism
Mongala Subregion, ix
Mouvement Populaire de la Révolution (MPR), 15, 16, 141; communications in, 33–34; as family, 1, 71, 72, 77; and Jehovah's Witnesses, 127–28; and the judiciary, 105–106
Mpinga-Kasenda, 75
Multinational corporations, 20
Mwabila, Malela, 13, 14, 28

Naipaul, V. S., 79
Nande tribe, 22
National Legislative Council, 43
Nationalism, 25–26
Nendaka, Victor, 39
Nguza Karl-i-bond, 3, 23, 94; on armed forces, 59, 67; and CND, 30, 39, 41, 43; on magistrature, 99, 114; and Mobutu, 81; use of paternalistic imagery by, 96
Nigeria, 9, 12–13, 18, 25
Nkrumah, Kwame, 16
Nyerere, Julius, 15, 92
Nyobe, Ruben Um, 22
Nzongola-Ntalaja, 143

Obbo, Christine, 28
Officiers de la police judiciaire (OPJ), 63, 64, 103

Parti de l'Unité National, 32
Parti Révolutionnaire du Peuple (PRP), 58, 60
Paternalism, 26–27, 71–73; abuse of imagery of, 91–93, 95–98, 141–42; ambiguity in imagery of, 90–91; and centralization of power, 94–95; colonial origins of imagery of, 84–88; and father as chief, 75–76, 78, 81; and father as gift-giver, 79–81; and father as nurturer, 89–90; and mother figure, 77–78; and nation as family, 76–77; pervasiveness of imagery of,

73–75, 81–82; post-independence origins of imagery of, 88–89; precolonial origins of imagery of, 82–84; use of imagery by opposition, 96–97
Peace, Adrian J., 9
Poulantzas, Nicos, 4, 5, 142
Price, Robert, 80–81
PRP, 58, 60

Receuil d'instructions aux missionnaires, 86
Religious groups, 115–16, 132–33. *See also* Catholic church; Kimbanguist church; Kitawalists
Rhodesia, 10
Rivière, Claude, 12
Rosberg, Carl G., 7
Rothchild, Joseph, 40, 66
Rubbens, Antoine, 105
Ruvuma Development Association (RDA), 15, 17
Rwanda, 13, 117
Ryckmans, Pierre, 101

Sadat, Anwar, 91–92
Sahlins, Marshall, 80
Sakombi Inongo, 3–4, 97
Salongo, 76–77
Samoff, Joel, 9, 25–26
Saul, John S., 14
Schildkrout, Enid, 9
Scott, James C., 10, 98, 141
Second Republic, 2–3; Catholic church's attitude toward, 118; First Republic politicians in, 23
Selassie, Haile, 23, 95
Senegal, 14, 92
Sennett, Richard, 90, 92
Senghor, Léopold, 92
Shaba I, 3, 32, 55, 60, 68, 141
Shaba II, 3, 32, 55, 68, 120, 141
Shagari, President, 18
Sierra Leone, 25, 26, 92
Singa, Colonel, 39
Sklar, Richard L., 19, 23
Skocpol, Theda, 4
Somalia, 25
South Africa, 17
Southall, Aidan W., 9, 21
Springborg, Robert, 17
Stanley, Henry Morton, 137
State: as class-based organization, 16–17, 28; communications and surveillance by, 31–35, 37–38, 42–43, 45–47; definition of, 4–5, 6–7; and ethnicity, 10–11, 21–25, 28; fluidity of, 10–11, 17–18, 27–28, 142–43; and ideology, 5, 25–27, 141–42; vs. independent bourgeoisie, 20–21; vs. independent organizations, 14–16; insecurity of, 3–4, 135–36, 137; interactions with populace, 143–44; local perceptions of, 5–6; and patron-client distributive networks, 14; as source of economic power, 12–13, 19–20, 28; as source of insecurity and scarcity, 28–29. *See also* Armed forces; Centre National de Documentation; Class; Ethnicity; Magistrature; Paternalism; Zaire

State Research Bureau (SRB), 51
Staudt, Kathleen A., 14
Stevens, Siaka, 92
Sûreté, 38–39, 40. *See also* Centre National de Documentation
Surveillance, 31–35, 42–43, 45–47. *See also* Centre National de Documentation; Information-gathering
Swainson, Nicola, 20

Tanzania, 15, 17, 25–26, 92, 131; invasion of Uganda by, 67
Tilly, Charles, 138
Togo, 26
Touré, Sékou, 16
Turner, Thomas, 53, 100, 140, 143

Uganda, 16, 51, 67
Union Minière du Haut-Katanga (UMHK), 88
Union Nationale Camerounaise (UNC), 16
Union pour la Démocratie et le Progrès Social (UDPS), 96
U.S. Central Intelligence Agency, 108
U.S. Congress, 41

van Velzen, Thoden, 15
Vansina, Jan, 9, 27, 80, 82–83, 90, 91, 92, 131
von Freyhold, Michaela, 15

Watch Tower Bible and Tract Society, 125, 126, 127–28, 136
Willame, Jean-Claude, 88
World Bank, 141

Yemo, Mama, 77, 79
Young, Crawford, 4, 9, 16, 53, 100, 140, 143, 144

Zaire: centralization in, 2–3, 18, 69–70, 136–38; and France compared, 73, 139; government coercion in, 138–39, 141; indebtedness of, 3; informal economy in, 140–41; insecurity and scarcity in, 3–4, 28–29, 135–36, 137; labor unions in, 14–15; as product of international nation-state system, 139–40; survival of *Mobutiste* state in, 140–42. *See also* Armed forces; Centre National de Documentation; Class; Ethnicity; Magistrature; Paternalism; State
Zairian National Police, 55
Zambia, 19